£40.00

KT-460-640

The Industrial Heritage

This book provides the first integrated approach to the assessment, conservation, interpretation, financing and management of the complex heritage of industrial cultures. It breaks new ground, as the authors (both active workers in the field) show how concepts of heritage defined to deal with pre-industrial cultures must be modified to deal with the very different demands presented by industrial objects and the societies which produced them.

And because the impact of industrialisation varies over time and between different societies the authors have produced a comparative international survey which looks at projects in many countries. They look in detail at the current revaluation of hitherto-ignored assets of industrial culture and assess their future viability. They also consider ways in which support and involvement can be obtained for industrial projects (drawing on a wide range of international examples) and also suggest how these programmes can be established and monitored.

The essence of this book is practicality, offering examples of the actual issues which confront those concerned with preserving and managing the industrial heritage. It will be of vital interest to all who are concerned with the industrial heritage, from museums and collections with only a limited holding to major industrial collections and heritage sites.

Judith Alfrey is a freelance historic buildings consultant, and lecturer in heritage management.
Tim Putnam is Head of the Centre of Applied Historical Studies at Middlesex Polytechnic.

THE HERITAGE
CARE
PRESERVATION
MANAGEMENT

Editor in chief   Andrew Wheatcroft

The Heritage: Care–Preservation–Management programme has been designed to serve the needs of the museum and heritage community worldwide. It publishes books and information services for professional museum and heritage workers, and for all the organisations that service the museum community.

The programme has been devised with the advice and assistance of the leading institutions in the museum and heritage community, both at an international level, with ICOM and ICOMOS, with the national and local museum organisations and with individual specialists drawn from every continent.

Museums Without Barriers: *A new deal for disabled people*
Fondation de France and ICOM

Museums and the Shaping of Knowledge
Eilean Hooper-Greenhill

Forward Planning: *A handbook of business, corporate and development planning for museums and galleries*
Edited by Timothy Ambrose and Sue Runyard

Museums 2000: *Politics, people, professionals and profit*
Edited by Patrick Boylan

The Past in Contemporary Society: Then, Now
Peter J. Fowler

The Industrial Heritage

Managing resources and uses

Judith Alfrey and Tim Putnam

London and New York

First published in 1992
by Routledge
11 New Fetter Lane, London EC4P 4EE

Transferred to Digital Printing 2003

Simultaneously published in the USA and Canada
by Routledge
a division of Routledge, Chapman and Hall Inc.
29 West 35th Street, New York, NY 10001

British Library Cataloguing in Publication Data

Alfrey, Judith and Putnam, Tim
   The industrial heritage.
   1. Industries. Antiquities
   I. Title II. Series
   609

Library of Congress Cataloging in Publication Data

Alfrey, Judith
   The industrial heritage: managing resources and uses / Judith
   Alfrey & Tim Putnam.
      p.   cm. – (Heritage)
   1. Industrial archaeology.   2. Industrial buildings – Conservation
   and restoration.   I. Putnam, Tim.   II. Title.
   III. Series.
   T37.A54   1992
   609——dc20   91–14017
                        CIP

ISBN 0 415 04068 X (hbk)
ISBN 0 415 07043 0 (pbk)

Printed and Bound by Antony Rowe Ltd

Contents

Contents

Acknowledgements

Much of the research for this book has been carried out through a programme of visits, interviews and informal discussions. Many people have helped us, by arranging meetings and visits, discussing ideas and practice, and providing source material. We would like to extend our special thanks to the following for their help and hospitality: Dennis Baker, Ed Battison, Stephen Bayley, Ola Bettum, Margareta Biörnstad, Ulf Boëthius, Britt Bogren, Klas Börjesson, Monica Borg, Val Bott, Barbro Bursell, Eva Bergdahl Bulukin, Pierre Camusat, Eusebe Casanelles, Nanna Cnattingius, Elin and Carmen Corneil, John Crompton, Jorge Custodio, Alison Cutforth, Barbara Czerannowski, Brian Daubney, Mick Downes, Jocelyn de Noblet, Eva Fägeborg, Steve Fletcher, Anne Follin, Jim Forester, Tommy Forss, Bernie Giffard, Mike Glasson, Dave Goodwin, Marc Goujard, Derek Green, Larry Gross, Örjan Hamrin and colleagues at the Ecomuseum Bergslagen, Tale and Hans-Jacob Hansteen, Cameron Hawke-Smith, Ann-Carlotte Hertz, Kari Hoel, Andrew Hood, Ellen Howland, John Hume, Ole Hyldtoft, colleagues and friends at Ironbridge Gorge Museum and Institute, Peter Jenkinson, Per-Andos Johannson, Walle Johansson, Stephen Kay, Therese Kelly, Phil Kiernan, Lars Larsson, Kevin Leyden, Per Lindroos, Svante Linqvist, Adriaan Linters, Eva Londos, Peter Ludvikson, Pat Malone, Marie-Thérèse Martin, Jean-Luc Mayaud, Jose Mende, Michael Mende, colleagues and friends at Middlesex Polytechnic, Jonathan Minns, Kersti Morger, Peter Nijhof, Staffan Nilsson, Marie Nisser, Lars-Erik Olsson, Mark O'Neill, Ola Øverås, Michael Parr, Peter Paul, Julia Porter, Mats Ramberg, Helen Rees, Reinhard Roseneck, Mat Roth, Bo Sahlholm, Paul Smith, Bill Startin, Annika Tyrfelt, Patrick Viaene, Steven Victor, Ian Walden, Anne-Lise Walsted, Luc Wante, Jan Westlund, Peter White.

We thank these people for the many insights which they have offered, some of which we have been able to incorporate into

Acknowledgements

this book. We regret that in a short book such as this there is not the space to do proper justice to the full situation and history, the problems and accomplishments, of each of the projects to which we refer or which we discuss. In choosing to single out certain aspects and themes we hope that we have not transmitted any false impressions.

Judith Alfrey
Tim Putnam

Illustrations

List of illustrations

List of illustrations

1 Industrial culture as heritage

Introduction

What is the industrial heritage? What does managing the industrial heritage involve? We have put this question to many people in several countries and received diverse answers:

- piecing together the remnants of long-lost (or not so long-lost) industry to understand how it functioned;
- protecting and caring for buildings, sites and machinery because of their technical, historical or aesthetic interest;
- finding new uses for redundant but irreplaceable elements of the industrial landscape;
- restoring disused machinery and working practices to use;
- recording the knowledge, skills and experience of industrial populations;
- using the results of the above to show how past generations lived and worked.

Each of these activities involves constituting a resource (selected traces and remains of previous activity) for one or more uses (study, care, representation). Making the industrial heritage involves managing the relationship between a range of such potential resources and their possible uses.

The range of potential resources is very broad – potentially the whole life and works of industrial civilisation. (In speaking of industrial civilisation we mean simply one which, however diverse and complex its course and contents, has industrial culture at its heart and as its constant presupposition.) The scope of this culture takes in medieval mineworkings or the musical consumption of a modern adolescent. Selection is inevitable: effective selection requires a well thought-out set of objectives to guide a programme of work (research, conservation, interpretation) that constitutes a resource of enduring value and usefulness.

The Industrial Heritage

This book is concerned with how potentially significant resources deposited by industrial civilisation can be identified and how they can best be exploited. Words like exploitation and use may sound strange in a discussion of heritage, where one is more accustomed to hear about protection for posterity. This is not as much of a contradiction as it might seem. The special cultural value which all heritage-making accords to its chosen resource is justified by, and specifies or implies a programme for, future use. While heritage management is often concerned with determining appropriate kinds and levels of use, its ultimate objective is to enrich the cultural resources which are available.

Those who have succeeded in extending the boundary of heritage concern to include the remains of industrial civilisation have had to demonstrate the cultural benefits of this 'new' heritage and have often been innovative in developing new programmes or cultivating new constituencies. They have accomplished some quite extraordinary things: a generation ago industrial heritage was virtually unknown, even in the academy; now it has become something to conjure with – even an element in the regeneration of areas devastated by the decline of key industries.

The concept of an industrial heritage can still seem contradictory, even nonsensical; many assumptions about heritage, and the institutions based on them, were formed in a period when an awesome industrialisation transformed familiar landscapes, disrupted habits and challenged established values. Most of what is today protected or celebrated as heritage has been chosen within industrialised societies as pre-industrial or non-industrial, as older, more rare, more beautiful, more traditional, more natural, more spiritual. Industrial culture has itself idealised archetypes of what it is not which can get in the way of recognising its own character, problems and achievements.

A civilisation unable to recognise itself would be a frightening thing. The demand for representations of all aspects of our common world is, however, voracious, and works to expand the heritage resource and extend its uses. Established 'treasures' are extensively reproduced while previously 'hidden' histories are ferreted out for public consumption. Heritage managers have to satisfy the demand for access while maintaining the integrity of the resource. This can only be done if we realise that our heritage is all around us and that the responsibility for recognising it, caring for it, and sharing it with others is ours, too.

In this sense industrial civilisation is coming to take possession of its own heritage.

Industrial civilisation, its characteristics and residues

Thanks to the work of a generation of enthusiasts, who have won increasing official and popular support, we now have windows into the industrial past. But it would be foolish to believe that we do more than catch glimpses through these windows – and then only of scenes which have been framed to suit present-day preoccupations and pastimes. The resource which is available as industrial heritage today may be voluminous, but it is still fragmentary. A prime task in its management is to understand the reasons for this and to be able to overcome their effects.

The first reason for the fragmentary record is to be found in the capacity of industrial civilisation to transform itself. In 1987 the ecomuseum of the community Le Creusot-Montceau-Les-Mines mounted an exhibition about the vast empty space overlooked by the main museum building. This 'Plaine des Riaux', already built and rebuilt several times in the course of the growth of the giant Schneider metallurgical company, was being flattened and rebuilt again. Fragments of industrial archaeology survived on a less eligible slope and the outlines of an early engine shed justified their survival by a twin reference to classical architectural rhetoric and the avant-garde status of the works at the dawn of the railway age. But the main theme of the industrial history of the Plaine des Riaux was to be found not in monuments, but in the array of photographs, plans and drawings to be seen in the exhibition. Its successive and continuing re-occupation spoke not only of the intensive development of the Schneider company and of the now world-wide industry in which it has been a protagonist, but also of the continual reassessment of resources essential to an industrial culture.

Not every piece of industrial landscape has been as intensively developed as the Plaine des Riaux. In the extensive northern forests of Scandinavia it is more usual to find the older works simply abandoned, perhaps surviving alongside the new. Yet the image of the Plaine des Riaux deserves a place at the head of any consideration of the industrial heritage resource. It reminds us that renewal and transformation are more characteristic, more emblematic, of industrial history than any monument. And, consequently, the fragments that survive are seldom representative of what went before.

The Industrial Heritage

The progress of industry produces a scrapheap: of redundant products, machinery, building materials and 'waste' certainly, but also of projects, performances and ways of life. What is abandoned though is seldom without value; much finds a new use, often in an unrecognisable form. What is left over becomes the raw material of the industrial heritage.

When managing the industrial history of today, or of the recent past, an active strategy which casts an eye over the entire scrapheap is possible – it can salvage much of cultural value which would otherwise be wasted, and record the overall shape and direction of industrial progress. The remains of the not so recent past, however, present a different challenge: their relative rarity value as artefacts is shrouded in doubts about their status as evidence – what, exactly, are they monuments of? and what of the histories for which the monuments are missing?

An important feature of the industrial heritage movement in several countries has been the emergence of a sort of historian intrigued by this challenge. As often amateur as professional, these historians have been relatively uninfluenced by academic fashionability, or the priorities of research councils. They have their own agenda – the material culture of the modern period and its modes of life.

Those academic disciplines that do study industrial culture have an important contribution to make in the development of proper understandings of heritage resources, whether their perspective is historical – embracing economic, social, cultural and political histories – or ethnological, or design study. But the directions of academic study will not always coincide with the prescriptions of heritage resources.

Historical studies have not been as much use in heritage management as might have been expected: whether their subject is defined as economic or social history, business or labour history, their discipline has concentrated on narrative order and causal relations. Selective focus and organisation of study, whether dealing with institutions, with people or with such apparently objective phenomena as national economies, has imposed an order which, concerned with stories and results, and with no place for particularity, may overlook the complexity and contradictions of heritage resources. Historical study which has attempted to embrace a total history containing the structures of everyday life, as the French Annales school has done, may offer a richer agenda to the heritage manager in locating and contextualising resources, but its broad perspectives may be impossible to represent in interpretation (for example Braudel 1981).

1 Cycles of use and re-use in the industrial landscape: Plaine des Riaux, Le Creusot, France

The Industrial Heritage

Industrial heritage has not been well served by any branch of historical study, not least because these disciplines have been heavily dominated by a nationalist perspective. This emphasis has spilt over into heritage management where resources may be identified only in so far as they illustrate particular themes relevant to certain periods or phases of development: monuments and machines become symbols of technological innovation; buildings appear on the historical stage newly built – the stubborn fact of their survival and continuing history conveniently overlooked. It is this very survival which is a starting point for the identification and study of heritage resources.

In the theatre of national economic development, images of what is and is not industry have also shaped perceptions of what industrial heritage can and cannot be. In Britain and the United States, for example, emphasis on heavy industry and technological innovation has encouraged definitions of resources focused on the factory, the machine and the technical monument. This heroic representation of industry as a largely male preserve has only recently been challenged by 'histories from below' bringing consideration of minor industries, the experience of work, the experience of industrial change for women and their participation in it.

Many branches of historical study have also tended to be ignorant, even contemptuous, of material culture. Ethnology, ethnography and archaeology are among the only disciplines that take as their starting point a concept of a whole culture. Having as their subject the integrity of a culture, and recognising the importance of material culture in that matrix, they have developed procedures for dealing specifically with material traces. These techniques have been developed to deal with unfamiliar societies, or those where documentary evidence is scanty, applying systematic rules for looking for and examining all sorts of traces and artefacts for a whole site or social system. Unlike historical studies, they must perforce engage with particularities, while seeking to contextualise them. Their disciplines are vital in heritage management.

In this connection, the work of amateur historians also comes to the fore. Although amateurs may have a weak grip on the general contexts and perspectives adopted in academic study, they may bring an energy to the pursuit of detailed investigation or documentary work, even sometimes saving artefacts as evidence.

Industrial archaeology has developed as an attempt to remedy the deficiencies both of academic study, and of amateur histories. Its programme suggests an alliance of particular histories based on artefacts, and a grand conceptual dimension – as the archaeology of the industrial period. In bringing these two things together, industrial archaeology is at once indispensable in curatorship and a key science for understanding contemporary society. However, industrial archaeology has tended to neglect one of the primary tenets of traditional archaeology, which takes a society and its people as its proper object of study; industrial archaeology has developed procedures for the investigation and analysis of technical monuments and machinery, but has had little to say about the experience and organisation of working life.

With its starting point in material or experiential traces of past activity, heritage management requires an interdisciplinary approach with a common agenda which may make use of the perspectives provided by these disciplines in generating awareness, understandings of and contexts for its resources. In turn, the prerequisites of industrial heritage may be able to influence the academic agenda.

Heritage resources refuse to be marshalled in the orderly narratives of historical study, and remain full of complexity and contradiction. Fragmentation of the resource is partly created by industrial progress itself and compounded by the absence of an integrated management strategy. Historical and other studies have only begun to establish a perspective using the new insights that greater involvement in industrial heritage is turning up – we do not yet have an integrated understanding of the varieties of industrial culture, so have to hold this out as a heuristic device.

For the present, what has been recognised as industrial heritage still faces inadequate appraisal of material and cultural resources on the one hand, and stereotyped ideas of industry on the other. Even so, we can already observe tensions between the outlines of an industrial heritage which are emerging and established ways of treating the heritage resource. These form the subject of this chapter.

Instruments of heritage thinking: planning for landscapes and sites

There are several institutional structures which have contained and shaped heritage values. The structures of planning and conservation have exercised a powerful influence on the direction and subject matter of heritage, encouraging a definition of resources heavily dependent on landscape features, and defining value according to particular criteria. Typically, conservation was introduced as one component of the larger agenda of land-use planning, and this context has served to shape the development of ideas about what heritage could and should be.

Conservation has typically been defined as the safeguarding of cultural assets, themselves more often seen as relics of a pre-industrial landscape, in a strategy which would enable certain classes of building, site or area to be removed from the normal process of development. Comprehensive planning takes land-use zoning as a key tenet, and although conservation does not have to be classed as if it was a particular land-use (as opposed to a general programme of land-management), in practice, effort has tended to be concentrated in certain areas, or on certain building types.

In Britain, specific and defined controls over the nature and direction of development concerning protected buildings, sites and landscapes were denoted from the outset, but, although the extent of assumed protection varies from country to country, general thinking about conservation conforms to certain paradigms. Its introduction in the context of amenity planning, with its concomitant ideas about order, tidiness and the appearance of things, has led to a clear conservation aesthetic, which has often been as much concerned with certain ideas about environmental design in general as it has with the specific qualities of individual buildings. Appearance has been (almost) all: assessment has been anchored to visual values rather than to any other than a superficial consideration of function or history (Smith 1974).

The orientation of this design process has been based on the validation of recognisable architectural aesthetics: buildings have been selected for conservation on the grounds of their stylistic content, with a bias towards the academic rather than the vernacular. The original design has been considered more important than the visibility of subsequent history – integrity of survival has been an important criterion of value (Suddards 1988; Ten Hallers 1985). Buildings have also typically been selected on the grounds of age, and in many places it is only relatively recently that serious attention has been paid to buildings post-dating 1850. There has been an emphasis on the rare rather than the typical, the exceptional rather than the traditional.

While the possibility of value for other than visual reasons has been admitted, historical criteria have been severely self-limiting, especially in relation to industrial heritage: in the

United Kingdom, for example, the original criteria allowed for the constructions of famous engineers, or buildings which represented technological innovations or virtuosity, or housed significant processes. There was little attempt at defining the scope of possible historical value outside the sphere of architectural history. A similar bias characterised interpretation of historical interest in the Netherlands, where importance in history of technology was steadfastly overlooked as ground for preservation (Ten Hallers 1985).

The dominance of conservation planning in establishing public definitions of heritage has led to certain assumptions: that heritage is largely concerned with building and landscape resources, and that these should conform to certain general standards of environmental design. It has generally encouraged a more or less tight selection of resources, which are bounded temporally as well as geographically. Heritage is set aside as a particular, and usually secondary, use of resources.

Industrial culture in conservation and renewal

It has often been hard to see industrial culture as heritage at all, since heritage has by convention been defined as relics from a pre-industrial history. Even where value has been accorded to industrial traces, there has been a tendency to focus on certain kinds of residue or to characterise them in certain circumscribed ways – as monumental, sublime, old, rare or technologically significant.

Established procedures and criteria for conservation may actively disfavour industrial buildings and landscapes. Industrial buildings may not be registered because they are too recent, too altered, or have no conventional architectural aesthetic. Industrial remains may be too untidy, too poorly designed and built to be deemed to merit retention. Selection by single item may not be responsive to context, to the complexity of form and the interconnections which characterise industrial landscapes and buildings. Separation of types of resource (building, monument and area or landscape), and the maintenance of different procedures for each make it difficult to register a detailed picture of the interconnectedness of the industrial landscape.

Visual values have led to emphasis on certain aspects of industry at the expense of others. Although there has been progress towards recognising the special qualities of industrial architecture, there remain problems of 'fit' when industrial traces are judged by standards intended for quite other

resources. J. M. Richards, in *The Functional Tradition*, identified the aesthetic qualities which were particular to industrial
architecture, and other studies have since taken up this theme
(Richards 1958). Although the essence of this industrial aesthetic was held to be the expression of function, in practice
only certain types of industrial building have been responsive
to analysis in this way: mills, warehouses, station architecture,
etc. – buildings which employ a highly visible architectural
vocabulary. This analysis has certainly helped to raise awareness of industrial buildings of certain types, but carries its
own problems where the functional significance of industrial
buildings is imperfectly understood.

Emphasis on particular visual qualities has sometimes led to
the misrepresentation of industrial heritage in conservation
registers, and severely limited their ability to foster any understanding of the significance of industrial sites and buildings.
Until recently, for example, Listing policies in the potteries
region in England focused almost exclusively on the protection
of bottle ovens, as significant emblems for the history of the
area, with special visual qualities. The policy demonstrated a
cavalier attitude to the functional integrity of the sites, and
has been revised to attempt the registration of working complexes in their entirety, but very few of these now survive.

Not all industrial processes have a visibility at all, let alone
one that conforms to a recognisable architectural aesthetic.
Selection based solely or largely on architectural qualities may
misrepresent industrial histories by identifying exceptional
rather than typical examples, and by registering superficial
rather than essential qualities. Emphasis on original condition
or visual integrity may not be very relevant for industrial
buildings which have been successively altered and adapted
to keep abreast of technological and economic changes as the
price of their survival. It is this pattern of change which is
often an essential feature of the development of industrial
activity.

Conservation planning as a strategy of heritage management

The value of conservation planning in a strategy for the
management of industrial heritage resources may be constrained by the basis of selection and recognition of value,
and by the way in which boundaries in planning and project
identification are defined. Conservation planning has limitations in what it can achieve as a tool in resource management: it has rarely been framed with industrial heritage

specifically in mind, and is anyway not capable of providing a comprehensive system of resource management – expectations exceed practical possibility, largely because of the great weight which has been laid on conservation as definer and arbiter of heritage values.

In practice, conservation planning is reactive rather than pro-active: heritage resources are often only recognised when under threat. This has been especially true of industrial traces, since there has been no coherent criterion set out at the outset (as there was for other building types). Eleventh hour assessments are limited in what they can achieve: if the original use has gone, the building or complex may be of limited historical value, yet, in its context of amenity planning, conservation is not constituted to make interventions in economic management for the maintenance of appropriate uses. Conservation tends therefore to be concerned with only a part of the industrial heritage – it can validate and help to protect the structures and appearance of things, but may not be able to sustain the patterns of use which have justified them. Even where there are integrated assessments which bring together notions of economic viability, they are likely to rely on new uses for old buildings.

In Britain, stringent processes of selection have meant that a presumption in favour of conservation will only be applicable to a limited range of local buildings and building types. The local authority may attempt to register the value and significance of a much greater range, but its ability to act upon this registration may be limited. In Stoke on Trent, for example, the local authority has used its ability to create conservation areas to good effect. There has also been good liaison with the local museum, which organised a comprehensive survey of buildings in the area. But it can be difficult to establish a presumption in favour of conservation outside the scope of statutory protection.

Defining a remit

Identification of heritage resources must be selective. However, if the basis of selection is drawn too tightly around a particular theme or area, traces of other histories may be overlooked and may lose out in a process of differential development.

New Bedford, in Massachusetts, grew up as a major whaling port, and is still responsible for the highest-value fishing trade in the United States. The importance of seafaring industries has left its stamp on the urban environment, not only in the houses of the whaling masters, the boarding houses and other domestic buildings, but also in a number of early nineteenth-century civic and commercial buildings. During the nineteenth century, however, the textile industry was at least as important to the economic growth of the city, and there are large late nineteenth-century suburbs and acres of stone-built mills which survive as a legacy of the complex economic and social structures of this industrialisation.

The municipality, the state and local civic societies chose to concentrate their attentions on the older history of whaling, and the boundaries of the historic district were at first drawn only round the original waterfront nucleus. A local buildings preservation society, WHALE (Waterfront Historic Area League), was also established with the specific aim of conserving the surviving fabric of the whaling landscape, and it is only now, nearly thirty years after its foundation, turning its attention both to the commercial heart of the city, and to the townscape produced by the textile industry (see chapter 3).

Definition of areas for special treatment through conservation planning may be apparently justified by the concentration of historical resources, but can also lead to problems of differential development. In the United Kingdom, for example, designation of the Ironbridge Gorge as a historic landscape within the context of a new town, Telford, has seen the concentration of effort and resources for conservation within a narrowly defined area, and the concomitant loss of historical traces from the wider area of the town. Alongside this, there is acute local awareness that not all the history of the town is validated. The Ironbridge Gorge is an exceptionally rich historical landscape, but its surrounding areas have histories of their own which are not given adequate recognition. Similar tensions in Halifax saw emphasis in a heritage and regeneration programme shifted to ensure that the results of enhanced investment in conservation were directed across the area as a whole and not simply focused on areas or buildings of high architectural quality (Lockwood 1988: 5–7).

Many new projects for the regeneration of industrial areas look away from rather than taking account of industrial culture. The industrial past is seen as something best forgotten. In Fall River, Massachusetts, a low estimation of industrial heritage resources and the destruction of many features of the industrial landscape have resulted in the importing of 'assets' which bear little or no relation to the history of the town. A Heritage State Park with a naval theme offers little in the way of interpreting the history of a town which owes its existence to the textile industry. Outside the boundaries of the park, neglect of the very real assets which survive from this industry is palpable. Ideas about heritage are being exploited in an income-raising attraction, which misses a real commitment to the care and management of extant local resources.

The problems of waste and decay which are left after the industry has gone are particularly acute in old mining landscapes. There is a not unnatural desire to make good, tidy away, and restore the landscape to its imagined former character. Economic renewal programmes may not take industrial heritage seriously, when it is the demise of the industrial base which is responsible for major local dislocation.

The Rhondda valley in South Wales is a landscape formed by coal mining: the narrow valley is lined with mining villages largely established in the nineteenth century, and punctuated by the surviving pitheads themselves. The last of these mines closed down in 1990. Local disquiet over the loss of historical resources found common cause with political concern to regenerate the area, both physically in the restoration of derelict land, and economically. Potential new uses explored included housing, industry and recreation, but it was decided to create a major tourism, recreational and heritage project to act as a regional resource. The project aims to assist regeneration by tackling dereliction associated with the mining sites through landscaping. It aims to attract visitors to the area, and to reverse a negative image representing the valley as heavily industrialised, declining and unattractive, in the hopes of attracting new industry. It aims to create an enhanced environment with new facilities for local people.

A key element in this assessment is the introduction of new uses to create new public amenities. This is the positive side: heritage cannot be a re-run of history when the economic base has failed, and this very failure can be turned into an opportunity to create access to new facilities. But a desire for regeneration does not in itself provide an adequate basis for the management of heritage resources, and their evaluation founders on an assumption that the best way to regenerate the area is to reverse centuries of history by turning back to some assumed pre-industrial character. Promotional literature and managerial opinion voice a desire to restore the valleys to their natural beauty. This fits ill with a concern to retain reminders of the industry which shaped the history of the area, and attempts to reconcile these tensions have resulted in a limited vision which has been highly selective of heritage resources, considering general historical themes rather than actual material traces.

Coupled with the desire to establish a heritage project as a major income raiser, this has effectively drawn a tight boundary round a 'heritage' site set in the middle of ambitious redevelopment and landscaping programmes. One of the ironies of the concept is that it proposes to reconstruct a village as if in the 1920s, but leaves problems of conserving the landscape that survives (and as built up over time) unresolved. The register of Listed Buildings offered little guidance to local planners, since it includes very few buildings in the area, and excludes many which were felt to have strong local value. Because of the fragmented and dispersed nature of the settlement pattern, it was not considered appropriate to extend any protection to the area as a whole so there is no conservation area. This means that attempts to manage the ordinary landscape beyond the pay boundary are fraught with difficulties.

In this case, a notion of heritage has been exploited as the solution for another problem (economic decline), and there is little detailed understanding of the history and character of the area. Resources have been appraised according to generalised historical themes, and landscape features identified to illustrate, rather than generate, these interpretive ideas.

In the Rhondda, 'heritage' has been consigned to a purpose-designed park, and only poorly informs the wider planning for the area. This problem arises at least in part from the inadequacy of current thinking about heritage in the planning process – in this case, it is seen largely as an economic opportunity, and not as a general management responsibility. The heritage park programme would like to extend an involvement in the wider issues of area management, and seeks to be consulted on development control outside its boundaries. Its project officer believes that there is progress towards a more generally conservation-oriented approach in planning, but it is a slow process, and its own interpretation of the local heritage does little to encourage the detailed appraisal which a more integrated approach would require.

A similar concern to draw firm pay boundaries round heritage resources at the expense of the wider landscape context has also beset smaller projects. At Swannington in the North West Leicestershire Coalfield, a local group has been working to ensure the conservation of a landscape which graphically illustrates a sequence of mining history from bell-pits in the seventeenth century towards progressively more sophisticated attempts to extract coal from deeper and deeper seams. Traces from each generation of endeavour are clearly stamped upon the landscape, as the geographical focus shifted with each new generation. In parallel to this developing technology of coal extraction, the evolution of settlement from scattered hamlets associated with by-employment to small but fully urban settlements established during the nineteenth century is also visible, and the landscape is also marked by a rich sequence of transport technologies associated with the moving of coal since the seventeenth century.

Local interest groups had gone a long way towards the identification of landscape resources, and their interpretation. They hoped to restore certain components of the landscape, ranging from the remains of a windmill to an early inclined plane, and wanted to restore access to old rights of way. They also sought to guarantee the long-term protection of fragile archaeological remains by taking them into direct ownership (see further discussion in chapter 3).

However, planning policies for the area did not support this kind of approach: the landscape features were apparently too dispersed to constitute an adequate basis for area protection, while a long history of adaptation and major structural change to individual buildings, exacerbated by current restrictions on settlement policy, reduced their apparent value for protection: and Listing, with its tight system of controls, was perhaps inappropriate for these kinds of building anyway.

The historical traces in this landscape ranged from settlement morphologies or individual buildings, to the archaeological scars of bell-pits, inclined planes and tramways. There was no system of evaluation, let alone of protection, which could simultaneously address these very different kinds of resource. When the interest of county and district administrations was aroused for the heritage of the area, it was channelled into a limited site in response to the closure of the last mine in the area. Concern for local economic renewal linked with the need to find a solution for derelict land led to the creation of a museum which could interpret the history of the area from within definite pay boundaries, but which would effectively channel resources away from the earlier scheme.

The exploitation of industrial heritage as a major visitor attraction/public relations tool can lead to the serious neglect or compromise of resources which are not within a pay boundary. In the recently opened 'Cadbury World' at Bournville, United Kingdom, the history of chocolate and the establishment of a garden village is told in a purpose-built quasi-industrial shed sited on the factory complex. Meanwhile, restructuring of the industry on the site has led to the abandonment or demolition of a number of the original factory buildings. A superficial commitment to interpret the surrounding landscape has seen the introduction of large and intrusive interpretive panels which serve as much to advertise the main event as they do to explain their environment. Major local buildings of undoubted historical and even architectural interest which do not suit the present purposes of the company are cynically ignored. The scheme points up the necessity to ensure that heritage projects are firmly integrated with the wider ramifications of local planning, even if this means co-operation between public and private agencies. Otherwise there is a serious risk that the heritage resources themselves will be compromised.

Adaptive re-use

An alliance of economic renewal with a conservation ethic may foster the adaptive re-use of redundant buildings. Given that many industrial buildings are only accorded value as heritage on becoming redundant, this would seem to offer an important opportunity to salvage at least something of their history. But many schemes for the adaptive re-use of individual buildings, apparently motivated by a concern for conservation, are only superficially responsive to the traces of industrial culture in its many aspects. Emphasis has often instead focused on certain visual qualities of industrial buildings. In a recent plea aimed primarily at developers, architects and local authorities, the organisation SAVE Britain's Heritage concentrates its attention on mills, warehouses, breweries and maltings – buildings with some architectural pretension, in settings of 'unexpected potential' (Binney, Machin and Powell 1990).

The analysis of particular buildings is almost exclusively focused on the external architectural qualities of the structure, with little reference to its previous function, and there are none other than aesthetic criteria to determine the extent of alteration which might be permitted in a new use project. But the industrial archaeologist might think that the addition of a pediment to a simple railway warehouse involved excessive compromise of its character.

Stress is also laid on the modification of the sites and surroundings of industrial buildings, tidying up and redesigning. The creation of water gardens from the water-power system of a Derbyshire textile mill, with the intention of 'wholly

2 (a) & (b) Cressbrook Mill, Derbyshire, UK: plans for adaptive re-use would demolish the weaving sheds in favour of a French-style water garden

transforming its surroundings', and the demolition of the weaving sheds, might again seem to compromise too much. It is the classical architecture of the mill, rather than its industrial purpose, which has provided the focus for a scheme like this, creating something which is more reminiscent of a French chateau than a former textile mill. Whatever else it might be, this scheme is not adequate as management of industrial heritage (Binney, Machin and Powell 1990).

Assessments of this kind are intended to create an interest in building types which may otherwise be overlooked by developers. There is a place for recognition of the superficial visual qualities of an industrial building, its role as landmark in a locality. But it is vital that the different possible registers of value are clearly distinguished, and related through to policy options. Had a more thorough evaluation of the building's worth and potential, a more detailed appraisal of its history, function and local worth, been carried out, different parameters both for acceptable new uses and for acceptable standards of design might have been suggested.

At the very least, such an appraisal would have been able to identify interpretive strategies which could compensate for what loss of character was unavoidable. There might for example be some account of the detailed operation of the whole site and its interdependencies, some reference to the function of particular components of the site, and an attempt to define its value according to criteria derived from this analysis. While literal retention of a building may not be viable, it is only when the reasons for the interest of a site or building have been clearly defined that it is possible to look for appropriate new uses, identifying ways in which they can be accommodated with least damage (Hume 1985; Putkonen 1984: 101–3; Roth 1984: 109–13).

It must be acknowledged that there are problems associated with the re-use of industrial buildings. Problems of size and scale tend to limit the possibilities of re-use. Run-down industrial areas have a bad press. How this can be reversed, and how people can be persuaded of the value of a new scheme, are the critical issues. The SAVE approach is to play down the industrial character of the buildings, and especially of their surroundings, but good practice elsewhere has shown that it is possible to introduce new functions without compromising the general character of industrial buildings. Textile mills have been re-used as shopping malls and offices while still presented as industrial buildings. Certain small new industries may even benefit from the low costs of minimal adaptation.

3 (a) & (b) A scheme for the re-use of gas-holders in Vienna includes a commitment to public access, interpretation and conservation of technical equipment (Photos: Michael Oberer, Manfred Wedhorn)

In Vienna, the monumental architecture and spectacular land-mark qualities of four gas-holders made their Listing relatively easy; their flexible internal space made adaptation to new uses relatively straightforward. Nevertheless, rehabilitation plans proceeded hand in hand with extensive research which resulted in an exhibition on the history of municipal works and services. The challenge for adaptation was to find a use which would enable interpretation and make the technology visible, and it was decided that one of the holders should be used as exhibition space. This assured the possibility of public access, and the use of a de-mountable internal structure did not interfere with the integrity of the technical equipment.

At Norberg in Sweden, the re-use of a pithead winding house as a theatre acknowledges the symbolic value of the tower – a greater landmark on the mind's eye than the church tower – and exploits its space and acoustic, incorporating extant machinery as sets, and sometimes using its local value as heritage as a point of departure in the creation of drama. The theatre provides instant use irrespective of long-term viability – many buildings are lost through irreversible decay for want of an immediate use, so that in itself is important; in Norberg, there are no strong competing uses for the site, so maintaining the structure is not necessarily costing other significant opportunities; the structure is robust enough not to require substantial immediate maintenance; use as theatre exploits the structural characteristics of the building with minimal alteration, and may help focus attention on its plight; the arrangement is an example of a well-developed Scan-dinavian tradition of partnership between a community and a voluntary group which may only use a building on a part-time basis; part-time and seasonal use reduces the necessity for the introduction of amenities which could detract from the characteristics of the site.

However, there remain questions over the long-term viability of such a scheme: how long can the present use of the building continue, what maintenance costs are likely to arise, and how can these be financed? Full-blown adaptive re-use, on the other hand, would require substantial investment which a part-time and seasonal theatre company could not justify – this might anyway detract from the dramatic interior spatial qualities which it is able to exploit at present. Whereas in Vienna it was possible to consider new uses which involved the investment of moderate amounts of money, such a course is not really open in Norberg, and alternative support systems capable of maintaining sites such as this one may have to be explored.

4 (a) & (b) A pithead winding tower in Norberg, Sweden, is the temporary home of a theatre company

The Industrial Heritage

Urban renewal

Appeals to a notion of heritage have successfully informed a number of urban renewal and regeneration programmes. In Oslo, the Akerselva project has worked to enhance the amenity value of a heavily used valley with a long industrial history. A mix of redundant and ongoing industry had produced a heavily polluted environment in an area which also had a high housing density. A long history of special planning culminated in the formation of the Aker River Environmental Park in 1987. It seeks a comprehensive planning approach treating the river valley as a cultural unit with its own character. While it distinguishes between areas of high heritage value and those where improvement or development may be permissible, it establishes a coherent framework for the management of the whole valley, integrating its consideration of heritage firmly into existing and projected patterns of use.

The Environmental Park, which is a joint venture of the Ministry of Environment and the city government, lays down guidelines for new development and general environmental management as well as the preservation of heritage resources. It recognises that in an area with a long industrial history, surviving industries can represent an important link with the past, and seeks to encourage the establishment of small industries in the area, while defining standards for their development. It has also introduced new uses for old industrial buildings, encouraged the restoration, maintenance and appropriate development of buildings in use, and renovated old housing stock. The river banks themselves have been greened, and although there has been extensive clearance, and some over-design in adaptive re-use, the scheme has retained vitality through mixed use, and has also introduced interpretive material to dramatise the history of the area (Bettum 1989: 46–51).

The Akerselva project is a locally focused scheme which aims to sustain an area while many of its industrial users are still in place. Heritage-led regeneration has also been aimed at wider markets where a substantially new economic base has been necessary. The dramatic change in the fortunes of Lowell, Mass. (see chapter 2) was founded on a commitment to the conservation and exploitation of its heritage (Falk 1987: 148–52). In the United Kingdom, the flagship project has been the Calderdale Inheritance programme which was adopted as a ten-year programme in 1985 by the borough council and the Civic Trust and re-launched as the Calderdale Fair Shares programme in 1988. It has mobilised public and private

5 The Aker River project in Oslo:
(a) the landscape of the falls

(b) rehabilitation of factories as offices

(c) conservation, re-use and new building

funding in an ambitious programme of conservation and regeneration. It is argued that industrial heritage is the town's best asset which can be used to attract investment as well as tourism (Lockwood 1988: 5–7; Patten, Whelan and Dixon 1989: 81–90).

The strategic plan of the Akerselva project contrasts with the more faltering approach to regeneration work exhibited in the Swedish city of Norrköping. The complex working riverscape of Motala Falls is the product of a long history of exploitation of the falls as motive power especially for the textile and paper-making industries. With the closure of many of the mills, there have been problems in securing an economic future for the town, as well as in defining a role for the derelict landscape, marked by a local struggle to recognise the area as worthy of preservation.

Now, although very few buildings are legally protected, the municipality has a commitment to conservation, backed up by detailed inventory work (Sylvan et al. 1984), and is initiating a major programme of work in the area and introducing new uses for industrial buildings. Assessment of appropriate treatment rests heavily on visual elements, such as lines of sight and river frontages. The use of conservation as one component in a general policy of renewal has inevitably led to compromises, and the loss of some buildings considered to be of some importance.

The large Holmans Bruk paper mill site, for example, is now in the hands of a foreign conglomerate after a merger, and no longer used for its original purpose. It has been agreed that it is important to open up this site for public access while protecting key buildings along the south bank of the river. The municipality hopes to take one large building as a concert hall and training centre for musicians, although it faces serious cost constraints. Another building is designated as a company museum, and the town museum may also expand into buildings in the area. Music and theatre groups may use the engine house and machine hall, though this might be partially demolished to create riverside open space. Other buildings further back from the river will be demolished to make way for new housing. Yet other industrial buildings will find new commercial, institutional and residential use.

These proposals lay the basis of a plan which would enhance cultural and amenity resources for the city, serving at the same time to monumentalise and dramatise the industrial landscape. The scheme will maintain a sense of the industrial landscape, while reversing several hundred years of private

(d) rehabilitation of workers' housing

(e) factory units refitted for new uses

ownership to exploit the site as a public resource. Yet even here, conservation cannot deliver an adequate interpretation of the industrial landscape – an integrated site loses its coherence when divided up for new uses, and if buildings are protected largely because of their contribution to the landscape, their wider histories of use will not necessarily be visible. There is a need for integrated strategies to compensate for what conservation cannot itself deliver. In Norrköping, the museum has played an important role, not only in leading conservation campaigns and in providing the knowledge to support them, but also in offering an interpretation of the urban history which begins to provide a complement to the conservation programmes undertaken by other agencies.

Defining an agenda

Existing structures for the representation of heritage through conservation planning provide an inadequate basis for an understanding of the complexities of past industrial cultures, while the coupling of heritage with conservation leaves out other aspects of heritage such as the histories of activity and use, and the contemporary landscape and culture. Divided structures of administration do nothing to promote integrated approaches to the assessment of resources, and it is often down to the work of a few individuals to ensure that some integrated strategy is actually instigated.

If conservation planning is to play its full part in the management of industrial heritage resources, definition and implementation of policy must fulfil the following criteria:

1. Adoption of systems of appraisal which are formulated specifically to deal with industrial traces, and not imported from other areas such as architectural history.

2. Thorough and detailed resource assessment or auditing: many of the weaknesses in existing conservation planning stem from a rigid and specialised system of appraisal which is unable to acknowledge value according to other registers. Inadequate intensive and extensive knowledge leads to poor decisions about what and how to conserve. A clear awareness of why conservation is desirable may form a basis for the determination of a more detailed heritage strategy, including documentation, recording and complementary interpretation programmes.

6 Motala Falls, Norrköping,
Sweden:
(a) 'German' wool spinning
mills disused in 1986 . . .

(b) being restored in 1989

(c) The 'Flat Iron': former
spinning mill acquired for
Museum of Work

3. Integrated planning for conservation, enabling all types of resource (building, site, landscape) to be assessed with an awareness of the relationships between them.

4. Flexibility in the administration of conservation – it should be integrated as a general commitment alongside the other functions of local planning, and not hived off as a specialist function.

5. Collaboration with other agencies of heritage management in an integrated strategy bringing together the work of planning with that carried out by museums and other agencies. While buildings, sites and landscapes are important, they may also constitute what Fritz Ten Hallers has termed a 'one-dimensional heritage' (Ten Hallers 1985: 1). Conservation, even literal preservation, is not capable of registering all the possible histories of a building or site.

Industrial heritage in the museum

'A vast tomb in which the exhibits are lined up like the embalmed corpses of the catacombs – still alive only in the eyes of the scientist, the archaeologist and the historian, but dead in the eyes of the common people' (Forsslund 1914; quoted in Rehnberg and Sörenson 1987).

By tradition, museums collect for display and edification. They have done so in the service of scientific enquiry, the preservation of treasures or pride in achievement. Their collections have been put together according to various paradigms – assembling cabinets of curiosity, arranging Darwinian taxonomies, making representations of aesthetic codes. Treatment meted out to collections in interpretation has ranged across the encyclopaedic, the narrative and the anecdotal or kaleidoscopic.

Organising knowledge

Museums have carried out these functions in the framework of a number of disciplines: science and technology, art, archaeology, antiquarianism, historical, ethnographic and folk-life studies. These disciplines have spawned separate departments or even separate museums, different disciplines matched against different collections. Even where the subject of a museum is multidisciplinary in scope, its interpretation has typically been channelled through limiting frames of reference.

Museums purporting to interpret an urban history, for example, may in practice only deliver a history of art or artefact: the museum of the history of Paris (The Musée Carnavalet) draws good interpretation of topographical and political history from what is largely a fine and decorative arts collection. But lacking a collecting policy which would seek wider representation of the history of the city, it depicts Paris as a bourgeois landscape. Confusion over whether the subject of the museum is an interpretive perspective (the history of the city), or a type of collection (paintings and drawings), acts as a limit on its value.

In several countries a strong tradition of public museums has elevated professional curatorship to a significant degree, although a hands-on self-help approach has characterised the organisation of industrial heritage. The strength of this professionalism has set high standards of conservation, interpretation and scholarship – it has also defined a particular pattern of relationships between museums and their public (Jenkinson 1989: 141–3).

This public is constituted differently in museums with different organisational bases. Nominally public museums may in fact have a more restricted legitimate public than some nominally private museums which have taken commercial marketing advice to improve visitor income. But both may treat their public as consumers, of either education or entertainment. It is only in the smaller institutions growing up from the concerns of local historical societies, or the community museums of northern Europe, built up around enthusiasm and voluntary support, that significant redefinitions of the relationship between professional and public have been formulated.

The heritage of industrial culture has fitted uneasily into this inheritance. Local history museums and collections have often been biased towards pre-industrial, craft-based societies – a social and economic order perceived to be threatened by industrialisation, which has therefore tended to gain representation only as catastrophe, a final chapter of decisive and irrevocable change. The municipal museum in Norrköping in Sweden, for example, was founded in 1946 with a brief for art and cultural history, and has only gradually redefined its role to represent the industrial history of the city.

When local museums and societies have approached industry, they are likely to have done so in certain circumscribed ways. Constrained to deal with what is collectable with small means and capable of display in small compass, attention has focused on certain aspects of an industrial past rather than others.

The Industrial Heritage

Collecting together the leavings of local industrial histories assembled as icons to a common past, such museums may be limited both in their interpretive possibilities and in their ability to generate and maintain external support.

Ethnographic and folk collections have had a similar predisposition allied to an interest in the exotic, the 'other', cultivating serious study of societies bound to agriculture and the crafts. But early on, some espoused a commitment to fuller understandings of social systems which led to the establishment of open-air museums primarily based on vernacular architecture, but enriched with folk art, craft, music and dancing. The most famous of these, Skansen in Stockholm, has been an acknowledged influence in the creation of a newer generation of open-air museums with industrial societies as their subject. The panoptic scope of the ethnographic discipline, and its humanistic perspectives, have come to provide a valuable basis for studies of industrial culture.

Museums have traditionally looked away from the recent past to classical archaeological or antiquarian pasts, or to the exotic other of anthropology. But the later nineteenth century saw the establishment of a number of museums specifically devoted to science and technology. These museums have dealt with aspects of industry, but not necessarily as culture, and possibly not even as technical culture. Foundations like the Museum of Industry in Prague and many municipal industrial museums elsewhere, have defined their subject as the history and development of industry, organising their galleries as chronological catalogues of innovation, classifying major industrial processes or products, showing the scope of power generation, developments in mining, metallurgy or textile technology, or evolution in the design of the motor car, for example. In their establishment, they have been influenced by a concern to provide a particular kind of engineering training, and have brought a Darwinian progressive taxonomy to bear on collections of specialised machinery. They have also espoused a particular aesthetic of industry – gleaming machines displayed as monuments. They are typically devoted to specialist connoisseurship, constituted as experts' museums, making small concessions to the unenlightened.

The encyclopaedic classifications of the eighteenth century, and the evolutionary filiations of the nineteenth, were designed to permit comparative examination of objects according to certain classifying principles often conceived as single disciplines. Even now, many 'traditional' museums of science and industry are organised on lines which would have been broadly identifiable in the nineteenth century: galleries of motive power, assemblages of particular types of machine or particular objects. Museums were multidisciplinary institutions, but the different disciplines each knew their own place and department.

Other foundations like the Deutsches Museum in Munich have been organised according to disciplinary codes. Departmental structure is arranged less by product or process and more by organisation of knowledge. Galleries are devoted to electrical or mechanical engineering, physical and optical sciences. The Palais des Descouverts in Paris sets out to explain the principles of science, the history of their discovery and their applications.

Museums and science centres like these can provide a valuable contribution to understandings of national industrial and technological development, with the disciplines and systems of knowledge that sustain it. The generalised and abstract nature of their discourse means that they are appropriately established as centres of regional or national expertise. But their progressive and synoptic range leaves little space for a local dimension, and cannot deal with geographical relationships or with those phases and types of development assumed to have been left behind by the march of progress, in reality perhaps still struggling to survive. They offer, in other words, a poor geographical scope, and only a limited historical perspective.

The South Kensington Museums complex in London owed its origins to trade exhibitions and was set up primarily to celebrate commerce. Eventual separation into Science and Decorative Arts museums made a decisive break between process and product, products coming to be seen as decorative arts, themselves anti-industrial. In Sweden, the Nordiska Museum was set up to be **the** museum of Nordic culture, but in its celebration of a pre-industrial folk culture it risked becoming increasingly anachronistic in an industrialising society without a profound change of emphasis.

In so far as industry was recognised here at the outset, it was only as craft, although 'dirty' industry was admitted in the 1930s under the influence of an ethnographer who collected workers' memories as a response to change, co-operating in the process with trade unions. There has been a division of responsibility whereby the Technical Museum deals with heavy industries, the Nordiska Museum with crafts and guilds, certainly as far as the collection of objects is concerned.

The Industrial Heritage

However, ethnographers on the staff of the Nordiska Museum have become increasingly involved with documenting recent or contemporary industry through interviews and photographs, since this dimension of industrial experience has never been seen as an appropriate subject for the Technical Museum. Different disciplines of enquiry have therefore been brought to bear on different industries and different periods of industrial history. These distinctions would not seem to be justified by differences in the constitution of the industries, their societies and the evidences which are available for them, but they do reflect the different constitutions of the museums themselves.

In the past, municipal museums have often hived off industry into separate museums or separate departments (Birmingham, Manchester, for example), arguing that this division is matched by the diverse specialist interests of their audiences. But such museum services have within their purview many more of the elements that could contribute to a fuller representation of industrial culture than specialised technical museums. They could therefore provide a basis for the rearrangement and reinterpretation of collections, breaking down old specialisms in a representation of industrial culture in its wider aspects, perhaps engaging with new audiences in the process.

Some museums have attempted this restructuring. The Museum of London, for example, has adopted a synoptic and kaleidoscopic view of urban life arranged by period rather than by category of artefact. Norrköping Museum takes a similar approach, balancing chronological with thematic perspectives, but bringing together different types of material and artefact in the representation of the city's history. An alternative approach advocated by some museologists would leave the traditional departmental structures intact, and route people through with information and study material, encouraging them to use the museum as a store-house of possibilities rather than having the themes and structures of knowledge predetermined.

The central problem which institutions like these are beginning to address is that there is small means at present to organise an integrated study of industrial societies through museums. Such a project would place artefact study in an important if not central position, but in relation to other cultural studies. But the knowledge base which is available to museums attempting to work in this area is limited and divided, bedevilled by collecting which has not been conceived to systematically represent a cultural matrix, and the fixity of traditional ways of looking at artefacts which may consider only narrow registers of significance. The categories used to structure museum functions may not be amenable to the initiation of such a project, hemmed in by entrenched departmental divisions and narrowly defined specialisms. Both archaeology and ethnography function as disciplines attempting the interpretation of a whole social order, but this synthetic approach is all-too rarely applied to industrial societies and, certainly in the case of archaeology, is hampered by the poverty of interpretation offered in museums which are often simply catalogues of artefacts assembled thematically.

Neither are attempts to revitalise the cultural role of museum collections helped by the underdeveloped state of material cultural studies in most branches of historical studies. Historical studies have typically been constructed as narratives, only sometimes departing from this into multiple linearity. Adoption of new narratives (history from below, women's history, labour history) has been able to make an important and decisive contribution to interpretation in museums. But recovering the cultural traces of objects requires their grouping in a multiplicity of contexts, using interdisciplinary perspectives. In many historical studies the multifaceted character of the sources can be comfortably subordinate to a primary theme: where the object itself is at the centre of study, its own histories, including the continuing history of its survival, the route it took to and through the museum, become of more than incidental interest (Vergo 1989: 41–59; Saumerez Smith 1989: 6–21).

New approaches

Since the early 1970s a number of new-generation museums have begun attempts to redraw the cultural heritage museological map in a way which favours a wider debate about industrial culture.

'Total environment museums' like the Ironbridge Gorge Museum have challenged the conventional boundaries between museum and environment by integrating on-site conservation and interpretation with the development of collections of artefacts ranging from industrially produced goods to whole houses, shops and workshops. In doing so, they have also stepped right outside the conventional departmental and professional structures of traditional museums, requiring traditional curatorial skills but introducing new, cross-disciplinary positions dealing with social history, and practical training in threatened skills. They have come to challenge conventional modes of display by integrating collections of industrially produced goods hitherto represented as fine art or heroic technology, with some awareness of the processes of design, production and use. It is worth remembering that the museum at Ironbridge began by making heroic representations of re-sited industrial monuments, gradually rethinking its strategy in the direction of interpretation which focused on the economic and social histories of the industrial past.

The ecomuseum movement originating in France seeks to redefine conventional organisational frameworks in its assertion that the ecomuseum is something which a power and a population make as a collaboration. The power has the experts, the facilities, and the resources, while the population brings in its own vitality, aspirations and know-how. The ecomuseum serves as a mirror to the population, permitting greater self-knowledge in the discovery of relationships to a cultural and historical landscape. In attempting to realise these ambitions, the ecomuseum redraws conventional boundaries both between the museum and the wider cultural landscape, and between professionals and public (de Varine-Bohan 1973; Scalbert Bellaigue 1981).

The French ecomuseum does not arise spontaneously from enthusiasts, but is instigated by politicians and sustained (usually) by professionals. However, it has popular culture as its object and proposes a continuing interaction. Recognising the risk that participation is offered merely as a sop to current ideologies, the ecomuseum of the region Fourmies-Trelon has been able to make effective use of its public in five main areas, ranging from decision-making through the constitution and presentation of collections, to documentation, interpretation and liaison (Camusat 1985). Similarly, the ecomuseum of the community Le Creusot-Montceau-Les-Mines attempted to engage its populace in the determination and constitution of locally oriented exhibitions, defining them, their histories and culture as part of its resource (de Varine-Bohan 1973; Scalbert Bellaigue 1981).

Transposed to the Swedish context – surprisingly in view of the strong traditions of grass-roots organisation, and the strength of ethnography as a discipline – the ecomuseum movement has lost some of its populist overtone. With its flagship, the Ecomuseum Bergslagen, it does however seek to revitalise the museum system and recapture a public by creating a 'total-environment museum' which aims to bring authentic environments to life and foster a sense of cultural identity. The museum aims to assist in the regeneration of

Industrial monuments are a focal point in Langban's new career as a holiday centre:
a) pithead gear and ore-crushing plant
b) derelict forge

the area by the development of tourism, and does so by dramatising its industrial history. In the early stages of its establishment, the museum is very dependent on the grass-roots organisations across the region, although how strong its commitment to these groups is remains to be seen. The Swedish ecomuseum draws on the vitality of these local associations in managing and interpreting a primarily archaeological heritage – unlike its French counterparts, it does not appear to see its local populations as themselves part of the heritage resource (Rehnberg and Sörenson 1987: 68–72).

Local history associations of the kind which underpin the Ecomuseum Bergslagen may be self-reflexive sustainable bodies which are not dependent on an external audience, at least initially. In the strong 'hembygdsgard' ('home' or community museum) tradition of Scandinavia and Germany, permanent exhibits – monuments, buildings and objects – may be uninterpreted, but are maintained for and by their communities, with seasonal activities primarily for a local audience. Possibly interpretation is not needed because the local significance of these things is generally recognised and does not need to be labelled. Some of these associations attempt to reach the wider audiences they may need for long-term sustainability, and a museum like that at Gnosjö in Sweden has embarked on an ambitious programme of expansion to guarantee its future at a time when local interest, know-how and commitment are perhaps waning. Similarly at Langban in Sweden, local commitment to the conservation of a mining landscape following closure of the mines in 1974 resulted in a collective project in which the village, with the support of its local council, has collaborated in preparing interpretive material, running a small museum and a programme of educational visits. It offers a practical welcome to visitors by providing ample accommodation for tourists.

In Britain, small local history museums have also taken on industrial heritage – sometimes very successfully, as exemplified in the weaving museum at Golcar and the framework knitters' shop at Ruddington (Shrimpton, Chambers, et al. 1986), but another local project faces a more uncertain fate: ambitious plans for an interpreted landscape of industrial heritage in the North West Leicestershire Coalfield grew out of an annual village festival, but have been unable either to sustain local commitment and involvement or to mobilise external support on a scale commensurate with their initial ambitions.

Industrial heritage has produced its own lively participatory project in industrial archaeology, which has grown from the

(c) pithead gear

(d) charcoal blast furnace

voluntary efforts of enthusiasts for field recording and investigation into a professional discipline. In countries where investment in heritage projects is less conspicuous than it is in Britain, the strength of these patterns of local involvement provides a very real resource for the management of heritage resources. In Flanders, for example, a small group of enthusiasts for steam engines has been active not only in the restoration and interpretation of engines, but also in persuading their owners to care for them.

Projects like these typically take as their object conventionally delineated components of heritage identified and pursued in a narrowly focused archaeological spirit. There have, however, been a number of experiments in heritage-making which have sought a greater integration of subject and object: John Greenwood, a block printer working in Kent, has carried out a project to document the work and world of the industrial block printer based on his own work in Lancashire and Kent, using oral history, manuals, patterns and blocks, and demonstrating processes live and through video (Greenwood 1990: 58–63).

A self-documentation project like this may not need external validation. But many small museums do need to create wider constituencies if they are to consolidate their achievements. Such museums may only be able to perform small things in relation to the whole potential scope of industrial heritage, but have unique cultural resources to do so. If local forms of heritage-making are to be sustained and enabled to contribute to the larger cultural project of industrial heritage management, there is a need for an integrated strategy which continues to enable these museums to function, while providing a framework of resources appropriate to industrial heritage in all its aspects. The need to address diverse audiences bringing differing cultural assumptions may be a vital part of this sustainability. It must also be founded on a full assessment of resources, taking seriously not only the traces of material culture but the lives and experience of diverse legitimate publics.

Industrial culture serves as a challenge to the heritage-making undertaken by museums in crossing specialisms and subject divisions. Because we are ourselves living within an industrial culture, it also provides a direct challenge to assumptions about the relationship between professional and public. The projects reviewed here can be placed on a matrix of 'power and population' – agency and legitimate public – and are concerned with different ways of travelling through the matrix. The care, constitution and interpretation of heritage resources are vital components of that relationship, and cannot be considered independently of it.

Both the museum tradition and the conservation-planning tradition of heritage management were developed originally to deal with an older heritage. Certain characteristics of heritage management have followed from that – the highly selective taking objects out of context, the separation of artefacts and built environment, the distinction between the creators and arrangers of collections and their consuming publics, the division of disciplines and types of collection. In working with industrial culture, heritage management needs to cross these divisions both in the interpretation of heritage and in its management as a resource.

What industrial heritage can do

2

The previous discussion began by asking what is the industrial heritage resource. We have found that the potentially significant remains of industrial civilisation are extensive, but also fragmentary. The most characteristic features have in the nature of things often been destroyed, and it is often a problem to establish a sufficient context to interpret the significance of what remains. Academic disciplines have an important contribution to make here but different disciplines have generally only taken up limited aspects of the problem, within the parameters of their current concerns; much of the most important work has been done by amateurs but without an overall framework or disciplinary development. Popular perceptions of the history of industrial civilisation have also been fragmentary; lacking an overall academic perspective, they have tended to mythologise affective (heroic or demonic or romantic) aspects of industrial culture. Those who have worked to conserve and interpret aspects of industrial heritage have thus had to orient their work in the absence of any central understanding of the nature of industrial culture or a 'map' of the growth of industrial civilisations. They have often had to work with definitions of heritage which were not designed for industrial culture and which tend to increase fragmentation.

To redress this fragmentation requires a different approach: more attention to systematic inventory and comparative evaluation, to inform a more balanced programme of documentation, collection and preservation; new synoptic interpretation of industrial culture to balance particular projects, and the targeting of research and conservation priorities. It would also benefit from conservation and curatorial strategies which are better integrated with ongoing environmental and cultural resources management.

The industrial heritage would therefore appear no mere supplicant at the table; to realise its potential requires research and innovative approaches to conservation and interpretation. But what exactly is this potential – the cultural significance of industrial heritage? As the previous discussion has suggested, the growth of an industrial heritage movement has been an important part of a general expansion and transformation of the cultural role of heritage, which has involved some new initiatives in conservation and curatorial policy. This chapter considers the causes and significance of this expansion and its implications for future uses of the industrial heritage. It finds that considerable cultural potential is being unlocked by innovative approaches, but that a new range of problems are posed thereby.

These questions cannot be considered without also asking what are the characteristics of heritage as a cultural process. For if one might say that the fragmentary remains of industrial culture get the treatment they deserve, as they have only qualified or specialised significance according to well established criteria, we are entitled to examine how such criteria are established and to what effect.

The expansion of heritage

The second half of the twentieth century has seen an enormous expansion of the phenomenon of heritage in the industrialised countries – the new initiatives discussed in the previous chapter are part of this (Hudson 1975).

There has been an expansion of what is considered a heritage resource: the number of things (artefacts, images, buildings, landscapes) accorded some form of heritage recognition and protection has increased dramatically and, more importantly, has diversified in type. Industrial monuments or the paraphernalia of everyday life in the recent past now attract interest and care alongside long-established 'jewels in the crown'.

There has also been a dramatic increase in heritage constituencies. Not only do a greater number of people take an interest in some aspect of heritage but the number of related groups, associations and charitable foundations has increased markedly. In several countries the most marked growth of constituencies has been in the area of industrial heritage.

This expansion has been accompanied by a transformation in the cultural character of heritage. There is a greater flexibility in ways of regarding and using heritage resources. The boundary around what is considered heritage has become somewhat blurred as strategies for use have broadened. Education and entertainment, conservation and regeneration, culture and commerce are no longer simply opposed. Conservation attitudes link care for heritage resources with ongoing environmental management. Public authorities enter into partnership with voluntary and commercial organisations to achieve common objectives. In several economies, heritage-related investment and trading have moved from a marginal position to attain considerable importance, linking the cultural industries, leisure and tourism, retailing and economic regeneration. Often, industrial heritage projects have been at the forefront of these developments.

Heritage, in becoming something to conjure with, has also become rather slippery; heritage phenomena often seem to have a life of their own, beyond the control of any one institution, and with rather tenuous links to any particular resource (Ousby 1990). This cultural volatility of heritage is attacked as superficial consumption of nostalgic myths, misrepresenting the past, trampling on the resource and obstructing cultural creativity. Contradictions appear, as when conservation investment which enhances apparent quality of life undermines it through attracting too much attention. In this new world, heritage management struggles to keep a grip both on its resource and on cultural purpose.

To understand the nature of this recent expansion we need to identify what causes change in the cultural role of heritage. Transformation of heritage is in part a response to recent change, but the qualities of this can only be understood by looking at the character of change.

Heritage resources may present themselves as self-evident and unchanging – but perceiving that self-evident stability depends on sharing a set of assumptions, more or less explicit, about values and orders of significance in general and the historical associations of the particular objects in question. These assumptions place the resource in a heritage and suggest a range of appropriate responses (identification, discrimination, veneration, pleasure, pride), which may be combined and elaborated in various pursuits (touring to view, seeking, collecting, conserving, showing and telling). Knowledge and awareness of the heritage resource arise in this larger matrix of value which has to do with the forging of individual and group identities; it is bound to be shaped by the processes which deal in or impinge on identities – processes which place people in relation to state power, the authority of knowledge, economies of production and consumption, and the array of communities to which real or imaginary affiliation is possible.

We have thus four kinds of heritage-making agents:

- individuals and voluntary cultural associations
- public authorities and political parties
- disciplinary and professional specialisms
- producers for consumption by others

What counts as heritage changes, therefore, not only because the potential resource is augmented or diminished by the passage of time, but because what may be done with it changes also. The designated objects which constitute the resource are doubly subject: they have significance as part of a representation which takes its order primarily from the work it does. When the parameters of that work change, the principles which constitute a heritage are redefined or broken up, and the meaning of the resource changes or is lost. Changes in the constitution of states and of the mode of political participation offered to subjects provide one set of parameters. The removal and public re-presentation of religious and aristocratic cultural property in serried ranks during the French Revolution and subsequent attempts to simulate its contexts of use after the Restoration provide particularly dramatic examples of this (Hooper-Greenhill 1989: 61–72). When subjects are to be mobilised, for example to fight, to pay, to obey the law, they are offered a symbolic representation of legitimate power, and a national heritage begins to take shape. The iconography of this heritage becomes more complex with moves towards representative democracy. One aspect of this is that power is legitimated in relation to a 'public' and this relation may be embodied in cultural institutions which codify heritage.

The distinctive roles of public sector professional heritage management thus come into being. The cultural project of public education and public participation in national sovereignty and aggrandisement which followed the French Revolution also instituted a break between the curators, monument protectors and their public – a disjuncture which has survived many subsequent changes of institutional organisation and interpretive practice. This public heritage sphere has not always been so decisively constituted in a moment of expropriation and legitimation of a new order, and the curatorial function has also been vested in philanthropic institutions of a patrician rather than a populist public (Hudson 1975).

The constitution of a heritage as distinct from the continuance of a tradition, the keeping of remembrances or the gathering of curiosities, may not require professional curatorship or state authority, but it does involve the existence of a public – for whom, if not necessarily of whom, it is constituted – its spiritual if not literal owners. Equally, there must be a knowledge which can assert that this is the heritage of that public. With this knowledge, in the name of that public, a heritage is constituted, by agents official or unofficial, voluntary or employed – things are bought, seized, moved, reworked or redefined to make this possible. This happens not only in the museum but also in the landscape.

Designation and exploitation of heritage have never, however, been brought fully under the control of official bodies or arbiters of knowledge, but have often been made to do other work. Studies of antiquarianism among the British aristocracy and landed gentry (Bann 1984; Bigmore 1990) show how such cultivation was used to gain advantage within elite circles – it was seldom the preoccupation of those unconcerned with justifying or advancing their social position. Local heritage knowledge in provincial antiquarian societies gradually grew to match the scope of its interests and social responsibilities: from family history to estate history and then developing specialisms ranging from regional topography and polity to church history or that of architecture. Gradually, personal and familial gentry histories became a heritage whose legitimate public was the antiquarian peer group but which stood for society as a whole. With publication, this complex process was offered simply as the result of discovery, shown for celebration.

Eventually, representative democracy was to bring into conflict the competing inheritances offered by different political tendencies and social interests. The invention of an aggregated 'tradition' for the political mobilisation of new peasant electorates has been well examined (Hobsbawm and Ranger 1983). The traditions of the peasantry such as they appeared in political symbolism or journalism were constructions; in order to mobilise people from different districts they deployed symbolic objects, stories and morals to represent 'peasant' life in a way that was recognisable as 'real' but conformed to no literal reality; through reference to this hypothetical 'tradition' new relations of political allegiance were instituted – and constrained the freedom of action of politicians. Comparable phenomena can be observed in the history of the 'labour movement'.

In the current expansion of heritage the character of these kinds of public address has been questioned. The ideas of 'county antiquarianism', 'peasant tradition' or 'labour movement' offer a ready-made heritage which implies shared future commitments. With the passage of time, their artifice has become evident and more likely to be experienced as constraining than as enabling. This usually arises from some sense that the heritage presented is socially circumscribed, which is often easy to support. The address may be limited by presupposed knowledge, sometimes by unfamiliar or abstract ways of thought and presentation, by discordant questions or idealisations, as well as simply an absence of treatment. The authority of ordered discourse or impressive iconography is not enough to prevent the question: whose history?

Such questioning of who is the legitimate public whose heritage is codified and represented poses problems for all heritage managers and especially for those whose job it is to select and present the official heritage resource. Didacticism has been the basis upon which public collecting and display exerted their authority over the preoccupations and practices of the amateur antiquary. In the museum which set out to serve a legitimate public, an educational programme held pride of place in determining what was accorded the honour of collection and exhibition, just as it disciplined the visitors. As an example we may take the Food Museum established in South Kensington, London, in the latter part of the nineteenth century, with the aim of teaching the working public the rudiments of nutrition; food substances were the objects on display, but the heritage unveiled was the power of the new science of chemistry over the array of nature's produce which British trade and Imperial dominion had put at the disposal of the metropolis.

That effect of the expansion and transformation of heritage can be seen by comparing the Food Museum with the Science Museum's 1989 'Food for Thought' Exhibition. Although the new gallery also purports to show the influence of science and technology on food, these instruments appear only through the benign omnipresence of the food processing and distributing industry. What is most significant about the display, however, is the way this vast apparatus of rationalised processes, livelihoods and products offers itself for public encounter. The *raison d'être* of science and industry – our inheritance – is presented as serving the desires of the consumer, but this is no expert proclamation addressed to an impersonal public; 'Food for Thought' addresses its visitors as consumers and attempts to lay out its wares in bite-size morsels corresponding to their anticipated tastes and predilections (Patrick 1990). This disingenuous strategy makes it difficult for the visitor to establish a standpoint from which to assess either food consumption or the food industry. But then the master narratives of earlier public discourse also prevented such a standpoint.

'Food for Thought' shows how industrial progress has fed the expansion of heritage. The display accurately depicts a world of technologically rationalised industry in which livelihoods arising in complexes of impersonal processes are fulfilled through choosing among the 'goods' these processes produce. People whose interdependence with each other is defined in a limited and abstract way have to produce the rest of an identity and the considerable resources with which to do so – in the sphere of 'leisure' and 'consumption'. The choices resulting from these desires may then be taken back into the productive system as demand for goods.

The communications industries have greatly expanded to provide cultural offerings of all sorts to fill the time and space once structured by contextual circumstances. The rapid circulation of cultural forms out of context by such media has been the subject of much discussion, and has in itself been held responsible for the erosion of meaning, the condition of post-modernity, etc., and they have undoubtedly been important, not least in enormously extending access to information and images of different ways of life, and thus increasing the ways in which, on one level at least, people can build their own culture (Harvey 1990).

To explain the transformation which is taking place in heritage culture, however, it is necessary to do more than explain access to new cultural resources. One must account for why and how these resources are used. Here, the relatively inconsequential nature of all contextual circumstances alongside the powerful logic of the technostructure is the central point linking a number of well-documented phenomena which bear on the demand for heritage:

■ the growing importance of leisure learning and a demand for cultural development in leisure of which a large part is heritage related – especially among social groups involved in the technostructure – yet at the same time a resistance to didacticism and a sceptical approach to official culture
■ an interest in ordinary things and aspects of life which would have been ruled out in a period when there was greater formality in relations between people – rather than the relations between people being formalised in the technostructure
■ the enormous interest in local heritage especially shown among those who have chosen to live in an area, rather than long-established inhabitants
■ the special interest shown in conservation in response to

recent change and loss of circumstantial context – especially in the landscape but also in relation to working practices and ways of life

Some commentators have almost entirely attributed the growth of heritage culture to a sense of loss and discontinuity, either as a positive reaction, or negatively, as a myopic and cowardly nostalgia (for example, Hewison 1987). One needs, however, to go beyond the simple fact of change or the extent or rate of change – which, in terms of livelihoods, domestic circumstances, or landscape, has often been greater recently than ever before – to the character of change and that of the resulting situation, considered from the points of view of cultural needs and resources. While it is certainly true that heritage managers must think about providing resources which will help people accommodate change, they have also to think about the reasons behind the continuing demand for heritage which is currently arising and likely to increase, not tied simply to the response to particular transitions.

It is necessary to focus clearly on these essential issues to avoid being distracted by polemics. As the previous chapter suggested, we are in a time of transition in heritage management in which paradigms clash. Defenders of the established paradigm which links univocal public address informed by expert knowledge with strict and consolidated hierarchies of value, and which wish to firmly separate, and even oppose, culture and commerce, have polemicised against aspects of the expansion of heritage – against the inclusion of new objects in the resource, against involving new constituencies, against experiment in extending the modes of involvement, mixing entertainment and education for example. Industrial heritage projects and even the idea of an industrial heritage have often been on the receiving end of such attacks.

Some of this debate has gone beyond alternatives in the practice of heritage management to take the public consumption of heritage representations as a sign of cultural decadence. Celebrated and popular industrial open-air museums have featured in a polemic by a British cultural critic against the 'heritage industry' (Hewison 1987; West 1988: 36–62). While the critics raise some interesting points, their aim is manifestly not to improve interpretive practice. They regard representations of defunct industry, somewhat tidied and spruced up, being offered to a paying public for leisured contemplation, as pathological. They implicitly accept an idea of heritage, and of truth to history, but they have difficulty accepting the demand by large numbers of people for a more or less casual access to such heritage resources on their own terms, to make of them what they will. This attitude has been characterised as 'sneering at the theme parks' (Wright and Putnam 1989). What appears as a progressive critique of the excesses of consumerism refuses to recognise characteristic cultural needs of large numbers of people and attempts to make heritage resources accessible to them; the implicit nostalgia for heritage as it used to be, which does not confuse the orienting categories mentioned above, cannot be realistically offered as an alternative heritage politics – so it amounts to disdain, to sneering at people who are 'taken in'.

Instead it would be more helpful to consider why 'heritages' are increasingly taking the shape required to be consumed as cultural products. They need not be literally bought, but discretionary identity-making and affiliation are the starting points, and the consuming paradigm is the dominant mode of satisfying needs. In heritage culture the dominance of this mode is evident in its wide use in relating to publics. While it is possible to find champions of voluntarism, public service or disciplinary education as preferred modes for constituting publics, most have accepted some of the major premises of the consumption model: specifically, they accept, in a way analogous to modern advertising, that address seeks to win public support on the basis of individual choice and its appeal has to start from where it imagines the recipient to be and to make the appeal in accordance with supposed motivations.

Such patterns are not entirely new. Individual motives have long been a starting point for the collecting and interpreting of heritage resources, and the long and intriguing history of amateur antiquarianism attests to this. Further, that such interest has long been served by commerce is attested by the very early development of literary and other forms of cultural tourism (Ousby 1990) which have established some of what later became prominent motifs in stereotypes of national heritage. In long-established areas of heritage culture there is a complementary and dialectical relationship between voluntary principle in heritage-making and that of consumption. This has also been a constructive dialectic between breadth of access and depth of involvement: the attempt to set up the former as the enemy of the latter (the popularisation problematic) is shortsighted; it isolates particular products for criticism rather than looking at culture-building over a period of time. In neglecting this, contemporary critiques of consumption are unduly pessimistic: the recovery of individual agency by the alienated social subject is possible and can be shown to happen for example in home-making, by a process of alteration and re-appropriation (Putnam and Newton 1990).

The recent expansion of heritage has been one of depth as well as breadth. The depth has been provided not only by official, academic and amateur specialists, but by people furnishing their lives. Such personal and familial culture-building has many motives and interrelated aspects: recognisable heritage concerns may on the one hand be connected to shared concerns about environment, community and the public realm, while on the other they blend into matters of taste and discrimination which have more to do with personalisation and social positioning. Because of the dynamics of taste, aspects of heritage culture can acquire and lose fashionability with particular social groups, and pass in and out of favour altogether. Sociological study has shown that certain groups will surround themselves with tokens of certified cultural or economic value while others prefer to demonstrate their knowledge of cultural results or processes. Recognisable types of collector, aesthete or connoisseur are reproduced (Bourdieu 1984). The uneven historical taste for classicism and sometimes related interests in Graeco-Roman antiquity and other period styles shows an interaction between taste formation of social groups and, sometimes, a more public and overtly political dimension of heritage culture.

As cultural objects and symbols so move in the field of tastes, they are inevitably transformed. Any preservation of aspects of ordinary manual work of the recent past creates something new, but the particular kind of 'museum effect' which results depends on a range of practical interpretive choices and the preoccupations of the using public(s). Those whose lives are depicted may be glad of recognition or critical of glamorised representations, while their children, no longer manual workers but members of technical or service classes, perceive this as their 'heritage' through an aesthetic rooted in their new habits and circumstances of life.

The map of heritage culture – what it contains, who is involved, their needs and purposes, institutional forms, etc. – has thus become extremely complex. There are more objects, more constituencies, more providers and arrangers of resources. It is no longer realistic to try to find one point – either within or without this complex – from which to be able to judge what the heritage resource should be, or one legitimate public which can be addressed in one particular way about it. Nor, however, can heritage management meet the diverse expectations of these publics simultaneously. Total history is a chimera even for the historians. There is however a great need for perspective on what are the key problems and points of development in the cultural role of heritage, which arise at the intersection of the different currents involved.

One of these, as discussed in chapter 1, is the interface between the professional heritage managers and the academy. The relationship between research, education, conservation and curatorship has been drawn together in several countries under the aegis of the state. But nowhere does it constitute a unified system. As the scope of the potential resource expands and the demands of different constituencies multiply and compete, heritage managers need help to bolster their knowledge of the resource which is the guarantee of its integrity and their professionalism. But the disciplines of the academy are not oriented to recognise, much less provide, the basis for an integrated knowledge of industrial civilisation that could be used in managing the expanded heritage. Unless heritage managers intervene in the academy to convene and stimulate interdisciplinary studies around an agenda of integrated assessment of cultural resources, to which they as specialists can also contribute, building and interpreting the resource must continue in the half-light.

Another interface is that between the voluntary movement and those who provide commodities for individual consumption. On one level, as we have pointed out, this is a symbiotic relationship of an unplannable market character. But there are antagonistic elements which threaten to destroy the balance. Producers want to add volume or value to their products, but if they do this in a way that removes or constrains the possibility of developing agency and depth of involvement then they undermine the development potential of their own business; this has happened to many companies which have got bound up in a volume leisure paradigm and have neglected the importance of cultural development and enrichment. The organised voluntary sector needs to attend to ways that interested individuals can extend their knowledge and interest through involvement, as well as being attentive to using and learning from commercial professionalism.

Perhaps the most important interface, however, is that between the public didactic–academic nexus on the one hand and the consumption–voluntary nexus on the other. It is sometimes suggested that passive consumerism or amateur enthusiasm are major threats to heritage interpretation and conservation. There is no doubt that public professionals have an important regulating and stabilising role to play in heritage culture. But there is a real danger that they will not be able to play this role effectively through failing to find a way to relate to new heritage constituencies; for all that is said about consumerism, the subject of today's expanded heritage culture is not only more numerous but also more active than the public which most public heritage institutions are used to address. The authority of the state or of knowledge must relate to this consuming–creating subject; education can no longer be neatly opposed to entertainment.

The drawing of everyone into a kind of perpetual education is connected with a polarisation around education/self-investment versus entertainment/self-gratification, but the latter is equally programmed and perhaps more monolithically so. It is in fact through a kind of leisure learning – pleasurable self-improvement – that the heritage phenomenon of the late twentieth century has expanded (in a situation of shifting co-ordinates, but not necessarily motivated by an urgent sense of loss or anxious quest for identity). This pleasurable self-enrichment, stigmatised as superficial by the critics mentioned above, embraces a quest for substance which the public and academic authorities could help meet if they accepted the challenge which consumer and voluntary initiatives present to established didactic strategies. Knowledge has not become obsolete, but new routes of exploration need to be defined. Nor has the public dimension of cultural process become any less important.

Expanded heritage culture can occupy an important place in contemporary political structures, which must be responsive to aggregate will while also overseeing the infrastructure of progress. To realise the full extent of this potential public significance, heritage culture must:

- show cognisance of important changes that are taking place and register awareness of expressed values; it may also become involved in promulgating values through 'recognition' of patrimony, while displaying its comprehensive healing command of change
- have a cultural dimension which can recognise difference, for example of race, generation or gender, and its implications
- construct meanings around place, and regulate disadvantage, so dealing with the geographical parameters of cultural identity
- ask whether its definition of the legitimate public excludes others or makes overlap possible: how can self-consciousness in this area be helpful in a strategy for widening its address?

There are pitfalls for public institutions as they approach a more diverse cultural initiative. For curatorial institutions, there is a danger of attempting to remedy past omissions by creating an overlooked heritage in a form which remains external, inappropriate to its intended constituency; a fatal flaw which some have attempted to remedy by participation (for example in Springburn Community Museum or Fourmies Ecomuseum: see chapters 4 and 5).

If heritage is to belong to people instead of being held out to them or administered for them, then they have to be able to share the moment around which this heritage is integrated, using results that are passed to them by commerce, cultural institutions and state educational authorities. Recognition of this has also been the starting point for much recent work in urban regeneration:

> Heritage is not just for toffs – it is not just high architecture and great houses. Most of us live in humbler surroundings. 'Everyday heritage' gives us our sense of place – continuity – stability. Our surroundings are a focus of identity. ... The future of everyday heritage will be determined by the decisions and resources of individual people – their enthusiasm for town life rather than moving to cottages in the country, their readiness to take on older houses, to look after them sensitively and well, their imagination in finding new uses for old buildings. Heritage depends on its valuation by people. (Bottomley 1989)

So established forms of heritage are transfigured. The subjects change as well as the objects held out for their contemplation or recognition. And as more can choose – and have more reason to choose – their own objects of identification, then the question of heritage management arises. It is a question not merely of more, more recent, more workaday, resources being admitted to a pantheon, nor even of more or different uses, resonances, of heritage phenomena, but of a much greater number of subjects engaged in cultural processes centred on heritage – neither just constituting their own object worlds nor being the passive recipients of some standardised identity, but being engaged in connected processes as choosing, determinate subjects.

Realising the cultural potential of industrial heritage

The industrial heritage resource that is recognised today has been built up over a considerable time by a complex of different sorts of interests. The interest of industrial heritage as history is relatively recent, however – only extensive in the last generation. The greater part of the technological and product collections until this time had been initially acquired because of their technological interest – models of mining machinery in the cabinets of princes, recording and public display of techniques and science and technology for didactic purposes, remains of expositions of products of diverse sorts, family transmission of the personal effects of trade or business. The conservation of redundant industrial buildings or monuments was hardly thought of. This means that much of the recognised industrial heritage resource as well as the potential one is a kind of scrapheap; the reasons why it was assembled are often as important or more important a resource than the artefacts themselves.

The historical awareness of industrial heritage has several roots. The obsolescence of collections acquired for contemporary purposes became evidence of progress, and, together with filling the pantheon of national heroes, prompted the recognition of landmark achievements. More recently, with the awareness of discontinuous change within industries, new groups of technical workers have sought to discover their origins in a different shop culture, while survivors of passing skills have been impressed upon to leave their testimony. Most recently, as millions entered into a new educational process, a broad awareness of undiscovered landmarks has been stimulated – indeed of the existence of whole cultures which have as little in common with our own as those of the peasantry and are yet recognisably industrial in character.

Thus the motives for interest in industrial heritage have been diverse – interest, pride or concern to promote an aspect of current industrial culture, a desire to celebrate achievement, an interest in innovation and ingenuity, or an effort to compensate for irreparable loss. As the management of industrial heritage becomes more professional, it is important not to lose that diversity of motive and of uses which has been a key to its vitality, and gives it a secure place in the current expansion of heritage culture. In cultivating an interest in various aspects of the industrial past we should remember how to use industrial heritage resources in connection with contemporary and future industry – and that this should be concerned with making evident the continuities of value in industrial culture as well as with points of technical knowledge. If industrial heritage should become used against aspects of contemporary industrial culture, this ought to be for a clear reason, for example, an intervention in contemporary debates about the ecological impact of manufacturing processes, rather than out of a general sense that older is better or more intriguing or that history, as culture, has a superior dignity to technical matters.

The Industrial Heritage

The growth of a more historical awareness of industrial culture has been part – perhaps the leading part of industrial heritage as taken in the broad sense used in this book – of the expansion of heritage discussed above. Industrial heritage has the potential to open up a panoply of objects to be considered as heritage – the everyday as well as the exceptional; the makers as well as the made; the mediation and representation as well as the use; the contemporary as well as the long-established; to consider not only artefacts but people and their associations, contexts and relations, sites and landscapes as objects. Many of these are undiscovered, others approachable; traces are to be found all around. There is a richness of interrelations between these objects and therefore of heritages, a plurality of stories, yet interconnectedness; they may show hidden relations, or forgotten ones. This heritage has a practical import, and yet, like all cultural resources, condenses experience.

There is a variety of things that can be, or need to be, done and which we have seen done with industrial heritage. These relations to heritage encompass attempts:

- to explore, to investigate
- to learn how to care for resources practically
- to share and to show
- to place one's self, one's surroundings
- to learn from, wonder at, be inspired by
- to remember, memorialise
- to possess
- to value

Such relations to heritage are not in themselves new, or necessarily unique to industrial heritage, but because these things can be done over such a diverse range of things and in such flexible ways, the access to this heritage is potentially very wide, though it may not be drawn so. It makes it possible to take the giving of value everywhere and connect it with management of the environment, of the workplace, of the home. But it is a question not only of wideness – also of openness to involvement.

We have observed examples of how quite ambitious things can be done: stories of reconciliation to change; of self-recognition; of discovering the no longer hidden; of acknowledgement of debt; of collective achievement; of autodidacticism, retraining; of education through entertainment; of resuscitation; of revaluation and regeneration; of symbolic exchange. It is often the case that work has been carried forward by innovative partnerships and collaborations; not only because the collaboration has been necessary, but because of a combination of interests. Realisation of the cultural potential of industrial heritage projects often depends on a strategy of creating constituencies. There is no doubt that this more adventurous style of heritage management involves additional difficulties and new management issues.

The following are typical examples of the new management issues and problems which arise with an expanded heritage, and the claims of access to it:

- dealing with an expanded object field; a problem of knowledge on one level – of inventory, but also of conservation policies – establishing priorities and extending responsibility for care
- recognition of new constituencies as legitimate; improving access to resources, adjusting to need; marketing
- reconciling and extending modes of use; dealing with clashes of conservation and developmental objectives, living with the reappropriation of heritage forms
- running hybrid cultural institutions and collaborations
- establishing a cultural resources strategy
- negotiating political conflicts

It is not really possible for the manager of the industrial heritage to avoid these problems, because industrial culture produces its past at an accelerated rate, generating a scrapheap of things, people, ideas, ways of life. The potential value of this resource – things, talents, techniques – has to be assessed in relation to changing needs – it does not automatically sort itself into hierarchies of importance in relation to unchanging values. Constituencies will contend for the preservation of different heritages, or, indeed, for the removal of what they would prefer not to acknowledge, as did the workers who wanted to be rid of the monuments of exploitation or the middle-class reformers who wished to obliterate 'sub-standard' housing.

Nor is the manager of industrial heritage often able simply to rely on the established heritage management strategy of removing things from use and protecting them with resources derived from elsewhere. There is a limit to the extent that such preservation can take place, even with plural funding, and the expanded heritage soon runs up against it. Conservation then depends on the ability to interpret potential resources to possible supporting constituencies, often in ways that compromise the resource to some degree. Some prospering industrial heritage projects are nevertheless so dependent on gate money that they run entertaining events programmes which are not really integral with the interpretation – and, more seriously, public relations programmes which carefully avoid negative connotations like factories and old industry. Compromises like this could make sense as part of an overall strategy to cultivate new constituencies, or be a sign of drift or lack of thought.

Projects regularly come to grief because coherent plans for conserving and interpreting a resource are poorly articulated with key constituencies. A fine collection of domestic art objects in a fine mansion may present opportunities for combining a decorative arts display with one more oriented towards the social context of use, supplemented by video interviews with makers. But if the decorative arts collectors are riled by social history interpretation for example, then the whole project can be destroyed. To address an international decorative arts audience, run a city industrial museum and serve as a focus for cultural animation in an old industrial neighbourhood newly populated with immigrants: is this possible in one project, as distinct from a whole area strategy?

Both the potential and the problems of industrial heritage reach their greatest extent in areas where the decline and disappearance of established industries or economic restructuring have placed renewal on the agenda. Where piecemeal or comprehensive redevelopment would have swept away the old landscape a generation ago, perhaps leaving some traces in a museum, it has been recently suggested (as mentioned in chapter 1) that, properly understood and used, the resources of the recent industrial past can play a leading role in a process of regeneration. Here the management of the industrial heritage can reach its apotheosis – or overreach itself.

Regeneration is a slogan behind which contradictory movements take place. On the one hand, consultants argue that building on a common appreciation of the qualities of local heritage is the most important point of departure for renewal, because a kind of pride of place is the essential subjective starting point. Other consultants consider that certain qualities of the local environment can be detached from their previous historical matrix and re-marketed as leading features designed to appeal to the tourist, to the volatile shopper, and above all to the executive's family, whose prospective quality of life is believed to be the key to corporate re-location decisions. In both of these approaches, the idea of basing regeneration on an industrial heritage resource seems out of place. In the first case, defunct industry is seldom remembered fondly in the immediate aftermath, especially if it has relocated elsewhere; in the other, producing executive quality of life with a collage made from industrial ruins seems an unlikely prospect.

In any event, property owners in such areas are generally more often attuned to the quick and sure gains to be had from slash and burn redevelopment than to any drawn-out gamble on subjective appreciations. Governmental agencies in regions which have experienced either significant transformation of the industrial structure or catastrophic decline are desirous of quick returns on macro-economic indicators and also favour quick, textbook solutions. They have been slow to form positive evaluations of the industrial past. Industry – especially that which may enter an area from outside – likes to start with a clean and, if possible, bright, slate. By contrast with the treatment of older heritage, it is quite common for even the most obvious industrial monuments to be bulldozed away even when they do not stand in the way of future development. Values of dynamism and progress, slick presentation and managerial control constitute a view of past survivals as a dirty disagreeable encumbrance, perhaps provoking a deeper embarrassment about upheavals and dislocations.

Likewise, many dispossessed industrial workers understandably resent processes of change which are beyond their control and may operate to their disadvantage; nor do they wish to memorialise a past in which and of which they were not possessors. Everything conspires to disregard and devalue what is thrown on the scrapheap until some are prepared to stand up and declare it of value – both to them and to posterity. This voice is usually small at first: a group of engineers or practitioners of old trades, a lecturer at a local college or a museum curator, someone who writes a letter to a newspaper about the symbolic importance of a local landmark. Even when a few such voices come together in a local group, they often have difficulty in being heard. As suggested in chapter 1, the conventions of conservation thinking do not accommodate industrial heritage easily. In Sheffield, England, the city government – controlled by the Labour Party – struggled to get national protection for its Victorian town hall but ignored the pleas of local industrial archaeologists to look after important industrial monuments and sites – like the Abbeydale forges – already nominally in its care.

This is a familiar situation, in which the pioneers learn to create and nurture constituencies who recognise and support the industrial heritage, or they remain marginal to the larger process, perhaps nevertheless bringing a specific project to fruition. In Sheffield, as elsewhere, the crucial turning point came when all, including the politicians, began to realise that the city might lose not only particular firms or industries, but its whole industrial base. Suddenly, the importance of the threatened industrial culture to personal and civic identity was acknowledged – something to be celebrated, taught to schoolchildren, shown to visitors, both tourists and prospective investors.

Often this realisation comes too late, after massive destruction, so that it is difficult to amass enough of a resource for any purpose. The problems of heritage management become greater, however, once the idea of industrial heritage as a resource for regeneration gets about. Habitual preoccupations and processes are not suspended because the word 'heritage' is mentioned, and a struggle ensues in which the partisans of the industrial heritage have to be clear-sighted and wily not to lose their way.

Managers of economic development who might wish that their population were as tractable as the landscape, and are not strongly motivated to memorialise a past they have not yet got under ground, can be persuaded that industrial heritage is interesting if it can fill vacant sites with tourist attractions, attract investment and generate employment. Because their fundamental interest is in this pattern of regeneration, they will accept any version of 'heritage' that is compatible with it. A simple caricature offered by theme park consultants will be preferable to a comprehensive assessment and valorisation of the potential resource because they are concerned with a device to fill a leisure attraction. What matters is how the project will fit with development grants, land reclamation and new infrastructure, and how it will be designed and run – that it will certainly be a big attraction. To accomplish this it must present something the like of which has never been seen in the area before, rather than something which is only too familiar.

It is possible – and often necessary – for heritage managers to work within such parameters. They may insist on the unique quality and spectacular attractiveness of a particular feature or groups of features around which the park will interpret and work to rigorously bring those to credible life. They may gradually introduce local character into their attraction while using its existence to recognise and relate to important aspects of local industrial heritage. They can do this only so long as their attraction is also successful in conventional terms. But if they cannot gradually introduce an agenda which recognises the value of indigenous resources, then they will become isolated.

The authorities responsible for an instant heritage scheme can be gradually drawn to take pride in a serious curatorial agenda for the whole area, but not overnight. While heritage management may initially be seen as purely academic and perhaps involving too serious (i.e. unprofessional – too 'soft') an attachment to the past, the ultimate success of such an attraction will be crucially dependent on aspects of curatorship. Furthermore, the image of the area will depend on the quality of presentation given – and this cannot simply be resolved by hiring specialists in theatrical effects. Once the profile of the project is raised then the connection – or lack of it – with the surrounding environment will come into focus. What should the park include, really, and is it really sensible to synthesise environments within the pay boundary when real ones outside are neglected? None of these questions – which link quality of visitor experience with local amenity and regeneration – can be answered outside a cultural management strategy that includes a curatorial perspective.

The landscape of industrial heritage as it is preserved and presented today is a landscape that has been negotiated. The simplest deals have been those struck with a single patron for a single site. With a shared understanding about how to work with those limitations much can be achieved. Most project histories are more complicated, and where area regeneration is concerned necessarily so. Not only are there more players and more resources at stake, but more complex choices. What is the boundary or, to put it another way, the relationship between heritage, living in the present and making the future in such an area? Is history safely in the museum? Saturated in the landscape? Mocked? Is the whole made a museum, or a mock museum?

Where the patrons are powerful government agencies with the powers and resources to remake the landscape, an extensive area may receive intensive treatment. It is then possible to make an impressive 'total landscape museum', which can be amenity, visitor attraction and publicity device as well as conservation and interpretation of industrial heritage although not, by the same token, heritage-led regeneration of the community. Most municipalities or civic projects seeking regeneration involve complex interactions of interests and perceptions. If industrial heritage enters into these broader discussions it will be pulled this way and that. It may get diluted into an expression of regional character in a scheme for built environment conservation which is oriented towards accommodating new commercial and industrial uses, and even then fought over as divisive, a newly proclaimed heritage that must be distributed. It may be shaped by a once economically dominant group which makes heritage exercise a kind of cultural power, or even a fleeting political gesture.

As industrial heritage can seldom simply be removed from the world and made immune to its processes and contradictions, as the possibility of augmenting and caring for it depends on the cultivation of constituencies, its managers must be armed with a clear development strategy, which connects an assessment of potential resources with one of potential uses. Otherwise they will be at the mercy of the established interests which they must bring together.

Having a strategy as such is not enough; it is crucial that the strategy identifies the potential cultural resources of the area and works out a programme of creating constituencies which support and draw on the work done on them. A clear result of our study is that the chief limits to what can be achieved are not what is left by history, although this is obviously important, but the possibilities for development which are aimed for or at least permitted when objectives are set. The Massachusetts Heritage State Park programme provides a good example of an attempt to adopt a clear strategy, flawed by an inadequate understanding of heritage resources and uses.

The Massachusetts Heritage State Park programme was born in the context of revival initiatives for decayed industrial areas – ones which had suffered out-migration or secular decline of the first-generation industries which had shaped settlement patterns, urban growth and culture for the last century at least. To a large extent this was a crisis of 'mill towns' and small- to medium-sized cities dependent on mechanised steam-powered manufacturing technologies developed during the nineteenth century. These industries were a diversification of the colonial mercantile economy, they were characteristically linked to external markets and raw materials (and, ultimately, external sources of labour) exploiting local water power and mechanical ingenuity within a factory system adapted from Great Britain. Nineteenth-century expansion was premised on exploiting improved land and water transport to move larger quantities of workers, money and materials through a factory which was progressively rationalised to achieve high-volume, high-productivity, standardised outputs. These were linked to particular styles of management, of innovations in supporting engineering industries, amounting to a distinctive kind of industrial culture, comparable to but not quite the same as that, say, of the English textile districts.

While growth fed on economies of scale, it encountered limits in power sources and diminishing returns to innovation before the end of the nineteenth century, and re-location of textile mills to waterfront sites within the region and a series of struggles over the wage bill indicated a sectorial climacteric which also exposed the fragility, even arbitrariness, of locational advantage. Migration of the more thoroughly rationalised and stable technologies to areas with lower labour, energy or transport costs was accelerated by financial agglomeration; competition with imitative lower-cost centres precipitated the decline and closure of remaining firms. Supporting engineering industry had already begun to orient itself towards the large metal manufacturing centres of the midwest. To add insult to injury, many surviving firms had their assets stripped by finance-oriented conglomerates to feed new generations of economic activity.

The fortuitous character of the development of the mill towns was exposed and they went into a long period of decline. The problem was symbolised by the question of what to do with massive redundant mill buildings which were once the centrepiece of economic and social life. Typically, they were re-let as warehousing or light industrial units at low rents, or torn down to permit new development or even just to erase an unpleasant memory. Many however have stood vacant; some have been burnt to become liquid assets. Advocates of industrial heritage have rarely wielded enough capital to do anything with enormous buildings with high operating costs from which in any case operating machinery had been removed. The sheer number of such buildings short-circuited arguments about the preservation of particular examples. Tax breaks encouraged the conversion of many into housing in the later 1970s and this opened the way to speculative conversion as retail or office accommodation, once the physical resources and architectural qualities of the mills had to some extent been revalidated, a development encouraged by a number of poignant photographic studies and essays on these industrial graveyards. Mill buildings thus began to become acceptable townscape elements in new guises a generation or more after the decline of the industry and after the economy had begun to be oriented towards new sources of wealth and employment, most especially in electronics and the tertiary sector.

There was little continuity in technology, entrepreneurship or work experience between the old industries and their successors. The textile culture of old New England now exists chiefly in the memories of old folk, and the collections of a few museums.

The interest of the US National Park Service in establishing an urban industrial history park in a mill city drew in the partnership of the state in Lowell, properly chosen for investment by the Service as the first mill city. The Commonwealth of Massachusetts under progressive Governor Dukakis sought to use tax revenues derived from booming sectors to ameliorate conditions in old mill towns, and they were open to a multi-dimensional approach which included a heritage direction.

The Massachusetts Heritage State Park programme, however, had only a limited conception of heritage. Its chief aim was to create amenity in old industrial districts; secondly, to contribute to regeneration; and thirdly, almost as an afterthought, to do something to recognise, preserve and interpret the industrial heritage. This schedule of priorities reflected partly the preconceptions of policy-makers, and partly those of the politicians whose support needed to be won.

The first aim secured the broadest support and provoked the least controversy. It promised a definite and lasting outcome, which could be regarded as an imaginative extension of state and municipal park-making traditions. The location of parks in depressed and disregarded industrial areas excited officials and politicians, who could see several birds being killed with one stone: landscaping and re-use of difficult sites, amenity and community activity for deprived populations, and a revalorisation through heritage-related tourism of the scrapheap of industrial history.

Municipal politicians from mill towns also got excited about the state park programme if only as a means of attracting funds for environmental improvements and assistance with civic boosterism. There was competition for nominations, and it appears that areas were chosen on the basis of their deprivation/lack of alternatives, with some attempt to get a geographical and thematic spread. For example, in southeastern Massachusetts, Fall River, a very large textile town which has experienced severe depression and lacked either dynamic new industry or much of a track record in heritage management, was chosen over neighbouring New Bedford, which has some textile industry survivals, a substantial fishing industry and a strong tradition of civic institutions dating from its earlier history as a whaling port which had spilled over into a programme of heritage-led regeneration in its waterfront area.

The park programme could itself make only a limited contribution to regeneration, however. Its direct impact on the landscape would be limited: specific sites to be used as visitor centres and public open space, some heritage street furniture and signing to indicate historic districts. While indirectly these might help create a climate favourable to building conservation, that would depend more on local civic atmosphere and economic projections. The direct contribution of the operation of the parks to the economy of regeneration would be small depending on what they could offer to attract and involve people; the mere creation of outdoor recreation facilities in the urban industrial context was not enough to attract visitors – so industrial heritage came into play.

In recognising industrial remains as heritage assets the Heritage State Park programme was attempting to extend an idea which was no longer new, but still controversial. The decision of the US National Park Service to establish the first national urban park in the Massachusetts city of Lowell – an early textile city built at a major water power site – was a catalyst as it drew collaboration from the state from which they gained experience. Two interpretive themes deployed in Lowell were to be extended through the park programme: use of buildings and features of the industrial landscape, and a focus on past experience of people and communities. To develop these themes effectively, however, required more investment in cultural resources management – specifically in curatorship – than the programme allowed. Crucially, the paradigm was that of a park (a resource which is set up and then serviced) rather than that of a museum (a resource which is continually being augmented and used in new ways).

After park designation, consultants were engaged for the park thematic programme, exhibition design, architecture and landscape architecture. Teams of state employees (Park Service – jointly funded by the locality) then managed the continuing public programmes/visitor services. The result entwines aspects of conservation policy, parks, museums and heritage centres, with even an overtone of community arts/neighbourhood centres. Because the formation of objectives, the definition of resource and the organisation cross established boundaries they become open to criticism from many points of view: as public parks, museums, etc.

At Fall River, for example, the visitor centre offers both an elaborate audio-visual and a thematic selection of old photographic prints – some blown up to life-size cut-outs inviting 'place yourself in history' snaps. There is a programme of cultural or historical events some of which are related to contemporary communities, albeit limited by the site's relative isolation from the city centre. But there is no evidence of any continuing curatorial function. Community relations and public programmes had been allowed for in the brief and, like the displays, the new hall, vaguely reminiscent of a textile mill, and the park, with its boating pond, have all been designed by competent professionals. In spite of that, the whole is less than the sum of the parts. The omission of curatorship from this programme may have been over-determined by budgetary limitations on continuing expenditure, the difficulty of locating, amassing and conserving a collection, the judgement that photographic verisimilitude was closer to life than 'mute objects'. Nevertheless, the resulting 'lack' at the heart of the park programme is very evident and is largely responsible for the lack of integration noted above.

The Massachusetts Heritage State Park programme is not the only place where curatorial roles in cultural management strategy have recently been eroded. Comparison or even competition with commercialised leisure has forced attention on visitor services and even insinuated model outcomes to flatter visitor expectations; at the same time the search for accountability and responsiveness among public revenue recipients has increased pressure to measure outcomes in relation to specified policy objectives and/or general income/expenditure balance. In established institutions, curators have been under pressure to produce more output, gain more revenue, while their management of collections has been stigmatised as unaccountable or actually out of control. The response has generally been frantic attempts to increase desired outputs, combined with a generalised defence of academic and/or conservation values.

It is important to identify and measure the full contribution of curatorial output to a comprehensively specified cultural management strategy. This would include, for example, the contribution to asset value, to a diversified 'goodwill', the indirect contribution of augmented knowledge, collections and connections to the success of particular interpretive projects, and the indirect contribution of participation in heritage activities to meeting other cultural and social objectives.

Policy objectives like amenity, tourism and regeneration have qualities which may in turn be quantified: for example, the amenity surveys indicated in chapter 6 below which may be extended to connect with other areas of social policy like, for example, care for the environment; visitors' experience can be similarly elaborated. Tourism quality may be seen from different perspectives – project revenue and area revenue, public relations and area image – and these relate dynamically to quality of visitor experience and profile of visitor populations. The contribution of both amenity enhancement and tourism to regeneration objectives depends – beyond the threshold effects of having any programme at all – on superior quality, which includes richness and continuity of enhancement.

Therefore it is not only curators, heritage enthusiasts, etc. who need to pay attention to defining their work in relation to objective-related measurable outcomes but especially those who are charged with the realisation of such outcomes. Curatorship, properly understood, is a key to asset enhancement and management, the qualitative and quantitative success of community and public programmes and many aspects of public relations.

Clarity about objectives and the design and direction of programmes to objectives is good management. But successful strategies of cultural management must also recognise the functional interdependence of activities, the interdependence of resources and uses and therefore the necessity of cultivating both in a developing process. Only in that way does one arrive at 'living' heritage. Now 'traditional curatorship' provides neither necessary nor sufficient means to this end, but the curatorial agenda represents a nexus of activities which cannot safely be disregarded:

- a continuing search to identify and secure significant cultural artefacts and documents
- the evaluation, study and care of this heritage

consequently

- extending a network of cultural recognition and guardianship
- augmenting the heritage resource

thus

- providing both the infrastructure for the success of more diverse and extensive programme of uses and
- enriching of interpretive programme content

By contrast, a strategy which regards the heritage resource as fixed, which fails to cultivate and extend it, offers little to justify continuing involvement and can do little to build understanding or relationships of care and custodianship. Its amenity and its tourism potential are cardboard (two-, let alone four-dimensional) and therefore the kind of regeneration for which it can provide a springboard is one which needs or desires only a stereotyped gesture towards the past rather than an 'organic' development from it. If the project itself and the representations which it makes and the relations which it cultivates are not capable of development then the result itself loses actuality and effectiveness quickly. The answer is not another face-lift in the manner of shop or cinema fittings but heritage management.

Such a strategy of heritage management must also strike a balance between:

- getting aspects of industrial culture recognised as heritage in well-established ways -as monuments, as points of significance, as histories worth documenting, studying, celebrating, preserving
- identifying distinctive characteristics of industrial culture and getting them recognised in ways specifically appropriate to them – with the management of change, with the rationalisation and elaboration of processes and products, different networks of interdependence and focal points of interaction.

The best general model of a complex heritage management strategy with the management of cultural resources at its core is provided by Georges-Henri Rivière's ecomuseum model. Here attention is given to valorising a diverse heritage dispersed in a landscape in a variety of modes, in an involvement with local populations as much as for tourists. If there is an over-arching objective here it is a kind of broad legitimation of the state as custodian of cultures. It involves a diversified concept of amenity and through mobilising people as much as collecting artefacts can play quite a strong role in a reintegrative regeneration; it also produces material for high-quality cultural tourism, but is not necessarily directed to this end (Rivière 1989).

The notion of an ecomuseum involves the whole of a territory, rather than a special district. It attracts attention to all its characteristic features, ways of life, landscapes. This inclusiveness and balance is a very important feature which is seldom found in the most ambitious heritage-led regeneration strategies. It is more usual that the legacy of industry is carved up, divided: history to the museum if it fits, and the buildings evaluated for their architectural or building stock potential, if any. It is necessary to establish the place of industrial culture in such an overall area strategy.

Outside the problematic of regeneration or some other totalising provocation, industrial heritage tends to disappear into established categories of architecture, landscape, artefact or cultural document evaluation. One consequent problem is the low place given to industrial culture in the hierarchies of value traditional in each area. In terms of such values industrial heritage may not seem of much worth or may be excluded by definition. However, it can be possible to validate industrial heritage in relation to each of these links with the older heritage, by showing, for example, how industry has been responsible for much of the pattern of urban growth (see further discussion in chapter 3).

In conducting this study we have encountered many projects which have established an active cultural resources and uses strategy with a solid curatorial core. They are of diverse sorts and levels of investment. They are not necessarily the most immediately impressive to the casual visitor, because they are oriented towards growth and involvement. They are recognisable by the following characteristics:

- they are continually building cultural resources – they are finding out more in scope and in detail, they are getting more heritage of diverse sorts recognised and cared for, and they are doing this in a proactive way to build an integrated resource
- they are creating and cultivating constituencies – involving people of diverse backgrounds and experiences in different ways: offering ways to learn, ways to help build the resource or interpret it for others, mobilising support and involvement in guiding the project, while regulating potential conflict
- they are good at developing new ways of using heritage resources that do not compromise their integrity; they offer diverse and open interpretive strategies while preventing undermining conflicts

We draw attention here to a few projects, discussed at greater length in other sections of the book, which have these characteristics. We have concentrated on relatively recently established projects because they will be of interest to others starting projects and also because they have more often been set out purposefully along these lines.

The Industrial Heritage

Springburn Community Museum

Glasgow is well known among social history curators for its People's Palace Museum, re-invigorated more than a decade ago by an active interventionist strategy of curatorship, and an accessible 'Grandma's Attic' style of interpretation. But a tiny community museum in its formerly industrial suburb of Springburn is the mecca for those starting new small projects in industrial areas. Springburn Community Museum shows what you can do with absolutely minimal resources, so long as the cultural strategy is clear. In a neighbourhood which had been stripped of many of its significant industrial monuments, carved up by infrastructure and redevelopment, the chief aim of the museum project has been to restore to people some sense of agency – so the work of the project leader has been in building up a network of human resources, chiefly in preparing exhibitions. The focus has been on documentary work rather than collecting, although it has recently acquired one of the Springburn Works' largest locomotives.

The community museum/community history project model has been very important for contemporary and near-contemporary work. Such projects have often been set up around personal involvement in documenting social historical themes, but might as easily undertake restoration and other related work. In many cases it is sensible to decide not to undertake many traditional museum responsibilities and it is possible to do this while still building up heritage resources. It is the absence of involvement in developing and using resources, rather than the absence of a collection *per se,* which weakens the Massachusetts Heritage State Park programme discussed above. Community care policies are possible without formal collecting. It is a model that can be effective with voluntary groups or partnership agreements with local authorities – these are common in Scandinavia and Germany.

The Workers' Museum, Copenhagen

The Workers' Museum was started by a group of people acting in response to the devaluing and destruction of their own part of the city of Copenhagen. After several years of lobbying, their energies elicited a response from the trade unions, which provided money for the establishment of a workers' museum. As the project shifted from a neighbourhood-based one to a trade union project, its objectives and direction were substantially changed, but the resultant professionally staffed and managed project has never lost contact with its roots. A 'Friends' organisation has been an

The banner, a product of the first community arts workshop, is an emblem of many of the dimensions of heritage which the museum is bringing to life in Springburn, Glasgow (Photo: Springburn Community Museum)

important means of retaining these contacts, but interpretive strategy has also kept faith with the founding ideas. The museum chose to make everything it did fit with a strategy about representation of living situations – more even than living conditions – reversing the usual approach of starting with the factory. Voluntary work has been blended into this strategy, and is integral with other uses of the museum building (the former Workers' Assembly Hall). In the words of a staff member, 'We are the professionals of the museum, and they are the experts of their lives, and we work together' (Anne-Lise Walsted).

Summerlee Heritage Park

As a recently established project, still visibly and actively being developed, interpretation at this ambitious industrial museum at Coatbridge near Glasgow may appear a bit chaotic to the casual visitor – part of a machine hall, some workshop stalls, display panels about local housing conditions, models of site archaeology, mobile transport and an incipient open-air museum. But the popularity of Summerlee, especially with its local constituencies, shows that developmental strategy is not the same as a 'designer' interpretive plan. Underneath there is a sound programme of resource building and care and good involvement programmes; the project was able to survive the demise of government employment schemes, and has proved so adept at offering ways for people to learn more and come back that the local authority decided to put in extra money in order to keep entry free.

The Ecomuseum of the Fourmies-Trélon region

Acknowledged as an ecomuseum now, though not originally officially so designated, the project has been a major recipient of various kinds of public funds, but is gradually earning more from visitors. It makes a very good implementation of the ideas of Rivière described above and effectively integrates past and present industries with local life. It makes good use of community involvement in actually making displays and is probably outstanding for drawing out and developing the experience of some of the volunteers over time, so that they form an integrated team with other staff. It has also adopted a gradual approach towards making a tourism attraction rather than a dash for glamour, and is doing so within the context of strategic economic and cultural resource-planning in its region. The ecomuseum offers something to tourists and local residents alike – that it is able to do so is largely the

9 (a) & (b) Summerlee combines the attractions of many different kinds of museum experience

result of the careful constituency-building and community work that characterised its formation. Now, with this work in place, the maintenance of local character can also be a resource for tourism.

Industrial heritage and the future of industrial civilisation

Our discussion of the expansion of heritage has suggested that an important aspect of this expansion has been in the cultural roles heritage is asked to play; and we have discussed various ways in which the use of industrial heritage resources can figure in life today, and even act as agents in forward-looking development. Heritage managers should be interested in securing as full a utilisation of such resources as possible, and indeed the possibility of maintaining the resource may well depend on this.

It must be acknowledged that this potential has only been partially realised. In fact, there is a danger that regarding aspects of industrial culture as a heritage resource may curtail or constrain their use rather than extend it. As mentioned above, one source of our recognised heritage was originally assembled for contemporary use – in scientific and technical education, as the specific embodiment of local pride in current achievement, or as a more general representation of power and progress. The limitations of such collection and interpretation strategies are well known, and they were for the most part restricted to contemporary resources (Basalla 1981; Chabal and Sclafer 1981; Putnam 1990; Clark 1990). But an industrial heritage which did not include the present and relate to the future, whose contribution to current possibilities and problems of development – technical, civic, ecological – was very indirect and limited, would be a hamstrung heritage.

It must be said that much of the contemporary discussion about the potential of the industrial heritage that we have surveyed here has been preoccupied with specific objectives which do not directly face the future. Extending knowledge of industrial history, preserving monuments to past achievement, acknowledging loss and recognising the everyday underpinning of our culture, and the contribution of these worthy activities to future choices, have been secondary to tidying up the scrapheap or compensating for the changes wrought by industrial progress. The interventionist use of industrial heritage resources in attempted regeneration has generally had the character of manufacturing a tradition rather than working from or within a history. A more direct use would

10 (a) & (b) Turn-of-the-century apartment rooms in the museum at Fourmies, furnished and arranged by volunteers

(c) An invitation to contribute to a collective photograph album, Fourmies

involve using an understanding of change in industrial culture to modify that process of change: innovation in technology and work organisation, processes and products, environmental management and design.

There have been a number of attempts to put industrial heritage at the direct service of industry and government. These have had only limited success and the problems they have encountered are instructive for further efforts in this direction. We may consider first the place of an industrial heritage function within industrial companies.

Companies vary enormously in the use they make of their own history; firms which have had continuity of ownership – especially if it is or has been family ownership – are more likely to maintain archives of some sort if not actually include an archivist on the payroll, and to have published company history in some form, and perhaps preserved elements of outmoded installations as monuments. Firms which have been closely identified with a particular range or type of product are more likely to have maintained significant product collections, and may often exhibit them to the public. In both cases a certain self-absorption and pride of achievement mingles with cooler assessments of publicity value; an additional element sometimes present is a paternalistic concern for the health of all aspects of company life. When these elements come together in, say, one of the family companies which became part of the first generation of corporations mass-producing consumer goods, then a substantial investment in company heritage could seem justifiable. The extent to which firms in different sectors have made use of their own historical resources in design and technical development as a matter of course is not known, as it is less visible to the public, but case histories exist which show that this can be important (Aérospatiale 1985; Fagerborg 1984b; Putnam 1988; Rydberg 1985).

In recent years, industrial concentration and restructuring have significantly eroded the number of firms which have at their basis continuity either of ownership or of product; for the same reason, the value of such continuity as a mark of distinction – to consumers, if not to bankers – has increased, where it continues to exist. While new ownerships or managements have often jettisoned archives and other paraphernalia of company heritage, the revival of historical styles in some markets has sent companies scurrying for discarded patterns and restored estimations of their usefulness. In parts of the engineering industries, old patterns have been recycled as intermediate or alternative technology. Interest has also extended to the revival of old techniques, although this has more often been taken up by new small firms rather than revived by old ones.

Such interest can provide a conditional ground for a more extensive appreciation of industrial history – conditional on the possibility of its envisaged use. The English hand block printer John Greenwood's efforts to record his disappearing craft have received some backing from his current employers, textile printers David Evans, since they began reviving their old patterns. Greenwood spends part of his time adding credibility to historical displays which accompany the promotion of the revivals in the company shop, where a video made at their expense documenting John's former work practices can be seen. Evans' historic patterns, however, are produced by modern technology. Revival (with varying licence) of pattern but not of technology has been the rule in the industry, although Sanderson's have brought back an exclusive block-printed range. Managers see this as the likely limit of the use they can make of industrial heritage, and even current levels of use have been questioned by new management who are more concerned with cutting costs and increasing efficiency rather than adding value to the product.

The way in which companies invest in history often reflects particular preconceptions about historical significance as well as about the potential contribution which heritage resources could make to operations, and this emerges clearly in company museums. The establishment of a company museum by UK glassmakers Pilkingtons was motivated by awareness of the pace of technical change in the early 1960s, and the original collections included substantial amounts of disused tools and machinery. However, as the museum became established in the new head office campus at St Helens, its focus turned away from industrial transformation to grander themes which reflected the company's world status: the uses of glass in history and the refinement of its craft into decorative art (which the company displayed but did not produce) and technology (in which past achievements led to today's products). The scope for curatorship, kept within the compass of a headquarters public relations function, could not engage seriously with the history of the company, its workforce or its landscape. These threads are being taken up in part by a new industrial heritage project which will provide a cultural attraction in a local regeneration scheme, but they are lost to the company itself.

A larger investment in developing an industrial heritage resource at the Dunlop Rubber Company demonstrated a much wider range of uses, although it eventually foundered in a management reshuffle. In the late 1970s Dunlop, which was undergoing considerable internal reorganisation and rationalisation, adopted a positive programme for managing its industrial heritage. A small professional staff invited volunteers from all parts of the corporation to join in an Archive Project. The object was to identify heritage resources of all kinds – objects, memories, photographs, documents – and make them available for use at all levels of the company. An Archive Project Journal was published to circulate articles based on contributions of employees, collecting began at a disused warehouse, inventories were established to guide this, archival material accumulated rapidly, and a number of special projects were initiated in response to openings and closures, changes of product, personnel and working practices.

Although it had been expected that the project would be good for morale inside Dunlop, few had anticipated how quickly interest would grow, or the extent to which participating in a heritage project would open up observations and expressions about the company. The Archive Project became like an agony aunt, collecting large numbers of unsolicited observations about current operations. What had seemed a harmless exercise in 'industrial archaeology', a hobby of the Chairman, was altering the company culture; in one view, for the better, because it enhanced the sense of a common history and a common effort, in another, a diversion from the tasks of work and management. As the project became responsible for the company's heritage it became subject to conflicting expectations, and project workers had to be careful to avoid being associated with factional interests.

The high degree of interest shown justified a larger expenditure which enabled the project to undertake more ambitious work. It developed a programme for factory closures which involved workers in extensive recording of their work, equipment and environment and especially of their experience; groups of workers discussed what was to be preserved and how this would be possible. This process not only generated a record and a resource but assured employees – in a difficult time of transition – that their contribution to the firm had been valued and was worth transmitting to future generations. Extensive self-documentation was also made of continuing work situations – something that would have been resisted had it been an exercise conducted by management or consultants. The Archive Project thus built up a kind of knowledge that was not possessed anywhere else in the company, to the extent that its resources were used in management training, especially for those going to new assignments in

11 An invitation to take part in the Dunlop Archive Project

12 Dunlop Archive Project: a published result – oral history, photographs and artefacts

This picture seems to symbolise our first journal. The tyre is a Dunlop – out of focus but identifiable. The family in Daddy's car is real enough but what do we know about their lives?

This journal hopes to tempt you into spending some of your spare time in helping the new Dunlop Archive Project. Join us in discovering our family history and bring into focus the Dunlop products these people made – and the Company they built.

SOME NOTES ON THE PROJECT

1 Why an Archive Project?

Many companies have archivists who do a good job in ensuring that the important documents of today find their way into storage for posterity. They do this with the experience of an established set of files. Dunlop has no such guide and its collection is dispersed inside and outside the Company.

Dunlop couldn't afford an army of full time people to make an archive and we firmly believe that people like us built up the Company. It is our history anyway, not to be entrusted to outsiders. Faced with this problem and because in Dunlop it is still true that the Company is the people working in it, we have decided that a tiny full time staff and the volunteer help of anyone, anywhere in the Company will produce better results. These results will reflect all our individual interests. As it is our past, these diverse approaches will discover things experts would ignore or not really appreciate.

We have presumed that those working in the Company now, would like to contribute to this work helping to recognize and record the contributions of those who built the Company.

2 What will volunteers do?

On another page in this journal you will find a list of hobbies and skills which can be useful to the Dunlop Archive Project but the only essential requirement is an interest in our past. Working alone or in groups, tasks are there for people's various skills, to investigate, to restore and record. To define these tasks is difficult but the following list shows the types of gaps which face us on almost every Dunlop site. But as we want our volunteers to enjoy their leisure, we will help them, wherever possible, to examine that which interests them.

Our list would include work with retired employees whose memories go back into the early days. (This is expanded in the Golfball factory article and the book review pages 37–38.)

We badly need lists of 'products made' with the 'date of commencement and conclusion'. One offs and short runs in particular seem to escape the published lists which are usually compiled at Head Office from old divisional reports

For products no longer made, we would like to produce descriptions and illustrations of machines used, the time it

Golfballs
A GLIMPSE AT THE PAST AND PRESENT

They did that all day?

THE ARCHIVE PROJECT MADE THE ASSUMPTION THAT THESE PHOTOGRAPHS WERE OF GOLF BALL PRODUCTION TAKEN IN THE EARLY DAYS OF FORT DUNLOP

MRS DAISY BLAKE AGREED TO RECORD HER MEMORIES OF SPORTS GOODS PRODUCTION AT FORT DUNLOP FOR US. ALTHOUGH HER MEMORY IS REMARKABLY CLEAR AND STRETCHES BACK EASILY TO THE MID TWENTIES, SHE SOON REALISED THAT THESE PICTURES DID NOT SHOW THE PLACES THAT SHE WORKED IN AT FORT DUNLOP. WE HAVE NOT COME ANY NEARER TO IDENTIFYING THESE PICTURES, THE WORKING METHODS THEY SHOW OR EVEN THE BUILDINGS . . . THIS IS A SMALL EXAMPLE OF THE KNOWLEDGE WE LACK BUT WHICH MUST BE SOMEWHERE WITH SOMEONE.

THE WORDS WHICH FOLLOW ARE PART OF THE TRANSCRIPT OF DAISY BLAKE'S TAPED CONVERSATION AND WE ALLOW THEM TO SPEAK FOR THEMSELVES. THE DRAWINGS WHICH FOLLOW ON THE NEXT FEW PAGES WERE DRAWN RECENTLY AT NORMANTON AND WE WOULD LIKE TO THANK THOSE DEPICTED IN THEM AND EVERYONE ELSE AT THIS ISC FACTORY FOR THEIR WILLING COOPERATION . . . BUT IN 50 YEARS' TIME THESE DRAWINGS WILL ONLY TELL A PORTION OF THE STORY.

PERHAPS THERE IS ROOM FOR AN ARCHIVE PROJECT VOLUNTEER WHO COULD RECORD TODAY'S WORKING LIFE AS WELL AS YESTERDAY'S

. . . in those days when they had the golf balls joined together and the core inserted, . . . they were put into boiling water or rather very hot water for 30 minutes. They then were put in cool water to cool off for 10 minutes. Then they were taken out of that and the girls would have, what they called 'trimmers', and they would have a little instrument with a wedge in it. it was only like thin rubber where they joined and they would take this little instrument round and just take it off.

Yes, that was their job. Then after that the paint went on. They used to put the paint in the palm of their hand and do that

So when that girl went home she had paint on her hands?

it was done by hand of course – and dropped on to a tray.

I don't know how they got it off. But that's all they did. They got the golf ball in the palm of their hand and they didn't touch it with their fingers, they dropped it on to a tray. Now, I am not sure whether that was allowed to sort of harden off. Then the girls were stenciling with the number, etc. They did that – my sister did the same stenciling also another sister did the paint so I do know that you see.

Were there hand tools in the golf and tennis department?

Oh it was all there, yes. Except for the core winding. That was on little machines and they held the rubber like that, you see, while it went round and round.

The picture of Mrs Daisy Blake, née Daisy Harris, was taken during her time at Fort Dunlop when she was a member of the sports and social – rifle club. It was kindly loaned by her to the journal. We would like to thank Daisy Blake for her help and cooperation in tape recording her memories of those early days.

unfamiliar plants. The recording work of the Archive Project enabled Dunlop to successfully negotiate the redevelopment of a protected factory of the 1930s, protecting the facade. Thus a higher level of investment produced results which could be directly applied to company operations.

Dunlop Archive Project began to find uses for the historical material it had collected – chiefly as a resource for publicity but also as a reservoir of material for design and technological study and adaptation. The project began to attract attention outside the company, both for the results and for the methods of its work. It began to be used by researchers in industrial history, social history and history of design, yielding results of great general significance on, for example, the relationship between increasing demands on tyres, scientific tyre design and the basis of corporate organisation (Woolaghan 1982).

In a climate of increasing public interest in industrial heritage in Britain, the Board approved a £2 million plan in 1980 to establish a museum, effectively hiving the project off as a charitable trust to which it would entrust corporate heritage and make tax-advantageous donations. Unfortunately, deflationary policy exacerbated Dunlop's already serious restructuring problems. Even the expanded project crew found itself unable to keep up with all the factory closures, or control the sprawling collection. Suddenly, the firm passed into new ownership and the project was summarily wound up, along with several more sizeable operations. Sadly, this took place only a short time before the vesting of Dunlop's heritage assets in an independent trust, and employees and supporters were powerless to prevent the disposal of the resource which so many had combined to create.

That it is possible for company heritage programmes to survive industrial transformations is shown by the example of Stora (formerly Stora Kopparberg). This long-established (arguably the oldest) industrial firm, which had its origins in the famous copper mountain at Falun in Sweden, had extensive and diverse heritage assets over which it had exercised careful stewardship for centuries. The utilisation of these assets for the benefit of the company and the public was skilfully developed in the 1960s and 1970s; the museum at the Falun mine was deservedly popular, a number of lesser industrial monuments were interpreted for the public, a rich archive and artefact collection were the delight of scholars and used by a number of branches of the corporation, which was able to display an unrivalled aura for its invited guests. Current heritage was not neglected, especially when the company's extensive metallurgical interests underwent restructuring in the 1970s. Suddenly, however, matters came to a head, and a new management decided to divest the company of virtually all its metal interests in order to concentrate on forest products, in which it held a stronger position internationally.

This change of strategy immediately threw in question the continued value of the company's heritage assets to the company because they were chiefly associated with industries with which it was no longer centrally concerned. More seriously, it cast in doubt the continued value of any kind of heritage programme; the new director saw it as necessary to make a decisive break from past traditions in order to address new challenges – he would prefer to spend money on sponsoring a hockey team than on the company's heritage. That the heritage operations of the company were not summarily closed down is due partly to their exceptional quality, which was widely recognised and supported, partly to the involvement of the Central Board of Antiquities, which had taken an interest in several of the monuments, and partly to the ingenuity of the director of the heritage programme. He found ways to personally interest the new director in history – through the history of his wife's family. He took on board a wider responsibility for cultural programmes and resources, and included representation of the company's current changes and new products. He developed new popular open-air attractions combining heritage and outdoor recreation. When in the general reorganisation heritage activities were made a separate cost centre, the diverse uses made of heritage within the company, its income-earning capacity and its low operating costs made it enormously profitable – even leaving out of account its effect on net assets. As it was accruing surpluses, it was re-absorbed into the corporate headquarters budget, and the immediate crisis had passed.

Other strategies have been applied to preserved historical resources in companies: modest projects in major corporations (like that at Boots pharmaceuticals in Nottingham, England) have been able to survive by keeping a low profile, relying on the use of spare time and facilities and adopting the style of an employees' club. However, the lack of continuity in company management and ownership today means that they are not reliable carriers for heritage responsibilities, and that the enthusiasm of one generation is not sufficient. Such problems may be attacked by vesting heritage assets in a related trust, by governmental regulation and responsibility, and by co-operation with museums and research establishments (Rydberg 1985).

The Industrial Heritage

Industrial concentration has sometimes led to deals in which family members have funds which they choose to apply to a continuation of the old family business as a museum, as in the case of the Berliet Foundation (Berliet 1985). Industry associations, like the Ironmasters' Association in Sweden, can play an important role in consolidating heritage resources, encouraging investment in them and devising programmes for their more effective use, so long as the industry remains reasonably healthy in the national context.

The extensive restructuring of industry in the past generation has done much to spark increased voluntary and public concern for industrial heritage and one must accept – much as companies can benefit from positive management of their industrial heritage – the necessity of a wider responsibility for the question of how these resources can best be put to public use. This seems quite widely accepted now as far as projects for interpreting science and technology are concerned. As was the case when museums first began to collect technical apparatus, it has been relatively easy to get both public and broad industrial support for educating the public in the principles of science and applied science and their benefits: large amounts of money have been thrown at devising techniques of user-centred learning to engage interest in science and technologies whose principles are less evident than those of a steam engine.

However, the science centres of North America, or the Cité des Sciences et de l'Industrie at La Villette in Paris, offer little opportunity to evaluate the place of technology in industrial transformation. These institutions are in accord with a governmental and corporate taste for the absolute and grandiose, which is hard to reconcile with the popular experience of the effects of technical change. The products and processes of industry risk appearing merely as outpourings of a technological cornucopia (Basalla 1981). Also, although it is accepted that there is a public responsibility for bridging industrial transformations and restructuring by helping displaced people find new work – and even quite extensive public support for retraining – in no country does manpower planning adopt an industrial heritage perspective. The potential value of skills and practices displaced in one location is assessed only in relation to current needs elsewhere. Who looks after the resources – the skills and experience, especially – for which there may be no current demand and which are for that reason as 'under threat' as any animal species or unique artefact?

There have been attempts to formulate this wider responsibility for the most readily perishable aspects of the industrial heritage – and the ones which are most relevant to renewal. The most programmatic attempt was that launched in France in the late 1970s under the title of Centres of Scientific, Technical and Industrial Culture (hereafter CCSTI).

A Centre for Research into Technical Culture was brought into being in 1979 by the French Ministry of Industry, following a survey of the state of technical culture in France, commissioned from Jocelyn de Noblet. The aim of the centre was at once to determine and promote awareness of the social and cultural impact of technical change in a way that would strengthen the development of 'technical culture'. This designation was taken to mean the competence necessary to make use of the environment and feel at home in the technical world. While a healthy technical culture was seen as a condition of national economic development, it also made for a public which would be less mystified by and dependent on 'technology' as an alien social power (Centre de Recherche sur la Culture Technique 1981: 9–12, 69). It was believed that the strength of technical culture in France was threatened by industrial restructuring as well as by an increasingly 'invisible' technology:

> The development of technical culture is necessary to give meaning to daily life in the modern world. Equally, it is one of the essential conditions for fostering innovation, whether industrial or individual.

> It is not sufficient to conserve and exhibit technical objects as though they were art or scenery or a spectacle. Though there will be objects to consider, these will be only one of the aspects of a CCSTI. It is equally necessary to propose an active and recreative pedagogy, activities which bring things alive and stimulate creativity and research centred on the national and regional industrial heritage.

> In this conception of the Centre, visitors are not abandoned to spectate, but will have access to a series of multi-sensory experiences requiring active participation. The key to this participation is the possibility of manipulating variables to arrive at a conclusion. Such practices are of both creative and cultural value, because they make it possible for visitors to communicate with each other and thus lose their anonymity (de Noblet 1981: 13–14, translated by T. Putnam)

It was recognised from the outset that the promotion of technical culture would require new institutional forms and a variety of means of dissemination. A broad network of contacts among educationalists, scientists, civil servants, engineers, designers and others was established. This provided a basis for local workshops, seminars and publications, in collaboration with colleges, companies and museums. Regional organisations were particularly concerned with research, teaching and the conservation and presentation of local industrial heritage, while a central office provided support services and initiated special projects.

An evaluation of contemporary museums of science and technology, especially in America, played an important part in shaping objectives, and clearly influenced the form of the regional CCSTIs established at Mulhouse, Roubaix and Annonay. Among American museums of science and industry, this evaluation found communication placed above preservation, the needs of the future above preservation of the past, the whole serviced by an imaginative educational programme.

Members of the Centre for Research into Technical Culture wanted the development of technical culture to encourage realistic technology evaluation, and were unenthusiastic about interpretive schemes heavily dependent on gadgets, favouring instead schemes which placed technology in a more realistic context. Bearing in mind the gross distortions which could occur in the simulation of production environments, thinking began to turn towards the development of 'living museums' on historic industrial sites. A concern for the 'ecology of the machine', which left contemporary technology to be studied in the factory and concentrated on the preservation and reconstruction of previous industrial and artisanal practice, diverged somewhat from contemporary practice in American museums of science, as the pursuit of historical values threatened to detract from the active educational outreach thought essential to the fostering of technical culture, and as the artificial environment of the museum abstracted science and technology from that real world context which constituted technical culture. These lines of fracture suggested the necessity for a more systematic treatment of the relations between culture, technique and education.

If museums have traditionally accorded cultural recognition to technical objects only when shorn of their immediate usefulness, neither is the everyday technical environment necessarily obvious to the casual observer. Machines do not clearly speak of how they work or how they are made, and the extent to which they depend on external systems is not always clear. Understanding of their operation is not given by general physical principles, but requires identification of their technological segments and their respective roles, connections and interactions, and the sequencing of their functioning. Regenerating familiarity with technology would require the creation of opportunities for 'hands-on' experience of the sort embodied in traditional apprenticeships but often absent from both general and technical education today. This was to be supplemented by analysis of the structure and workings of the object and its place in relation to energy, material and information systems.

These reflections on the relationship between culture, technology and education reinforced the importance of rethinking the museum as a place where people could gain 'hands-on' experience with technical objects, and familiarity with the systems on which they depended. This conception had a central place in the priorities for the proposed CCSTIs, and informed the choice of electrical energy for the first such centre at Mulhouse. The search for modern analogues to and substitutes for apprenticeship arbitrated between the aims of conservation and interpretation, serving as a criterion for the selective emulation of contemporary science museums and museums of industry. The purpose of the centres was educational, and the value of objects held to relate primarily to their educational use. Conservation became more important as an educational activity than as an end in itself.

Although this education was intended to be oriented towards the future, it used historical materials and drew on historical research. The focus of this research and preservation was the working environment, both material and cultural, involving the social history of industry and its archaeology. No value was given to the reconstruction of the past as such, or to the preservation of technological or architectural monuments for their own sake. Reconstruction and preservation were deemed necessary in so far as they enabled machines to be situated in real-world contexts, and a broad historical context was considered important to the capacity for evaluation of technology which the centres wished to foster.

The CCSTI programme aimed to directly address the important question of public appreciation of and basic competence in the technical underpinnings of contemporary society, an area of great importance both to those concerned with the regeneration of creativity and economic growth, and to those concerned with the social, economic and political consequences of particular paths of technical and industrial development. But the programme eventually lost out to La Villette, in which the history of industry and technology has a subordinate place – not only a small place, but firmly in the past. This regrettable decision has not blocked the emergence of a number of centres of science, technology and industry, often run by industrial archaeologists or ethnographers of industrial culture and based in the remains of depleted or defunct ways and places of making. While these preserve a highly perishable resource, with the drive of the initial programme gone, few address effectively the question of innovation within industrial traditions.

It may be that the objectives propounded for the CCSTI were impossibly ambitious. Because they bring together things which are usually held apart – past and future, hand and eye, learning and doing, technical and creative, public and private – they are difficult for many people to understand, let alone implement. However, initiatives are still being taken. In France a national programme still exists and it is proposed, for example, to establish a CCSTI for textiles in the ecomuseum at Fourmies. This will be concerned especially with the use of electronic technology in contemporary textile design – the demonstration of and training in such new applications will take place in the context of the museum's extensive collection, and will be accompanied by an exposition centre for new textile designs. While it is not clear how this plan will realise that part of the original CCSTI objectives which has to do with the recovery of already existing skills and experience, there clearly is a sense in which both the museum and the proposed centre within it do support and encourage a 'technical culture' in the local population and among visitors.

In other countries there is no one project which quite parallels the concerns of the CCSTI. The place of applied science and technical education in regional industrial renewal is addressed directly by Bologna's Casa dell'innovazione e del patrimonio industriale. Building on the work of the Aldini-Valeriani technical institute over the past century, this 'museum–laboratory' has developed a coherent approach to technical culture focused on the relationship between knowledge and the division of labour. A strategic view of 'mind' and 'hand' on a social scale provides an effective means for relating past and present, underlining the continuing relevance of industrial heritage (Poni et al. 1980; Curti 1988; Curti et al. 1988).

More often, industrial heritage projects aim to conserve aspects of a particular technical culture. De Noblet was impressed with Brighton's Engineerium, a collection of mechanical and electrical engineering apparatus and models housed in a Victorian steam pumping station, because of its attempts to keep alive the kind of training that would once have been conveyed by an engineering apprenticeship. Behind the scenes, the Engineerium has a fine conservation workshop which has helped transfer skills and experience, chiefly to those learning conservation techniques. This is an important kind of function, as the danger of losing irreplaceable expertise is real and the crisis has already arrived in certain mechanical arts, like watchmaking. Such work also takes place in a less advertised way at a number of other industrial museums and could be developed as a learning network.

If the Engineerium has had limited success in involving the public or addressing the future in the way the concept of technical culture implies this is part of a larger failure on the part of educationalists, training boards and companies to be able to come to terms with its 'hands-on' resource – itself a testimony to the decline of technical culture. Government unemployment training schemes appeared to open the possibility of transferring technical culture to new generations, but have been chiefly viewed by heritage projects as a subsidy in kind rather than as an educational responsibility. In the UK the managers of such schemes have responded by restricting placements to cases where the training offered precisely fits current industrial vacancies. Nevertheless there are cases where learning on such schemes has opened up new vocations making adaptive re-use of techniques and experience which are currently being displaced from industry. If governmental agencies wake up to the fact that the maintenance of a broad skill base is an important element in regional regeneration, then industrial museums could play a more direct role in renewal.

Several museums have stepped in to record, preserve and exhibit local industrial cultures on the point of their disappearance – a fine example was the work of the Geffrye Museum with the remnants of East London's furniture trade, which effectively captured a way of life and brought some publicity to the work of surviving firms. The experience of recent restructuring has made some municipalities and regional governments more willing to intervene to maintain the health of industries on which they are dependent. A recent initiative of this sort has been taken by the town of Walsall in its Leather Centre. Although the town's long-established leather trade has adapted many times to changes in markets and circumstances, incorporating appliances into what are basically hand and eye processes of cutting and stitching, the industry has become increasingly bound up with the supply of certain 'traditional' items. High-quality small leather goods are provided to retailers in London and abroad, while other areas, ladies' handbags for example, have been lost through failure to meet foreign competition on either design or price.

The Industrial Heritage

The local government decided that the time had come to revitalise the trade before it declined irreparably and initiated the Leather Centre in a restored leather goods factory adjacent to the technical college where leather goods making is still taught.

The centre serves to make the trade visible in the town, so that it is open to more diverse influences, while demonstrating the importance of the trade in the area and thus bringing out a formerly invisible aspect of its character. The largest part of the building is devoted to historical and technical exhibits, of which the most effective is the workshop in which the making of leather goods is still carried on, and the oral history testimony from current workers in the trade, which indicates some of its problems as well as its pride. The active education programme brings aspects of the trade into school at every level, and, in association with the college, has promoted the work of contemporary leather designers, whose innovative work is shown alongside the 'traditional' output of the industry in showcases and the shop. The small size of the shop underlines one basic problem of the relationship between the trade and the town which the centre has not been able to transform: people who want established leather goods would find them too expensive here and would get them if at all privately from friends in the trade; the designer leather goods are way beyond the reach of local people, and leather workers especially.

The kind of intervention being attempted in Walsall is also at play in the project to create a museum of glass in Coimbra in Portugal. In this case the desire of a socially conscious municipality to dramatise the vibrant political culture of the glassworkers seems to blend with eagerness of manufacturers and dealers to assemble and exhibit collections of the town's diverse production, and the industry has enough economic importance and historical interest of a technical kind in a national perspective to attract some investment from national agencies as well. This goes to indicate not only that the possibility for using industrial heritage to write a new chapter of industrial history will vary in relation to such factors but that the time when an industry can make the most effective use of industrial heritage is when it is healthy.

3 | *Creating constituencies*

Heritage as a service

The manager of heritage marshals and protects a cultural resource and interprets it for the public. Much thinking about heritage, from those who talk about preservation for posterity to those who talk about producing and marketing a product, starts with the finding or making of a resource and prepares it for predetermined uses. But it is as appropriate to view the process of heritage management as arising from the formation of these uses in relation to anticipated or expressed desires and needs, and to look at the work which is done in constituting the heritage resource as part of a service to the public or a more specifically defined constituency. The quality of constituency-building is probably more important than the resource in determining the character of the result.

There are many 'product'- or 'resource'-oriented texts in heritage literature, and few which start from the service which it performs. Yet there can be no doubt that the vast majority of people who are engaged in industrial heritage-related work view their work as a service. The overwhelming majority of people, both voluntary and professional, with whom we have spoken, feel and act as though engaged in a vocation of public trust. Those who depend on revenue earned and contributed and whose self-conception is more entrepreneurial are also keenly aware of the importance of the service they provide.

Relatively few managers, however, have a conception of service which is sufficiently articulated to guide them in choices they have to make – it tends to get swallowed up in general definitions of what it is to be a public sector professional or to run a business. In both cases the relationship to the public served can be rather impersonal, abstract and one-directional, characterised by purely functional visitor services and impersonal didacticism. Neither shows much depth of thinking about heritage management as a service relationship. Volunteers can often more readily give an articulate account of how and for whom their heritage work is performing a service by analogy to what it does for them.

There are different modes of creating constituencies which tend to be associated with different kinds of organisations. Voluntary groups may give a priority to finding those who want to become actively involved in a project, or contribute useful sponsorship, perhaps in kind. Public authorities need to show that they are benefiting the generality of their constituents, and perhaps paying particular attention to groups that have been highlighted by other public programmes, for example old people, schoolchildren, the economically or culturally disadvantaged. However, to the extent that they are professional providers of a service, they may not prioritise active involvement. According to a commercial model, creating constituencies is a matter of marketing and public relations. In this paradigm, heritage is a product, not a service, and commercial organisations may have a more distant relationship with their constituencies, seeking extensive, rather than intensive, involvement. Trusts, and value-based enterprises, can combine aspects of the above ideas of constituency in varying proportions (see chapter 6 for a fuller discussion of these different approaches).

There are certain formulae which recur in discussions about the service which heritage work performs which tend to get in the way of any serious examination of what benefits people do or might derive from it: the focus on preserving for posterity, which removes one's attention not only from present use, but from any use; claims about the status of the heritage resource also often make extensive presumptions about benefits to be derived; for example, the idea that something must be preserved for future study, without consideration of the possible applications of the knowledge that might thereby be derived; vague conceptions of benevolence – or equally general educational obligations towards an unspecified public; threats to stimulate people's imaginations – these may betray patronage if not contempt of the actual user rather than any practical relationship of service. As suggested in chapter 2, this distancing may be partly explained by the practical difficulty of coping with the enormous demand for heritage services which is still only partially expressed. The great demand for information and recognition which workers in heritage institutions experience often renders difficult the completion of other work and may for example impede the introduction of active collecting, with time taken up in answering queries and giving opinions rather

than launching public community or educational programmes.

Investigation of what service actually is performed and for
whom in heritage work, and assessments of its effectiveness,
are seldom incorporated in actual projects and rarely investigated on a comparative basis. This lack of clarity and rigour
has led both public sector and commercial managers (in,
for example, public enquiries or sponsorship discussions) to
regard heritage as a 'soft' field lacking in professionalism.
There has been some discussion of the benefits of conservation
and regeneration – enough to establish in a vague way that
enhancement of self-esteem in an area can be achieved through
heritage work – but aspects of this work – subjective recognition, additional knowledge, investment, focal point for
association – are hardly differentiated. In heritage attractions,
generally only attendance statistics are used as feedback,
although many organisations have given some consideration
to reaching new constituencies or markets (Hooper-Greenhill
1988: 213–32).

Patterns of museum use are known to vary from country to
country, with age, class, gender, etc. What are we to infer
from this? As Merriman's survey among others shows, attendance and positive views of museums vary with social position
(Merriman 1989a: 149–71; Merriman 1989b: 153–71). More
importantly, heritages are prioritised differently by different
groups, and this relates both to their different orders of experience and to their ability to participate in the processes
involved. Those of high status, with an elaborate cultural
formation and involved, at least imaginatively, in questions
of domination and order, consider world history as more
important than national, regional, local or familial, while
those with little cultural or economic scope have the inverse
culture of particularism. Intermediate groups may focus on
national or regional identity, but this does not mean that there
simply exist differently geographically focused heritages for
different social groups.

Such survey results aggregate several elements which enter
into the constitution of appropriate heritages. As Bourdieu
would have it, the acceptance or refusal of reified systems
of abstraction plays an important role in distinguishing the
particularism of the powerless, but positive reinforcement
may also be given to certain face-to-face histories by established patterns of association and dependence – but not only
in conditions of deprivation. There may be senses of constituency which involve symbolic mediation by class or nation

for example, and yet which involve a kind of face-to-face immediacy in extensive organisations (Bourdieu 1984).

The lack of attention to the benefits of heritage work as a service would be more embarrassing were it not evident that interest and involvement in heritage-related phenomena are increasing steadily, for the reasons we discussed in chapter 2, and that heritage managers have often had to be concerned with the pressure of this interest on irreplaceable resources. Nevertheless there are several points at which this lack impinges on heritage projects and policies:

- in mobilising and organising the key elements of support for launching and sustaining projects
- in canvassing a broad consensus supportive of heritage policies and projects
- in determining project aims and objectives
- in identifying the heritage resource
- in making the best use of voluntary contributions of all kinds in projects, and of voluntary initiatives in support of public policies
- in designing interpretive materials and public programmes
- in extending opportunities for involvement

Recognition and understanding of the industrial heritage have grown sharply in several countries over the past quarter century and are now rapidly growing in others. There are several indices of such growth:

- publications and periodicals
- inventories and documentation
- societies and group participation: study, conservation and interpretation
- conservation and adaptive re-use
- recognition in planning policy
- visits to museums and sites and landscapes
- related hobby and leisure pursuits, for example, canal holidays, collecting
- academic recognition of new specialisms

This expansion has been achieved through the growth of a number of constituencies. It is underpinned by the growing interest in industrial artefacts and industrial archaeology among the technically educated, and the broader interest among those who have been through expanding higher education in an enlarged heritage which reveals previously hidden histories and connects with immediate surroundings.

The key source and in many ways still the core of industrial heritage culture is to be found in specialist societies and local avocational groups. Here are the largest numbers of people involved in making heritage. They may be held together by a common interest based on a specific monument, plant or ensemble of features in a locality or in a particular category of object. Such groups usually arise from the enthusiasm of one individual or a very few people. This interest, fixed on a visible object or category of objects, stands in the place of a strategy of resources and uses; groups get off the ground depending on how well the founder's enthusiasm can be communicated to others. This is mainly done informally and the project takes shape through the early interchange between those who agree to get involved.

Finding the appropriate people who are responsive, and can and will contribute something valuable, is crucial. Usually this has to be done using personal contact, and speaking or writing at well-chosen points of communication, taking advantage of meetings of any groups, using appropriate openings given by local or specialist publications or broadcasts, publishing notices, or convening meetings.

In this process, aims and objectives are defined, linking an evaluation of resources with an often implicit programme of uses and constituencies of users. The choices made are not trivial: unclear or impractical objectives are soon exposed, and narrowness in conceiving relevant constituencies will become a mid-term problem if not corrected in a process of growth. For example, a programme of work which is primarily based on machine conservation on the one hand or documentary or oral history research or writing on the other will limit the interest and ability of people to take part; lack of awareness of the likely perception of the project by potential supporters such as public agencies can also have a stultifying effect. Early decisions about organisational form and direction are important and really constitute different kinds of projects as much as their putative objects. A campaigning body or pressure group which seeks to provoke public authorities to take or prevent certain kinds of action has a very different dynamic from a hobby group which undertakes projects within its own compass – though these aspects can be combined.

With the exception of the would-be community spokespeople in local amenity societies, partisans of industrial heritage have seldom been tribunes. They have communicated best to those of related persuasion. For a long time the still clearly recognisable circles of specialist interest (for example in steam railways) have made up the lion's share of industrial heritage projects in most countries. 'Industrial archaeologists' appeared more like another such grouping than a group which commanded a sovereign intellectual agenda or held the keys to a wider public address, but their work has made it possible to claim a place for industrial heritage at the table of knowledges. A wider public has been gained through the efforts of a few crusading publicists, through campaigns to save buildings and monuments and, above all, through the opening of industrial heritage attractions, interpreted sites and museums. Recognition of the industrial heritage by government agencies, industry and cultural institutions, prodded by backstage persuasion and growing public awareness, has now been established to some extent in most industrial countries and continues to grow. A few people have even managed to make a living by it.

As discussed in chapter 2, certain social trends connected with the expansion of heritage have contributed to the growth of industrial heritage constituencies and have also helped to shape the movement in particular directions. These trends include increasing leisure time; conflicts between expanded educational horizons and employment constraint; expansion of hobbies and active day-out leisure; awareness of history arising out of rapid technological change, etc. – this is contingent especially on the passing of certain generations of industrial development as well as a shift in the relative importance of types of industry in some regions; discovery of disregarded value with partial overcoming of industrial stigma.

Those who have been involved in managing the industrial heritage have been more aware than most of the need to recognise, create and cultivate constituencies, for a variety of reasons which relate to the expansion of heritage discussed in chapter 2:

- the strong contribution made to many projects by groups of enthusiasts
- the need to persuade others of the value of recognising industrial heritage
- the necessity of devising innovative means for financing projects to conserve and interpret industrial heritage resources
- the vitality of popular interest in representations of past working and living practices and environments
- the contribution which raising the self-esteem of old industrial areas can make to their regeneration
- the difficulty of obtaining appropriate advice for innovative projects and the value in this context of a peer support network

A wide range of specialisms are required to identify, conserve and interpret the industrial heritage, and the success of the movement as a whole and often of particular projects has depended on an ability to foster mutual understanding of these specialisms. For example, in cases of adaptive re-use the sympathy and support of architects and clients are as important as those of planners and developers. One weak link in the chain can spoil the whole thing. Equally, proposals to establish a new kind of museum, or redefine a planning policy, must be able to call upon a range of specialisms brought into collaboration.

Failures to identify or win essential elements of support are a major source of project failure or blockage. The failure to engage at least moral if not financial support from local government has been a problem for the American Precision Museum, Vermont, the Hanomag industrial museum proposal in Hanover, the Swannington project in Leicestershire; failure to address wider publics – 'marketing failure' – has been a serious problem for the Bowes Railway, Tyne and Wear, and a number of other projects. State-supported projects may be able to hobble along but for trusts this is crippling. Failure to cultivate important knowledgeable interests who can give personal patronage and voluntary support is another pitfall – again fatal in the formation of a new project but also an oversight made in the name of misguided professionalism in either public or market-oriented projects. Conservation policy-makers are now learning lessons from regeneration and community architecture about the importance of tapping such sources of initiative.

Key constituencies in the formation of a project

In creating a new project it is necessary to consider what kind of heritage it will produce and effectively whose heritage that will be – who will be consulted in making it, who will support and be involved in this work and to whom the results will be most readily accessible. These questions arise first in forming the initiating group and support structure, but must again be addressed in defining the resource to be maintained and interpreted, and the service which this offers. Decisions which commit the project are often made tacitly, or are shaped by assumptions brought to the project from another sphere, or by the preponderant influence of a major contributor or sponsor.

In certain sorts of project such decisions must be faced explicitly; these can serve as instructive examples. A would-be community museum which takes the cultural needs of a hypothetical community for heritage as a starting point has to discover what those needs are; so the constitution of a resource is integrally related to the creation of the prime constituency from the beginning. Many things readily flow from this, as one can see in Springburn or on a larger scale in Fourmies. At Springburn, for example, few people belonged to socio-economic groups which felt themselves possessors of a general social heritage, and older residents had been dispossessed of most of their immediate local heritage in living memory: the local engineering industry, once the centre of European locomotive building, had been decimated and most of the area's older housing and commercial and civic building demolished in comprehensive redevelopment. A modest project was initiated with government support to deal with this massive loss of heritage. All work had therefore to start with the memories and traumatic experience of dislocation, to involve people in a process of shared enquiry and expression which would re-create a sense of having any heritage at all, and of being able to have one.

All historical resources produced had to be evaluated in terms of what they could contribute to this process of re-enabling a dispossessed population. There was much ambivalence of feeling to be dealt with, for example in relation to Springburn's involvement with industrial history: it seemed important to remember the past and acknowledge aspects of longing for it, but equally important to understand and articulate intense feeling about the reasons for change. Therefore, a succession of exhibitions and events programmes were mounted dealing with major issues or focusing on major elements in the population, covering this period of transition up to the present day. Each project was based on widespread oral history and borrowing of objects and photographs from the population, guided by appropriate groups of volunteers working with the project staff. Professional historical interpretation was balanced with opportunities for self-expression and creative interpretation by community artists. The emphasis has been on building up heritage resources in the community rather than collecting them in a museum, which acts more as a documentary centre and point of community animation. Longer term collecting policy will be determined in relation to the needs of these constituencies. Many of the same elements of practice have been employed at Fourmies, where it has also been possible to preserve, collect and interpret on a larger scale – eventually producing a resource which can be shown to a wider constituency, while remaining soundly based in immediate constituencies.

Problems can easily arise in locally oriented projects, perhaps

13 Passing skills between the generations at Springburn Community Museum (Photo: Springburn Community Museum)

14 Primary school children interview the older generation for an exhibition about play, Springburn Community Museum (Photo: Springburn Community Museum)

15 Brome, Lower Saxony: the results of co-ordinated collecting and documentation from traditional trades

especially in voluntary projects which are perceived to be dominated by particular groups or views. The small museum in Brome, in Lower Saxony, is one example – the burghers who were used to being the keepers of the town have worked hard to collect and interpret its traditional crafts which had survived until relatively recently, and have assembled a comprehensive set of annotated tools and work-benches, used in the museum to say something about the history of the trades in the economy and society of the town and region. But the municipal leaders have been puzzled by the lack of interest of the crafts-people in their own heritage – attempts at a programme of interviews and recorded demonstrations have not been very successful; a cultural gulf between tradesmen and burghers seems to be indicated, exacerbated perhaps by the resentments of redundancy and retirement.

At Swannington there was a divergence between constituencies which could not be held together. The project was initiated by a few people who were aware of the complex industrial history of local mining and its effects on the landscape; a small group inventorised the features of this landscape and succeeded in getting these accepted as significant locally by linking them with wider landscape appreciation expressed through civic pride in a range of participatory activities such as clearing and marking paths, conducting oral history work, issuing guides and having a village festival. Money and involvement raised became sufficient to buy small parcels of woodland containing seventeenth-century mining ruins to be held as a landscape park, and also the site of a pioneering early nineteenth-century inclined plane. The broad participation at parish level was not consolidated with public support at district or county level, however – partly by choice, partly through adverse personal politics, and partly because the district saw only a limited return from a substantial investment in the conservation of a blast furnace in a nearby locality as a museum.

After about five years the project began to encounter difficulties: it had achieved basic objectives in landscape interpretation, and these, together with its community festival, were seen as sufficient by some of those involved, while others wanted to push on to more ambitious projects like the conservation and restoration of the inclined plane. For these people, running the festival was not an end in itself and was beginning to become tiresome, but in the larger community the goal of restoring the engine and incline and making it work seemed too ambitious, contradicted other uses and introduced the controversial question of tourism. A government unemployment relief scheme made it possible to push on with this larger project in spite of these misgivings and let the annual community festival lapse. There were additional arrivals and departures to the key group which had carried out intensive voluntary work at this time allied with tension and confusion about the best way forward. As the Community Programme proved only temporary and neither local voluntary nor governmental support was forthcoming, the inclined plane restoration fell into abeyance and the group into eclipse. The county council decided to place its resources into a major mining heritage centre at the recently disused pit in nearby Coalville, and there remains some prospect of accessing the inclined plane and other aspects of the local industrial landscape as linked outdoor extensions of this museum project. Those of the original group most interested in industrial history have been drawn into the orbit of the new scheme.

The chief lesson of the case is that it is important to be clear about the different reasons why people get involved, as these will resurface as limits to commitment. While many residents were prepared to get involved in a landscape industry exercise, their commitment to specific mining or railway heritage conservation and interpretation was understandably limited because it did not form part of their personal experience or interests. For those more deeply committed to industrial heritage, the decision to seek community involvement instead of programme-dedicated support from government was good from the point of view of landscape appreciation, but provided insufficient support for more ambitious specialised projects, which were probably never thoroughly vetted as viable openings in their own right, and might better never have been attempted, although it was understandable and necessary to see the need for a next stage with a concrete and more ambitious result. The county and district could be faulted for failing to have environmental and cultural policies which could collaborate with Swannington to some extent and find appropriate forms to institutionalise its efforts.

It is often local or regional government that directly or indirectly provides the crucial support to establish a public access venture (abetted by philanthropy and visitor income) and accordingly the question of locality as subject/local constituency as object becomes important, if it was not already. The character of the local supporting constituency, how it was built up and around what issues or personalities, has a very important influence on the orientation of the project at the point at which it first acquires a public profile and formal existence. The project can be pushed into alliance with tourism in making representations of the locality, or it can be drawn into what it can offer to residents, schoolchildren, etc.

The project at Swannington was unable to articulate the relationship between a local history interest, local government, specialist interests and tourism. Other projects have been more successful in striking a balance between these constituencies, although most often where there is some overlap between them – for example where local history or specialist interests have direct representation in local government.

A society (probably not a trust) which has some collections can sometimes enter into a partnership with a local authority, whereby it provides wholly or mainly voluntary services for their care and interpretation, the local authority taking financial responsibility for long-term upkeep, and sometimes educational resources and publicity (for example, J. E. Hyltens Museum, Gnosjö, Sweden; Passmore Edwards Museum, London Borough of Newham). According to this model, the local authority bears a limited commitment, and does not have to invest in staff or curators, which are provided by the operating society. Sites organised on this basis only need open when they are going to be used by a particular and known constituency.

Where the communities are small and the sites and number of visitors small also, then the 'heimat' or 'hembygdsgard' ('home' or community museum) model seems to be most common, in which the public opening of the building or site is only seasonal – that is, the season of tourism, of holidays. There may be other days and times of opening but these are really intended primarily for the community and are known within. There are several degrees of development between this and something which is still a partnership but is run to be open nearly all the time, is more likely to involve paid staff and is intended to serve a larger number of people; this is more likely to be found in a conurbation or in areas with extensive tourism. There are other questions than partnership here – although partnership facilitates degrees of opening because the division of responsibility involved in a formal or informal agreement helps to specify programme objectives and may also compartmentalise budgetary responsibility.

Technically oriented projects may be able to command a specialist audience, but often have difficulty in establishing a local base. The pumping station at Walthamstow, East London, is a good example of this. It is a Victorian pumping station, forming part of an extensive network of sites in the

Lea Valley feeding East London, but now disused. The station, together with rights to restore it, was leased to a local voluntary industrial archaeology group, which restored it to working order. In spite of its London location, the site is relatively isolated, and the group has no rights over adjacent land, restricting the possibility of development or enhancement. A secure future for the project can only be ensured through visitor income or local authority subsidy, but the society is unable to persuade the authority that the station is of sufficient benefit to the locality to be worth maintaining as a visitor attraction. Its best way forward would be through promotion as part of a regional network of related sites, possibly through the auspices of the Greater London Industrial Archaeological Society. The benefits of a co-ordinated approach can be demonstrated from another extreme in the Netherlands, where the Federation of Industrial Heritage has given priority to securing a future for newly redundant pumping stations, but where large numbers of similar sites, all generating considerable local interest, threaten to overwhelm both immediate financial resources and long-term touristic potential (Nijhof 1990b).

The Bowes Railway, Tyne and Wear, is a double inclined plane associated with the transport of coal, and using a mining winding engine, which worked until the 1960s. It has been restored to working order by a group of volunteers, some of whom had worked there during its primary working life, with substantial and sustained financial support from local government. The project attracts only small numbers of visitors (less than 5,000 a year), and has been open to the criticism that it is in fact a government-subsidised hobby for local enthusiasts, with insufficient cultural output to justify the expenditure of public funds. Its difficulties in attracting a larger public can be traced to real problems concerning the resource – safety requirements mean that while it can operate, it cannot carry people – and it is unlikely to be able to attract other than a small, already interested public, unless it can establish links with other industrial heritage sites in its region.

Such projects may well have a choice about prioritising constituencies but if a technicist project fails to gain either political support, corporate support, voluntary local support, or a broad public appeal as a visitor attraction then it is in trouble. This is not to neglect the importance of an array of special constituencies which break down on technical lines: canal, railway, steam engine, technology enthusiasts can often provide a great deal of support to a project even if they do not live locally. Specialist enthusiasts will travel and pool resources to tackle projects of conservation as well as make visits, and beyond this regional orbit form a constituency of tourism and publication which is extremely important; it may be practically sufficient to sustain certain kinds of restoration and operation or demonstration projects on its own if they are modest or – at least in the case of railways – to operate public attractions.

Opening to the public involves commitments which may not be chosen by all such voluntary groups, but in many cases opening is a condition of restoration grants or other sponsorship or subvention, and the number of visitors at least may be a criterion of this support. It is far better to have a plan to attract an appropriate public and one which can be easily won. Steam engine enthusiasts have discovered the appeal of steam days with the public, but few have been able to do much with the occasional wider appeal in between. The Kew Bridge Engines in London are much more successful than many pumping stations in pulling crowds every weekend because groups of all kinds of mechanical restoration enthusiasts are invited to come and meet to display their wares. While the meetings often do not have much to do with understanding steam engine technology or its place in industrial history, this is a sensible strategy of constituency-building because it taps a network of people with similar kinds of heritage interests who happen to have fixed on different objects, and their friends. Publicity through this network is very efficient indeed, and a more general public knows there is always a kind of 'mechanical carnival' at Kew Bridge.

Overcoming local opposition: constituencies for regeneration

Winning interest and support on such a broad basis inevitably involves encountering opposition – active or passive. It is necessary to remember that for many people the very idea of industrial heritage is a contradiction in terms as the concerns for heritage were defined in opposition to the changes wrought by industrialisation. This distinction can be expressed in many ways: as recognition of or interest only in the supposedly pre-industrial (which can still involve industry), in a distinction between greater and lesser heritage, as well as an outright opposition to industrial culture being given heritage treatment.

Accordingly we have to consider strategies for overcoming these sorts of oppositions. One approach is to argue from what industrial heritage can do for you – that is, to stress some of the wide-ranging possibilities from the extension of the notion of heritage. Another approach is to dwell on continuities between industrial and pre-industrial heritage in relation to one aspect or another – as has been done in relation to urban development in Thessalonika.

Here, the problem was how to validate industrial heritage perceived as a lesser inheritance in a city rich in the traces of a far more ancient history. Two exhibitions were mounted at the French Institute of Thessalonika, before finding a permanent home at the Technical Museum. Their aim was to reveal the first stages of industrialisation in the city to a wide public – not just specialist interest groups. They did so by connecting with perspectives used in thinking about the older heritage, showing how profoundly the image and life of the city have been re-formed under the impact of industrialisation over the last century.

Presenting this industrial history as a common inheritance, the exhibition organisers aimed to reveal the technological and aesthetic qualities of particular areas and activities, hitherto overlooked; to demonstrate the learning potential in old machinery; to present the richness of information and evidence which the industrial heritage was capable of offering. Researchers used and presented local material – maps and plans, photographs from municipal and company archives, and written histories and guides detailing industrial activity. Revelation of the particular history of industrialisation in the city is a necessary first stage in getting the industrial heritage taken seriously, which must be followed by more specific and directed research, conservation initiatives and organisation (Deligianni 1990).

It is important to be able to understand as precisely as possible the seat of specific oppositions and to work round them as Peter Nijhof (1990b) suggests in relation to understanding the interaction of heritage hierarchies and development pressures in Dutch towns. Here, in pre-industrial cities, the historic core is seen as the primary heritage resource, and restrictions in the central area push development to the periphery, precisely where it impinges most on industrial heritage sites. In industrial cities, industrial heritage sites may fare better in the concern to promote and enhance the civic townscape, but are highly vulnerable to shifts in the relative costs and benefits of public and private transport. Cheaper private transport serves to encourage development on the peripheries, leading to intense pressure on industrial heritage sites; when the benefits of public transport systems are in the ascendant, it is the central zones which face the strongest development pressures. It is only by understanding these shifts, which in themselves have nothing to do with the quality and character of heritage resources, that threats can be anticipated and forestalled.

In other cases as with architecture and urban design it may become necessary to give special publicity either to new ways of working or to shocking neglect. Photographic exhibitions have often been used to dramatise examples of each, sometimes forming the turning point in a campaign for protection for example, simply by showing an attrition which had not been widely registered hitherto, or drawing attention to the particular qualities of industrial buildings and sites previously hidden behind assumptions and negative connotations. In Britain, 'Satanic Mills', an exhibition mounted by the organisation SAVE Britain's Heritage, aimed to do this for textile mills by conveying the often accomplished and monumental design of the mills – showing that they did indeed have architectural qualities of their own – and discussing their often considerable local value. In Flanders, the Flemish Association for Industrial Archaeology (the VVIA) launched its general campaign for industrial archaeology (discussed below) with a photographic exhibition drawing attention to the diversity of form, style and purpose encompassed in industrial building. By encouraging a re-evaluation, such exhibitions may serve as a useful starting point for a deeper campaign.

The importance of constituency-building is well recognised in regeneration work; the outstanding question relates to the status of different constituencies. Regeneration consultants recognise the importance of cultivating and motivating groups whose interest is crucial to the success of a project. If you are in the process of stimulating additional investment in an area, then your initial preoccupation is likely to be with either local or external sources of that investment – the well-known split among regeneration consultants between orientation towards the executive and towards the 'civic' spirit represented by the local chamber of commerce (see chapter 2). However, such projects inevitably have to extend to embrace and motivate others.

In New Bedford, Massachusetts, for example, where the initial focus was on a particular waterfront area which had been associated with the whaling industry, on the one hand it was necessary to involve existing and potential new owners, including the old bourgeoisie which was linked to the whaling interest, but it was also necessary to cultivate officials in the local government, and win the support of political elders representing now dominant constituencies associated with other industries and heritages. To find a new future for this

5 (a) & (b) Architectural conservation in the ship chandlery area of New Bedford's historic waterfront area

old area it was necessary to cultivate new constituencies alto-gether – cultural and heritage tourism, and those who could become interested in living or working or trading in a restored waterfront area. In this process the personal moral and financ-ial commitment of certain key members of old whaling fam-ilies (who had already created the non-public municipal museum) was crucial.

That this was more than a process of historic area con-servation has been subsequently proved by the election of the former director of the Waterfront Historic Area League (WHALE) to be the Mayor of the city and the extension of related lines of thinking – with WHALE support – to the actual waterfront itself, in association with the state and federal government, and to the business district, which has several fine examples of brick and steel-framed blocks. Each of these programmes introduces special problems and requires a new array of agencies and constituencies, each with their own specific objectives.

Schemes for the port area offer the opportunity of connecting the city to the water again and so undoing some of the damage done by a highway to nowhere that sparked the formation of WHALE in the first place. But developing these plans will involve careful relationships between different visitor attrac-tions and the living waterfront with its transport bustle. Plan-ning has required delicate negotiations between several constituencies in order to establish mutually satisfactory objectives, and success will depend in any case on public investment, which for the present is uncertain.

The downtown revitalisation plan will involve a different balance of constituencies than that for the waterfront historic areas as well as different objectives. The main aim is to promote commercial investment in and use of the downtown in ways that are essentially consistent with its robust build-ings: rather than thorough-going restoration or conservation, extensive internal adaptation is envisaged while keeping the overall flavour of the area. It also involves creation of new appropriate instruments – partnership agreements, redevel-opment consortia, incentives – and some common ones such as street infrastructure.

In Calderdale, UK, the emphasis has moved on further still, from retail areas and re-use of major factories to peripheral centres and estates, amenity projects and small scale industrial units – the Fair Shares programme responding to criticism of the initial programme being narrowly drawn, yet spending public money. In New Bedford, what has happened is in effect the continuation and a revival of a civic culture. This has centrally been about focusing existing concern on new tasks but equally about involving others in that concern – so it has been managing a civic heritage constituency. Extension of interest into the commercial and manufacturing areas of the city, and also into its residential districts, has at least in part been led by a growing awareness that it is questions of 'whose heritage' as much as 'what heritage' that must be addressed.

A civic spirit has also been revitalised through the Ecomuseum of the Fourmies-Trélon region. The old civic leadership had decayed and a new one had to be synthesised through the museum project, with the leadership falling more to engineers, foremen and schoolteachers. People in Fourmies had already decided that they wanted to give a value to the disappearing industrial heritage, and had been rescuing textile machinery with a view to forming a museum. They were greatly helped in their efforts to do this by the ecomuseum concept (which had not in fact been designed specifically for industrial heritage). Establishment of the museum was assured not just because the programme was able to get financial help under a wide array of government programmes, but also by the way in which general objectives and strategy were defined – the community-wide integrated approach to the whole landscape, the validation of monuments and traces of many significant ways of life, the central place given to a dialogue with the local populations by the curators, and the importance of drawing people into a process of 'making heritage'. These were not only important in organising a programme of work and resources, but also provided an agenda in terms of which constituencies could be addressed.

By comparison, elsewhere – where similar problems on a similar scope have to be tackled, and the integrative approach has been lacking – progress has been more difficult, though still possible. For example, in Norrköping, Sweden, it was possible to build up a constituency about Motala Falls, to extend the remit of the museum to represent industrial history, to enlist the city in a landscape study, following which the city did hold the ring for some key re-use projects to preserve the landscape of the falls with support from the Central Board of Antiquities. But there is still a stark comparison with the situation at Fourmies – one indication is that the city of Norrköping's current publicity – to attract visitors or workers or employers – makes no reference whatsoever to its industrial heritage. In Fourmies, on the other hand, the museum is now leading the promotion of the Avesnois region, using the heritage resources and local support it has marshalled as the basis for attracting tourism and investment.

The Industrial Heritage

This comparison shows that it is necessary to have not just a conservation policy for historic areas, or a museum service with a broad remit, but a strategic approach which invites broad involvement in a heritage which is inclusive of the main ways of life in the area, and validates these as assets. This strategy must have a broad validation of resources and the nurturance of a heritage movement as its central tenets. A governmental museum or park programme in itself is not sufficient. The benefits of this approach can be summed up by looking again at a North American comparison: the Massachusetts Heritage State Park programme, plus a weak heritage movement, produced limited results in Fall River, whereas in New Bedford a strong heritage movement has spawned a series of programmes with increasingly wide remits, producing a continually expanding agenda of revitalisation. But, as we argued in the previous chapter, the focus and content of public heritage programmes play an important role in enabling or frustrating civic initiative. This consideration seems to have been taken on board by those responsible for the Massachusetts programme – in their new plans for a heritage park in Roxbury, community history curatorship is to be given a central place.

Addressing a wider public

Small projects sustained by a core of voluntary effort are correctly preoccupied with their immediate constituencies: they must keep up momentum and development through having a succession of objects or forms in which to produce the work, whether they be conserved objects, publications or whatever. The question of how to offer this work to a wider public inevitably arises, but often almost as an afterthought. A key decision is whether to simply produce and display results or to 'open' a facility for the general public. 'Opening' requires not only interpretation as well as conservation and study, but continuing commitments of time and money which are difficult to sustain on an avocational basis alone. Formal organisation of internal and external relations is likely to follow, as are external support and commitments, the question of paid staff; all this amounts to a fundamental change in the kind of organisation, the implications of which we discuss in chapter 6.

Many groups with substantial continuing support have pulled up short of opening on a regular, let alone continuous basis, or have fallen back from the commitments involved. And it must be said that this may often be a wise choice: a very active programme of work with concrete results can be achieved without attempting to establish something like a museum. Other voluntary groups have been able to establish a partnership with local government or possess an endowment which enables them to maintain premises and collections which are 'opened'. Such decisions must be related to an assessment of the best way of reaching key constituencies.

A large number of industrial heritage projects provide facilities which are opened for the public without very clear conceptions of who would use them or how they would be invited to do so. The chief reasons for these elementary failures of marketing are assumptions about the self-evident importance of the resource, preoccupation with immediate constituencies or other aspects of project management, or lack of experience. Such marketing failure has received much attention but the remedies for it are often abstract: marketing is not just publicity – but identifying publics, not just for targeting advertising, but for meeting needs. Much marketing advice to museums is of low quality; there is an implicit message in it which is dangerous (for heritage organisations) – that large potential numbers of visitors, with money to spend, justify a large investment, which in turn must be aimed at the lowest common denominator of the large potential numbers.

Large investments are obviously not appropriate where they will be little used and may in any case compromise the project's basic objectives; it may swamp the resource or cause it to be extensively altered to accommodate the requisite of success in the mass leisure industry. Those who commit large investments will wish to reduce risk, and this will lead to the adoption of production values thought to guarantee success, irrespective of the particular qualities of the resource – and also at the expense of any detailed consideration of the needs of constituencies which are central to the cultural purposes of the heritage project. While there is room for heritage attractions of a variety of types, such decisions should not be taken without due consideration.

One project which has given these considerations explicit attention in its development is London's Design Museum. This project grew from an art historian's enthusiasm for commercial design as the 'legitimate art of the twentieth century'. His initial proposals that design objects of diverse sorts should be collected and exhibited along with accounts of their production, sale and consumption encountered as much opposition as they did enthusiasm. While some designers, manufacturers and retailers were interested in dramatising and enhancing the cultural significance of design, many academics and curators were doubtful both about the kind of status to be accorded to ordinary objects and also about the proponent's idiosyncratic enthusiasms – the proposed museum seemed more likely to become a monument to one man's taste than anything else.

The progenitor, however, showed a remarkable ability to continue to nurture support while incorporating many of the ideas and objections of critics. With substantial backing from a design/retailing group a foundation was established which, with the co-operation of the Victoria and Albert Museum, established an exhibition and education project which treated significant moments in the relationship between the design profession, industry and consumption, taste, and national characteristics in design, as well as playing host to a range of commercial exhibitions of product design by major corporations. Again, controversy generated by the shows was used to build a support structure and incorporate new ideas. This culminated in the opening, in July 1989, of a Design Museum as part of the redevelopment of Victorian riverside warehouses by the chief sponsoring corporate group. The local government was persuaded to accept this as the public interest 'planning gain' often stipulated for consent to such developments.

The Design Museum proved to be no ordinary museum. For a start it had no collection in the ordinary sense. A long process of consultation had established that the design collection originally envisaged was neither feasible nor necessary. To select a few objects for posterity would require criteria of selection too narrow to allow the museum to engage with a wide range of issues about the place of design in industrial culture; a more comprehensive collection would be both logistically impossible and unnecessary, with objects of industrial production. A strategy of uses strongly influenced the definition of the resource: public access space was divided between a small graphics exhibition space which doubled as foyer/coffee bar, a space for 'review' of current innovative products from around the world, a small temporary exhibition space and a large study collection – arranged around selective comparisons – supported by a computerised documentation system referencing large numbers of other significant objects; these were supported by a small library and viewing/conference theatre. Backstage space was overwhelmingly devoted to office accommodation.

This allocation of space accurately attempted to both reflect and influence design's cultural role. It was decided that, in order to do justice to issues and change in the relationship between designers, industry and consumption, it was necessary to involve professional designers, industrialists and retailers, design educators and historians and the 'general' public. Museum staff were set to cultivate each constituency – to invite attachment to the museum through membership schemes with special programmes of events and access to facilities, with costs and benefits tailored to each group. This meant a substantial amount of direct-mailed publicity, both of special programmes and of the quarterly public exhibition and events programmes, which have also been tailored to the needs of these constituencies. Regular monitoring of responses has been fed into planning, underlining the service orientation of the museum. The museum's board, though, represents professional and corporate interests in design rather than this full range of constituencies.

This commitment of the museum to explore design issues in a differentiated way attracted additional initial funding for education work (corporate sponsorship from a multinational company which wished to enhance and diffuse its image) and its attempt to interest industry in design quality and innovation attracted governmental support. This enabled a 'high profile' launch, with the aim of rapidly adding to the circle of sponsors and attracting a wide variety of visitors and building up repeat users for its programmes.

Early progress was somewhat uneven. Although the museum opening attracted considerable public interest, there are contradictions involved in representing the museum as specially suited to the needs of different groups. Elements of the design community were suspicious of the provocative (and somewhat obscure) opening exhibition, which possibly impugned their integrity in proclaiming the unity of 'commerce' and 'culture', while the business climate generally has become less charmed by the notion that design is a 'magic' ingredient. The initial response from education has been enthusiastic, although repeat visits will depend on the museum developing a learning resource in greater depth, while continuing to innovate its programme offerings. The 'general public', rather neglected in the cultivation of specialist interests, itself breaks down into a number of constituencies whose requirements need further study: tourists, for example, require a compelling and easily dramatised reason to find a stunning but less than easily accessible site, while those who are not already convinced that design is really significant have not really been addressed since the opening exhibition, and may be confused or even alienated by the general aura of stylishness which has drawn the sobriquet of 'yuppie' museum.

The Industrial Heritage

With these questions in play and continuing funding uncertain, the Design Museum cannot yet be regarded as securely established. The project of promoting understanding of how design works in industrial culture in order to have an impact on these processes is challenging and courageous. The strategy of prioritising the needs of key constituencies for this task is clear-sighted although its implementation involves contradictions. One problem is how far to go in parcelling out programmes in pursuing particular constituencies – this can be rather artificial and can sap vitality which would arise from their interaction in public programmes; another way of putting the problem is how can the museum offer something substantial to such constituencies without nurturing expectations about how far all the work of the museum is oriented towards those interests. The complementary problem is that serving special constituencies can create subtle barriers to public involvement.

A second problem is the delicate balance between responsiveness and challenge, costs and benefits, which must be struck in engaging each constituency; the enthusiastic response from education reflects the fact that they are offered a flexible range of programme service and useful if limited learning resources for little or no cost. Like many other revenue-earning industrial heritage projects, including the Museum of the Moving Image a mile upstream on the South Bank, the Design Museum regards free or heavily discounted educational group services as a good investment in building constituencies of the future as well as an important function in its own right. Such access programmes are often also supported by education authorities, other foundations or corporate sponsors.

The tactics employed in cultivating constituencies at the Design Museum are not in themselves original. Cultivating constituencies is not guaranteed by a marketing formula of mailings and specially promoted events. The Design Museum strategy requires staff to produce a stream of differentiated programmes and exhibitions while amending the study resources – a prodigious cultural output for an institution of its size. Success depends on producing strings of appealing ideas and offering scope for degrees of personal involvement in the work of the museum. If the concept of heritage management as service is to mean anything fundamentally different from offering heritage as a result or a product, then it has to permit degrees of appropriation on the part of the user which extend to taking part in making the heritage.

Extending opportunities for involvement

It has to be accepted at least as a starting point that there will be an unevenness in response: some will not want to be involved at all through feelings of general social marginality; others will stick closely to their particular heritages, and beyond this consume what is offered to them; others will feel more confident about overseeing a community's heritage, or indeed the heritage of an industry.

Industrial heritage projects and programmes of all types can be evaluated in terms of the possibilities for involvement they offer. The quality of such involvement is a major factor in the development of constituencies. In a service-oriented perspective, the point of departure must be the various ways people are continually engaged in making their own heritage, in personal or unselfconscious memorialising or participating in the continuous adaptation of tradition. Such heritage-making, which does not depend on public or academic sanction, nevertheless embodies cultural norms: the arranging of family photo albums is done in relation to expectations about usual family milestones and experiences. As we discussed in chapter 2, it uses various kinds of heritage resources to locate this personal heritage in a wider frame. The address which industrial heritage projects make to their intended constituencies is selectively received according to these personal agenda.

A strategy for developing crucial constituencies is beginning to be adopted by many heritage organisations and reflected in their organisation of work. Some established industrial museums have, like the Museum of American Textile History, made a distinction between public programme development, which produces events and exhibitions for a general public as a product, and outreach or community relations, which is thought of as an interactive cultivation of and co-operation with particular constituencies, whether they be defined geographically, socially or culturally – including a kind of public relations function.

While such programmes can always be 'tacked on' to an existing resource-oriented structure, the interaction of the parts has to be determined: Can they initiate projects which change what is to be collected as well as exhibited? May they be a route whereby people may become involved in voluntary work in the museum or a related Friends group? What are the implications of inviting involvement in learning, making, caring, sharing for managing the industrial heritage?

One implication concerns what counts as history and its connection with the present. While many professionals have difficulty in recognising or dealing with the near present as heritage, cutting off all that can be touched through living memory has serious consequences for involvement and possible benefit, as does the identification as significant of only stories or survivals pertaining to a particular and remote period. Of course there are many things which can be learnt about techniques of research about all historical periods and interesting results produced thereby. In the industrial heritage as in other areas, a rich diversity of projects is possible, but one should suspect disavowals of the recent past, as this disregards living memory and those who hold it, or those who live in recent buildings; it blocks off the possibility of expressing feelings or articulating views about historical change, and obstructs a continuing programme of contemporary documentation for future use.

What is constituted as a heritage resource and how it is made is also affected by perspectives of involvement. It may be a mistake to conflate all collecting around a small series of motives or even assume a particular status for collecting, in the sense of making a public collection. Some institutions today invest a great deal of effort in methodical collecting on behalf of a hypothetical posterity. Studies of the history of private collecting – or indeed the history of public industrial collections – show these to have been amassed for a variety of motives (Bann 1984). A significant part of what would now be considered heritage, for example in nineteenth-century collections, has been assembled in its own time for didactic purposes or pride of work or ownership, another form of public dissemination. This heritage was assembled more as domestic keepsakes or things which get put in the attic.

Few museums acknowledge this diversity of motive or draw attention to the basis of keeping and collecting in past showing, presenting and making representations; ones which do, like the People's Palace in Glasgow, seem to tap a wider and deeper emotional response in the visiting public. The natural extension of this approach is to invite public participation in the making of collections or designing objects or features of heritage significance. At Fourmies and the People's Story in Edinburgh, voluntary committees not only played a leading role in establishing collections but also arbitrated guidelines for their exhibition in working context. In the early days at Le Creusot, neighbourhood exercises of docu-

17 Summerlee's steam roller travels as ambassador to local events and has become the symbol of the museum (Photo: Summerlee Heritage Trust)

mentation and exhibition of old domestic objects were carried out – with the idea not of collecting the objects out of the community on a permanent basis but of determining the collective mentality about significance, making a record of this and of material culture for future use, and confirming the value of culturally significant objects in the minds of owners who might otherwise discard them unknowingly (perhaps under the onslaught of advertising). Extending opportunity for involvement in public collecting does not diminish the role of the professional or make 'passive collecting' a necessity, but altered priorities change the emphasis in the work.

An involvement perspective affects not only what is preserved and exhibited, but how. As we saw in chapter 2, it has become progressively more difficult for museum display to carry out didactic functions: on the one hand cultural authority has come to depend on a more complex knowledge, while on the other an increasingly wide range of cultural offerings attempts to engage the attention of the potential museum visitor. In this changing context the use of museums became restricted to those who saw their contents as 'their' heritage and brought the knowledge to use it. Museums were in danger of becoming the preserve of cultural elites and justifying their public status by tourism. Three problems had to be dealt with sim- ultaneously:

- to involve a more diverse public
- to involve each person on more 'levels'
- to maintain and extend opportunities for self-education, repeat use and further involvement

In response to these developments two contrasting display strategies developed. The first was the idea of subordinating presentation to the strong story. In often confused attempts to adapt the conventions of film and print, liberal doses of graphic design linked images, objects and dioramas in a narrative sequence. Anyone could follow the basic storyline in dramatic headlines and large-visual effects, while those who wanted to look more closely could find diverting detail. Preparing display in this form is an exacting discipline capable of being executed to high standards; done well, it can provide a reasonable range of address for temporary exhibitions of limited scope. As a basic display strategy for a whole site or museum for the medium to long term, however, the storyline lacks flexibility, and is crucially weak in opportunities for further use. Attempts to build in reasons for repeat visits through investing in spectacular production values compound the problem (see chapter 5).

There are special situations where such story-telling can be effective as part of a larger scheme: as an introduction to a more complex site (best made optional, as at the Black Country Museum or gestural, as at Wigan Pier); in contextualising and regulating flow past intensively sought-after exhibits (important for such sites as Jorvik and Bayeux, less tried in relation to industrial heritage); or, most suitably, when allowing the visitor to follow in the footsteps of others' experience, as in the Emigration Experience gallery at the Merseyside Maritime Museum. Where the user can play at being the subject of the story, then the logic of exposition and the logic of discovery are congruent.

The second, and in many ways opposite, strategy adopted to extend involvement is that of presenting an environment 'as if' and allowing users to make of it what they will. Simulated contexts in the sense of room sets are a long-established and much discussed display tactic (Saumerez Smith 1989: 6–21); the more recent development has responded to the total immersion offered in film or in Disney-style theme parks by extending the boundary to make the display a 'world of its own'. The golden rule is that no direct address to the user may be incorporated in the display itself, for fear of transgressing its 'authenticity'. As awareness of an 'industrial past' has increased, managers of the industrial heritage have been able to draw on the practice of open-air museums and archaeological reconstruction to simulate environments on a large scale. Vigilant curators have been able to secure industrial works or habitations complete with effects, on or near the point of last use, as inimitable testimony to past ways of living and working (for example, at Gnosjö and Klevfos – see chapter 5).

Environmental simulation offers many opportunities for inviting involvement: four-dimensional immersion in strange surroundings without an explicit guide or storyline is an adventure, heightened by the raw, unprocessed nature of many industrial sites and remains. It can offer complex appeals to the senses, stimulation to the imagination and challenges to understanding. It is capable of being used in several different ways simultaneously, catering for visitor diversity and inviting repeat use.

There are, however, contradictions to be managed. While historically minded interpreters are chiefly preoccupied with the pursuit of a perhaps chimerical 'authenticity' in such displays, the distinction between theme park fancy, scholarly reconstruction, animated assemblage and preservation intact is often lost on users. If many of the joys of experiencing another world arise irrespective of its historical accuracy, does authenticity matter? More to the point, if heritage managers want to maintain that it does, how can the ability to probe for it be stimulated without disturbing the seamless surface of the simulated world? Theme parks and museums may have been designed starting from different ends, but the ability to tell the results apart and find the difference interesting must be acquired. It may well be that quite different resources are used in a museum and in a theme park, that authenticity is in play in all sorts of ways which may be disentangled by the historian or museum critic, but how will this be evident to the first-time visitor in such a way as to prompt further interest and enquiry? How, in this context can support be given to the interests of a repeat visitor to encourage a deeper level of involvement? Not only do objects not speak for themselves but in environments, too, although they communicate a suggestive aura and can condense a set of clues, the questions are missing, and must be brought or supplied.

One strategy to encourage repeat visits is simply to extend the range of attractions on offer so that they cannot be surveyed in one visit. This superfluity creates an impression of richness. More to the point is to make the interpretation more dense and offer pathways of involvement which take the 'shop window' as a point of departure. Questions which problematise the surface appearance can be offered by actors, demonstrators, broadcast or printed guides, and can be offered as an optional extra adapted to special needs and interests. Devices of this sort have been naturally resorted to in attempts to enliven galleries and museums whose interpretive schemes are fundamentally classificatory; it is both easy and necessary to demonstrate the validity of such referencing systems by using them as a starting point for a number of different paths of discovery. In set-piece interpretation, the demonstrator can be a point of departure for more complex enquiries, and workshops places of reconstructive experiment, or repositories of connoisseurship.

These strategies are based more on work developed in museum education contexts than in the display practices aimed at courting first-time visitors. Inviting involvement means extending the scope of education services to encompass all users, and shifting to a user-centred, resource-based learning strategy. Beyond the visible differences in address between projects which have been exaggerated into an education versus entertainment polemic, there is a quite striking convergence of thinking between leading educationalists and those setting the pace in the marketing of cultural attractions: both agree that continuing education or leisure learning will become even

18 Visitors can witness the making of the museum: at Summerlee they view the machining of bushes to be used on the overhead cable system used to power the tram cars (Photo: Summerlee Heritage Trust)

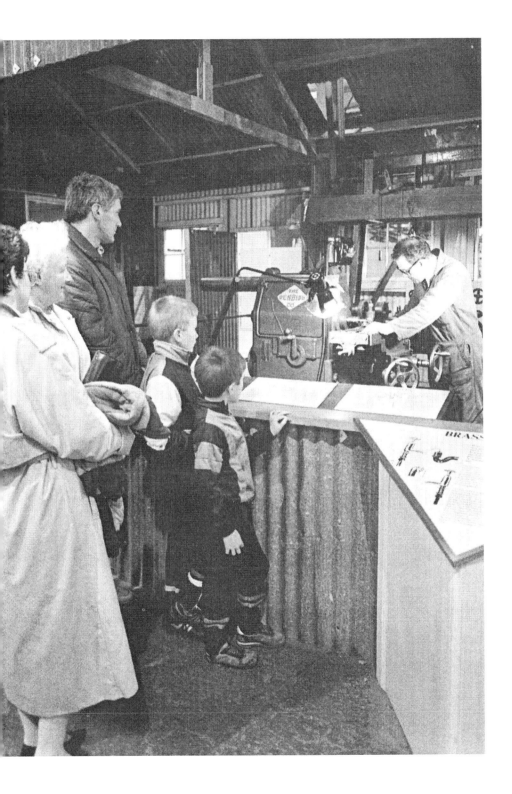

more important. Museums, which are supposed to be central institutions in this area, need both new investment and a re-invigorated approach to continue this traditional role; heritage attractions not perceived or presented as traditional museums have been relatively more successful in gaining a wider audience and in developing some new strategies for involvement.

Contemporary educational strategies which emphasise student-centred, resource-based, open learning, and which recognise a diversity of interest and aptitude, are compatible with much market-oriented thinking and would be perceived by many people as incorporating pleasure as well as discipline. There may be a greater consensus here between educationalists and marketers than there is among curators; in the industrial area it is noticeable that those involved with community museum work seem to share many assumptions with marketers about the primacy of an active and complex relationship between the museum – and the curator – and current users, whereas there is another sort of curator who prefers to deal with machines and objects than with the public. Industrial heritage has made its contributions to this development – in the opportunities for voluntary work which is more ambitious and challenging than average, in extending the open-air museum tradition and the practice of demonstration to new areas, and often in extending the recognition of heritage into new territory and building links from the museum into the community.

Areas for development within this new paradigm would seek to balance attention given to the initiate and to the novice to pathways of involvement. One model is placing museum-based project work within curricular contexts in school or adult education. This latter seems particularly well developed in relation to Swedish study circles – where there is a high level of participation in adult education networks, especially co-ordinated through the trade unions. Programmes of studies are particularly strong in industrial history, labour history and the history of work, as well as in environmental considerations, and, typically, winter studies are followed by summer site visits. The Museum of Work being developed in Norrköping has undertaken surveys of the courses dealing both with work, and also with the related issues of the various projects dealing with similar subjects. One of its objectives is to improve the communication between the work carried out by study circles, and that done by museums and sites, and it has recently published a directory of Swedish industrial museums (Geijerstam 1990). It also intends to develop programmes in relation to study circles itself, aiming to service and sustain them wherever, and in whatever way, it can.

Another model of good practice would encourage pre- and post-visit work – notably for school parties but perhaps for other groups, which could also make use of learning resources publications, which could be much more developed and varied than they are at present. There is quite a gap between literature which gives you the interpretation supports and things which invite you either to learn about some category of objects or phenomena, or to actually engage with how to study or do something. Dramatic re-creations are a way of entering into this and could be done on or off site, or be the basis for a continuing relationship – one aspect of giving students and other interested parties roles within the museum. Interactive catalogues are an adjunct which could be developed. 'Hands-on' experience – if taken as more than trivial – is already a strongpoint which could be developed. When it can be mixed with learning to do and demonstrate and can culminate for those who wish in a voluntary role doing something like driving a steam engine, for example, or learning how to do quite difficult things, then it gets interesting and the whole project begins to become oriented around personal develop-ment explicitly – quite different from the conventional use of volunteers or many education programmes which slot out-siders into some self-referential piece of museum work or give them the finished history rather than the resources to make, discover or present their own. Museum staff who are involved with demonstration or equally with education could take this as their main focus – enabling, not giving too much or controlling too much, but encouraging and underpinning – with the availability of a good range of supports, more path-ways to involvement could be opened up.

Equally, in interpretation things have to work on several levels; they can't just tell 'a story' and may close off interest by 'over-explaining', although they should suggest enough of relations to enable contexts to be imagined. Instead of synthesising results, the juxtaposition of different kinds of evidence, or different aspects of a problem, or perspectives on a historical situation may invite greater involvement. Dem-onstrators show, actors engage, and exhibitions can be designed to place visitors in a position to imaginatively re-create or identify with the experiences of others.

Access must address the breadth and depth of involvement respectively; both are important. Breadth of access in terms of visitor numbers has been much discussed in recent years, both as a direct source of income and as justification for subvention or other support, and access (to disadvantaged groups in particular) is increasingly discussed in a more qualitatively sophisticated way; this trend reflects a more serious consideration of the cultural roles of heritage projects. That role depends centrally on the possibility of cultivation in depth. We return to the contention that heritage concern is justified by what it enables people to do. What is becoming outmoded is the polarisation between education and entertainment, where the former means didacticism and the latter means themed experience – disproportionate investment in inflexible theatricality is perhaps an appropriate risk for niche retailing, but quite misplaced for an industry which lives by cultural creation.

Extending the scope of industrial heritage

Today it is possible to talk of an international movement for the conservation of the industrial heritage, to survey the landscape of industrial archaeology (for example, Trinder 1982) and to assess achievements in conservation and interpretation to indicate key problems and issues for further work as we do in this book. This movement has sprung up almost overnight: extensive interest and initiative in industrial heritage are only a generation old and the sense of an international movement guided by an integrated concept of the industrial heritage only arose in the late 1970s.

This book is primarily intended as an aid to managers of particular projects and programmes, and we have concentrated on issues likely to be important to success in such projects. But interest and involvement have not grown only through the work of such projects; there are other dimensions which we might call a culture of industrial heritage and a movement. In the culture we refer to the servicing of shared interests by publishers and broadcasters, and parts of professional conservation and curatorial and academic networks. By the movement we refer to those organisations which actively campaign for the recognition and expansion of industrial heritage. Practically speaking the one often blends into the other.

Publications

Publishers in several countries have played an important role in extending the scope of industrial heritage culture. There are several different kinds of publishing activity which have been important.

19 (a) 'Doing the washing' at Summerlee (Photo: Summerlee Heritage Trust)
(b) 'Doing the ironing' at Fourmies

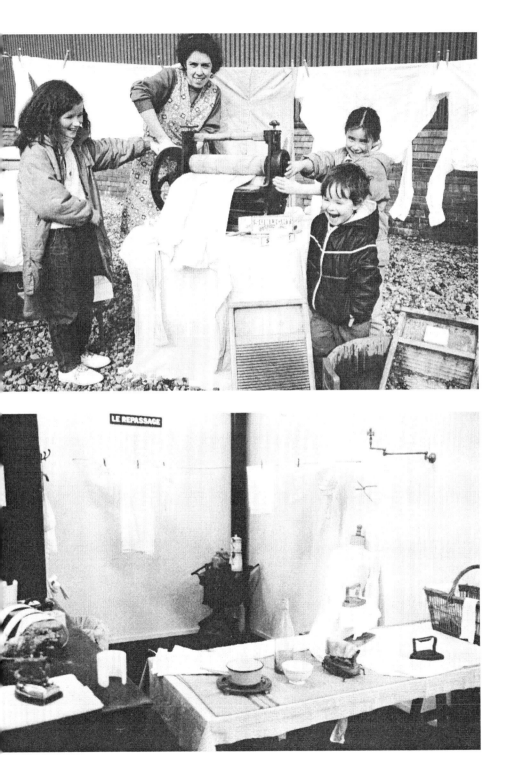

Specialist series or presses have documented key aspects of industrial culture using various sorts of evidence. This has only really worked where there is a fairly extensive market given by the existence of readily identifiable subcultures of interest, and some means – by societies or museums or specialist shops – of distribution. Areas with a particularly high degree of development are those in which fairly large numbers of people are involved in collection, restoration work or study, like aspects of transport history, clocks and watches, or ones which are highly visible – transport again, aspects of industrial architecture and monumental structures such as watertowers. These are object-oriented literatures for the most part – often examining the resource in great detail – yet they still achieve economically feasible circulation, while other artefacts, buildings or structures are comparatively neglected, and it remains a problem to see how this imbalance can be remedied. The market for the books has also to be created, and it will not in any case be viable in every language.

An important phenomenon is self-publication on a limited scale by societies and local groups. Distribution is an important problem beyond the society, but technology favours the extension of self-publication. Local and thematic societies have published the results of industrial archaeological survey work and conservation projects for the attention of other enthusiasts. Local or community history projects have also produced publications in which photo history and oral history have featured extensively (see, for example, Brecher, Lombardi and Stackhouse 1982; Hutchinson and O'Neill 1989). All such publications are potentially usable both in the immediate constituency and to feed wider interest, and some have been bent more one way and some another. A number of museums have also been able to bring forth periodicals of considerable substance. *Tools and Technology*, produced by the American Precision Museum, and *Scuolaofficina,* from Bologna's Museo–laboratorio Aldini-Valeriani, have reputations which far exceed their modest budgets. Museum yearbooks can offer more than an annual record: those of the Nordiska Museum, Stockholm, and the Workers' Museum, Copenhagen, for example, have often achieved a thematic focus of value in their own right.

Research institutions and governmental bodies have played an important role in publishing the selected results of inventory work and exemplary studies from a methodological point of view, sometimes in collaboration with commercial publishers. This is an important way in which models of work can be passed on and discussed as well as results of enquiries accumulated (see, for example, Brelot and Mayaud 1982;

Morger 1985). Consideration of how results should be published should be taken into account when any research or inventory project is planned, as a contribution to knowledge in a general sense. Consideration should also be given to whether aspects of the results can be presented in publications with a broader remit – newspapers, journals or television – or distributed via specialised newsletters and journals. There does appear to be a lack in any country of a centre to co-ordinate distribution of such publications or to fill gaps such as training literature which are not covered by existing museums services.

Protection organisations in some countries or localities have become aware that the information gathered in inventory can be used to beneficial effect – both as a research base on the history of the building stock and as a basis for spreading information to encourage responsible attitudes towards maintenance and conservation in particular and good environmental management more generally. Such an information strategy fits with the need to invite broad involvement in the extensive conservation responsibilities entailed by the industrial heritage (see chapter 4).

In Sweden, for example, inventory publications are developed as part of a cultural heritage policy for an area which is itself published. This has prepared the ground for assuming conservation responsibilities for suddenly threatened buildings and landscapes and also for responding to technological emergencies: the need to produce higher standards of insulation and energy conservation posed a direct threat to historic buildings, which the Central Board of Antiquities was able to forestall, mobilising information gathered through this inventory programme, and going on to produce advice tailored to the particular needs of owners of historic property.

Important initiatives towards interesting the general public in visiting industrial heritage sites and monuments have been taken by automobile clubs in Sweden and Italy (Touring Club Italiano 1983; Svenska Turistforeningen 1989) as well as by regional tourist authorities and by specialist academic bodies and societies such as regional ethnological institutes or industrial archaeology societies (for example the VVIA in Flanders, and the Association des Arts et Traditions Comtoises in the Jura) or, in some cases, by special regional heritage projects which give a prominent place to industrial remains and landscape – like Pennine Heritage or associations of related museums like the CCSTIs. These are extremely important initiatives and well worth establishing on a collaborative basis to connect with the best circles for general tourist information as well as specialist circles of distribution. A few writers have seen the possibility of a wide audience for industrial heritage from an early date and have made an invaluable contribution to extending public awareness: important instances are the early texts by Rix (1955), Raistrick (1972) and others spreading the idea of industrial archaeology and those by Barrie Trinder (1973, 1982), which spread the idea of industrial landscape, as well as Kenneth Hudson's (1975), Georges Henri Rivière's (1989) and Sven Lindqvist's (1982) work to expand people's conception of what heritage might mean.

The journals of societies of industrial archaeology and industrial history have attempted to connect amateur and professional contributions and audiences and also to extend interests beyond discrete areas of history in the range of articles they carry; nevertheless there do appear still to be lines of fracture between those whose studies are object-focused and those whose studies are people-focused in the sense of oral history or ethnography.

Societies, networks and associations

Those involved in industrial heritage seek out ways to develop mutual interests. The Social History Curators' Group, Women's History and Museums in Britain and the association of CCSTI in France are good examples of networking among curators around programmes of common museological interest. These networks are not simply expedients – they also further the extended heritage discussed in chapter 2, drawing in new interpretations with each new constituency reached. Professional and amateur associations – societies for the study of labour history, transport history societies, local history and oral history societies, restoration groups – are all involved in some form of history-making, while in museums themselves, professional affiliations – concerning the place of social history, ethnography, or women's history within the museum, for example – may foster reinterpretation and extended access.

It is crucially important to get industrial heritage concerns registered on the agenda of general museum or heritage authorities – not always the easiest of tasks. Where, as in Britain, the new generation of museums dealing with the industrial heritage have been nominally 'independent' trusts (albeit often public revenue recipients), some of the leading thinking about their heritage management problems has been sponsored by the Association of Independent Museums (Walden 1991). In Sweden, a co-ordinated programme of collaboration in contemporary documentation (SAMDOK) involves all museums in the country and has provided an important way of extending treatment of the industrial heritage throughout the country. As a voluntary programme it was established only after long discussion and debate, which was undoubtedly made easier by the existence of a national policy which decentralises much heritage responsibility to county level but with a clear remit to develop integrated regional cultural resources policies. In Britain, the area museums councils and arts councils attempt to serve a regional provision which has great diversity but little co-ordination. The Scottish Museums Council is presently considering how better support can be given to the recent expansion in industrial heritage.

The growth of independent industrial heritage projects in Scotland has been sparked by its still current de-industrialisation and the rather weak commitment of public museums in this area. The Royal Museum of Scotland's original connections with industry, diluted and then long neglected through 'congestion' of collections, were in the 1960s revived in response to the growing interest in industrial heritage, and in particular in response to the work of the Scottish Society for the Preservation of Historic Machinery, whose collections it eventually took over. In 1980, government reports which pointed to the creation of a unified Museum of Scotland indicated a more central place for industry and its products, but this has been overtaken by rapid developments in the voluntary sector which have included not only museums of specific industries based on interpreted sites but the New Lanark restoration and the development at Summerlee of a general industrial and open-air museum of the Strathclyde region, albeit strongly supported by a district council. While the development of the integrated Scottish Museum proceeds, the initiative in many ways has passed to the independents, and the national museum has recognised this in loaning to the independents machinery from its stores.

The achievements and problems of the independents must now be central to any discussion of what a national network should seek to provide. If the industrial heritage needs a 'synoptic institution', one can no longer assume that this role would be best played by the Museum of Scotland. Its new building offers neither optimal scale nor character, and, despite its recent definite contributions to conservation and attempts to re-cast its interpretation of Scottish society, it does not command the full confidence of the industrial independents. They would prefer to be the dominant clients of dedicated national funding, alongside the national museum. Independents of all sizes and local authority museums that have taken on aspects of industrial history will be hopeful of new support to consolidate and extend their own projects, and needful of improved co-ordination for industrial collection, documentation, conservation, interpretation and public relations. It is unclear what collaborative infrastructure is needed in each of these areas, and what implications this has for the boundaries between different areas of museum practice or between those responsible for the movable and immovable heritage.

The somewhat abstract character of the discussion about the need for a synoptic centre will be re-examined in the context of the priorities institutions wish to establish among this wider range of issues. The precise nature of the complementarity of such a centre with the nurturance of existing and desired developments will be closely scrutinised in competition for potential funding, and both the way in which this is done and the scale of the support likely to become available will depend on how widely the circle of discussants is enlarged beyond the museum world, to include conservation and education agencies, for example. The possible tasks of a nationally co-ordinated overview of industrial history may well, in the end, be parcelled out to different institutions, with, for example, the Museum of Scotland giving an overview of the place of industry in modern life, New Lanark being invested with a museum of industrialisation in the sense of a mill or factory system, and Summerlee being a museum of the metallurgical–mechanical engineering complex of Strathclyde which for over a hundred years was the lion's share of Scotland's contribution to industrial history.

Such a division of responsibility would not just be a matter of convenience to existing institutions, although it would help secure their future and support a more diverse programme of educational and touristic visits. While there are national stories to be told which have claim to national support, they aren't necessarily best told together in one place, because the historical and curatorial resources to do so aren't so distributed. It is of course possible to argue for a synoptic interpretation of industrial processes in the spirit of those national centres for science and technology which inevitably developed an historical dimension. But such a comparative overview necessarily abstracts from many relationships which can best be conveyed in museums and interpreted sites, and such comparison can now also be disseminated in a variety of media with better effect than through centralised collections and displays. Current thinking about science centres, which are less context dependent, favours the use of such media to facilitate geographical dispersal of multiple centres in an attempt to improve access.

Most of Scotland's industrial independents face serious obstacles to their development or even survival; all are under-capitalised, with inadequate reserves to underwrite current, let alone projected, conservation responsibilities, and are over-committed to ambitious schemes of restoration, for which state support has been patchy at best and private sponsorship (from industry or locality) negligible. Only Summerlee, less in thrall to the demands of an interpreted site and with a broad base of local support, has managed a balanced expansion. Yet all can show achievements in conservation collection and audience response, and claim good access and resource poten-tial to justify further investment. But there is no doubt that the problems are serious and do demand more than mutual help, current area museum service programmes or injections of tourist board marketing advice. Recent UK government policy, in pursuing the revenue-independent trust as panacea, has failed to reassess the nature of public responsibility in relation to the the changing public expectations of museums, and the burgeoning of industrial heritage forces attention on this deficiency in public policy.

It is important to remember that industrial heritage was not chiefly created by museums, let alone public agencies, and the voluntary societies continue to play a leading and formative role. Such societies often co-ordinate thematic public events (for example steam days) and may play an important role in contextualising work on particular projects for the par-ticipants as well as outsiders, amass important collections in their own right, acquire sites, issue important publications or make an input into conservation processes. However, they rarely enter into the running of sites or museums, although it does happen (in Belgium, for example – see below).

The management of larger societies also involves charac-teristic problems of organisational form and personal dynam-ics. Meetings are both more difficult and potentially of more exceptional benefit, so need to be planned more carefully, and relations between the activities of the society and the range of concerns of its members and their involvement in other projects needs to be considered. There is the real danger of lack of co-ordinating initiative on the one hand or, on the other one, exercise in a partial or even partisan spirit; the danger of decline through an ever-narrowing circle of interests is a real one, as is fracture. There is no formal answer to such problems, which can only be avoided with fortune and some foresight. Motivation is the bottom line in voluntary groups, and the critical question is what defines people's willingness to form a common project; locality, shared experience of work, similarities of formation, common interest in the subject, society, the possibility of achieving something otherwise impossible, or of learning, are all considerations. In general, it is possible to make a polarity between given bases of association, like shared experience or locality, and artificial or chosen ones, like interest in the subject, which are more likely to be important in conurbations or in national or regional specialist groups.

The idea of a movement for industrial heritage requires a different kind of society than either the locally based or those consecrated to particular interests. It has not only to embrace a wide scope in terms of the resources with which it is concerned but also to touch the constituencies whose support is necessary to the study, conservation and interpretation of this heritage. In several countries such groups have come together around the idea of industrial archaeology. This idea has been developed and understood in different ways and while it promises an ambitious programme of interdisciplinary study there is no way in which this can be carried out, both because of the limits of public resources and also because the industrial heritage actually requires an integrated approach by different disciplines which cannot simply be merged together without loss of valuable discrete perspectives. It may be, though, that heritage managers have a role to play in instigating appropriate projects in collaboration with academics.

The most important and promising aspect of industrial archaeology – apart from its willingness to search for hidden history in the most obvious, but also the most arcane, places – has been its ability to involve amateurs and professionals together in the same or related enquiries. Although there have been some fiascos in the organisation or lack of organisation of information projects involving loosely co-ordinated amateurs, the involvement of amateurs is crucial to the possibility of extensive future documentary or investigative work, as well as being important in its own right. The association of industrial archaeology with enthusiasts has not always helped the status of industrial heritage with professional academics or planning officials, but it is a constituency which should be encouraged to grow and develop in its responsibilities.

Industrial archaeology is however primarily focused on the study and in some cases the preservation of industrial remains – and this is only one element in managing the industrial heritage. There is a whole parallel culture of academic professionals and voluntary societies which are focused on ethnography and oral history – in many countries these links are stronger than the ones focused on artefacts. All of the research and preservation groups have to be linked to the constituencies which engage in environmental and cultural management, which are crucial to any programme to manage the industrial heritage as an integrated resource for a broad audience on a continuing basis. This broader constituency has never met as such in many countries but was brought together on an international level in 1973 through the formation of The International Conference for the Conservation of the Industrial Heritage (TICCIH) – a very important initiative which has through the contacts established not only spread the movement from country to country but through this exchange given it an overall character and direction which would not otherwise have appeared. TICCIH itself has now grown and become established to the extent that different concerns and focal points have grown up within it and it is beginning – so far as a loose association without substantial funding can – to develop a more differentiated programme to further agenda of research, conservation and interpretation. At the moment, the academic dimension especially is developing in a way not catered for by discipline-specific international associations, but its continued effectiveness depends ultimately on the extent to which it can continue to bring together the whole range of people and issues which are connected in the management of the industrial heritage.

TICCIH can only be effective if it makes links between different sectors and is not just an academic body for co-ordinated historical study. The specific functions of national and special interest bodies such as this have to do with information and communication, but not only with the gathering of material. They must also make propaganda, take initiatives and be able to offer advice. It is on this basis that great steps forward can be taken in enlarging the constituency for the industrial heritage. One dramatic example of what an active national society for industrial archaeology can achieve is provided by the Flemish Association for Industrial Archaeology (VVIA) which in 1990–1 dramatically boosted public awareness of industrial heritage through a year-long campaign.

The Flemish Association has a largely but not wholly federal structure; it aims to complement the activities of local groups and groups of thematic interest, such as those concerned with steam engines, breweries, etc., by programmes which promote public awareness, pooling information and expertise and co-ordinating advice and education. Members can belong both individually and through local groups – this permits degrees of involvement and helps maintain the national association as a specific entity which is more than the sum of the parts. As a society it is largely supported by members' donations and those of affiliated groups, though also by sponsorship and foundation grants. As a registered charity and association it keeps independent from substantial government sponsorship, preferring the role of advocate and adviser to government.

The association understands industrial archaeology to mean the study of the material culture of the modern period, including its working and living practices as well as artefacts. It promotes an active and critical interest in this history – a resource, not just an object of nostalgia. Unlike some heritage groups, it is interested in conservation, for example of buildings, not for its own sake but in so far as they are significant in this history. The association believes that it is important to encourage regional strategies for the study, conservation and interpretation of industrial heritage so that the sum of individual projects is more than the parts. It has encouraged the formation of regional ecomuseums or other co-ordinated projects connected with the mines of Limburg, the Rupel brick fields, and the flax region of Kortrijk. It has also been able to advise local groups on how to direct their efforts (for instance in the conservation and interpretation of a brewery at Alveringem), and has been called upon to give advice to companies interested in heritage projects (for example in the conservation and interpretation of a power station at Zwevegem).

The association has attempted to pool the information which its members and affiliates possess through establishing its own database of industrial sites and monuments, in consultation with official and academic bodies. It also attempts to pool experience by a series of thematic seminars and workshops whose programme is agreed and shared between some twenty constituent groups. Officers of the association can tap this network of knowledge and experience when they advocate and advise on problems which arise, or when taking initiatives such as the promotion of tourism. The association is on the point of opening its own centre of documentation and information.

Officers and active members of the association work relentlessly to promote public awareness of industrial heritage; they pool and cultivate contacts, especially in the local and regional press, to invite interest in neglected buildings and sites, tours and visits, conservation projects, etc. From this basis they ask local government and companies to take or support initiatives – in conservation, or in collaborative promotion of industrial tourism. Careful attention is paid to groups such as chambers of commerce and tourist organisations which are important in reaching powerful interests or broad publics. Travelling exhibitions, brochures, etc. support this effort. A special industrial tourism programme has been developed, with sponsorship from a major bank, which includes factory visits, site tours and self-guiding programmes which were promoted by a rally, backed up by an enquiry service.

Although this programme had been developed with increasing success, the association also found certain limits to the success and impact of industrial heritage in:

■ the health of the regional and local economy: heritage is likely to be more favoured in economically flourishing areas but these also have pressures of land value, etc. which can threaten conservation
■ the risk of conserving only the nostalgic, where pervasive influences needed to be counteracted on a large scale
■ the difficulties of preservation in the case of large industries, which required private capital or public investment beyond the reach of the association's affiliates

In order to breach these barriers and reach the 75 per cent of the public not aware of industrial heritage, the association decided in 1987 to launch a Campaign for Flemish Industrial Heritage in 1990–1, with an enhanced programme of temporary exhibitions, guided visits, publications, media, brochures and open days. It negotiated to get over 120 industrial monuments and sites included in the National Monument Open Day and took advantage of the presence of the TICCIH conference in Brussels to gain extra publicity.

The association mustered all its resources and contacts in preparing this campaign. Local groups worked to prepare projects for public attention, with voluntary effort and donations of goods and services from local firms. The association pressed these concrete personal stories into the hands of journalists along with material of another kind: basic material about the campaign and the significance of industrial heritage, accompanied by supporting statements from forty public figures representing a wide range of interests and perspectives – officials and politicians of different hues, educationalists, entrepreneurs and tourism promoters, guardians of the cultural heritage and experts on regeneration, engineers and trade union officials. Industrial heritage had raised a national profile. Throughout the year the atmosphere of campaign continued to mount.

The biggest single event occurred on National Monument

Open Day when sixty-five mills and sixty other sites were open and each attracted at least 500 visitors, with the largest – the mining area near Limburg – attracting over 10,000. Such numbers were a shock to the public authorities, who then began to receive representations as a result. By the next month the VVIA had been invited to advise or act as consultants on a number of dossiers about sites and monuments proposed for protection or re-use which had previously lain dormant. These included a power station and the large tile-drying sheds near Kortrijk which are now to be re-used as units for small industries. The crowd-pulling potential dramatised on the open day has led to the VVIA being invited to consult with a local authority on plans for a transport museum.

Another important change which the campaign has brought about is the readiness of industry to offer sponsorship for industrial archaeology projects. The VVIA has always actively sought industrial and commercial sponsorship – often asking for contributions in kind or of products at reduced prices, rather than cash. By these means the cost of a major photographic exhibition accompanying the campaign was reduced from £30,000 to £10,000, and many events were able to proceed with donated bus tours, facilities, brochures, refreshments, etc., and groups of volunteers got necessary raw materials. This strategy is easier to follow in regions with a diverse industrial culture of small and medium-sized firms of various branches rather than one concentrated and centralised.

But in 1990–1 the possibility of cash sponsorships – small ones of around £5,000 for concrete projects – increased enormously and the chief reason for this was the extensive and favourable publicity which the campaign had in the local and regional press. Firms could recognise not only the objectives of the campaign and in many cases their particular projects but more importantly that the campaign had news value and that therefore sponsorship has some publicity effect. The association itself secured sponsorship for their newsletter which was being re-launched with an enlarged and improved format and also for an annual Flemish Industrial Heritage award.

Looking back over the campaign as it drew to a close the Secretary of the VVIA, Adriaan Linters, said there was no reason to be afraid of a campaign of publicity like this which cost very little in financial terms, and expanded the organisation and its constituencies in several directions. The number of people who joined VVIA-related groups increased markedly throughout the year. If there is a problem area it has been people-planning. It is never possible to plan exactly with volunteers, especially for the more casual sorts of work which are nevertheless important for setting up stands, etc., but the rapid expansion of events, enquiries, new members, etc. has been difficult to organise. Nevertheless in October 1990 twenty local groups met to agree a shared programme of events, including training, and they also agreed to pool the cost of a stand at the Brussels industrial fair in the spring of 1991.

Defining heritage resources: protection, collection and documentation

4

A strategy linking resources and uses is a prerequisite of good practice in heritage management. The effectiveness of such a strategy can only be ensured by thorough evaluation, not only of the resource, but also of its possible uses. The management of heritage resources is a dynamic process of making and sharing meaning and value, and it is only by detailed study that it is possible to set parameters for management practices which are capable of enhancing the understanding – and enabling the care – of resources, whether through conservation or interpretation.

In relation to industrial heritage especially, many potential histories may be hidden – literally obscured physically, undervalued or unresearched. A careful programme of identification and study sets the agenda for heritage management, enabling better recognition of resources, and helping to identify appropriate strategies for their care. This chapter surveys techniques which are employed in the identification of heritage resources, setting out typical patterns of choice and fields of value. Different classes of resource are identified for diverse purposes, but it is in relation to buildings and sites that the techniques of appraisal have been most highly developed, largely in the interests of servicing systems of statutory protection. It is therefore with these inventories, and with these protection systems, that this chapter begins.

Inventories of heritage resources are traditionally organised according to certain classification systems – the separation of buildings from landscapes and from archaeological remains, and the separation of all these from other aspects of material (or other) culture. Each system has its own specialist disciplines and modes of study, any or all or which have their place in a heritage strategy, but attempts to bring them together in an integrated evaluation of resources are few and far between.

Landscape resources

The inventory is a well-tried technique for assembling information about landscape resources. It is at once a means of organising and structuring research and a means of presenting results. Field-based study is capable of recovering histories which other sources may not be able to reveal: the adoption of new structural technology and new systems of power transmission, for example, or conversely the adaptation of existing, leaves an imprint on surviving fabric but may leave no other form of record; the context of industrial production, the structure of its settlements, the ancillary processes and support services of an industrial economy, may also register precise physical traces which can be retrieved through detailed study.

A structured programme of field research, presented in a coherent way, may therefore provide a valuable database serving interpretive programmes designed to enhance understandings of particular landscapes, sites or buildings; it may also only be through the comparative evaluation of a number of different sites that an adequate basis for protection decisions can be reached. While an inventory which is designed to meet the needs of a particular planning policy may necessarily be structured within a tight thematic remit, the interpretive agenda may be wider.

Whichever the case, an inventory programme must find a convenient method to gather and register this information: most would include some textual component – describing the building or site, detailing its history, giving sources – and an illustrative element, which might be photographic or measured drawing. In arriving at an appropriate survey technique and style, there are a number of problems to be overcome: there are types of historical evidence which will leave no particular physical trace; the site-specific nature of inventories can focus attention too much on particular elements of systems and contexts without looking at their interconnections. For large built-up areas or complex industrial plant, the itemised process of research and recording may not be cost-effective. As a method of organising the assessment of resources, inventories need to be able to give attention to the wider context, and may also need to evaluate what survives against what does not. It is important to establish links between individual sites and infrastructural elements; it is also important to study links between sites and the urban space to which they give rise.

Determining boundaries: geographical, thematic, chronological

All inventories must have certain defining parameters, although the priorities of these may vary with the uses to which they are to be put. In the service of knowledge, or the enhancement of interpretive programmes, the broadest chronological, geographical and thematic range would ideally be incorporated into the survey, but, in practice, administrative convenience and costs are likely to fix quite precise limits. These limits may also need to be drawn tightly to meet the stringent, and possibly urgent, requirements of conservation planning programmes. The following discussion focuses on alternative ways of establishing boundaries – geographical, chronological and thematic. The subject of survey may be defined either as an industry or industries, or as a particular site or building type, or as a particular area or landscape. Choice of remit will depend on anticipated use.

Some surveys have been organised with the industrial heritage of a particular region as their remit. In practice the determination of geographical boundaries is likely to be dependent on administrative convenience as much as on historical morphologies. The larger the geographical area, the more selective the inventory process must be. Different approaches must be adopted according to the scale of the area surveyed. Working for state and city administrations in Connecticut, Mat Roth undertook extensive state and intensive city-wide inventories of industrial buildings. In carrying out extensive surveys, he gathered together as much background knowledge as possible first, in order to have a context from which to select certain examples to study in more detail.

This selection was drawn up with the aim of ensuring a cross-section of industrial buildings which could serve as an evaluative context for other examples. It was hoped that results would be of direct benefit to planners trying to gauge the value and interest of particular sites or buildings, where questions of relative quality, rarity or typicality are important, and expected that these results would be of more limited use to the historian: results were likely to advance understandings of the buildings of particular industries, and the broad historical development of industry in the state, but would not be able to say very much about the formation of industrial economies, cultures and landscapes as a whole (Roth 1981).

In more detailed local surveys every site where some form of industrial production took place could be identified. To some extent, the geographical area forms the subject of the survey, since the results may considerably enhance an understanding of its history and development. Subsidiary functions can be illustrated, the organisation of an industrial society at the micro-level traced and the impact of industrialisation on the physical environment explored and illustrated. This type of detailed survey provides more information than is needed simply in the administration of local planning decisions, and may be of more value to the historian (Roth 1986: 54–60).

These survey types were both specifically defined as surveys of industrial buildings, although their geographical remit helped to determine the differing levels of information that they could give: other inventories have been organised looking at the buildings and sites associated with particular industries, or with the traces of an industrial society or landscape as a whole. Others still have not distinguished industrial from any other building type. In Flanders, a general architectural inventory was launched and industry had its place within it (Van Aerschot 1986: 69–80). Similarly, an inventory of post-1850 buildings commissioned by the Dutch government as the basis for a revised conservation strategy, did not make distinctions between industrial and other buildings (Docter 1987: 32–40; Nijhof 1990a). Swedish local authorities are required to undertake comprehensive inventories of their built heritage resources before making conservation decisions. Small-scale local surveys have sometimes taken as their subject not a particular industry or a particular period, but a landscape itself (for example Alfrey and Clark forthcoming).

These inclusive strategies have a number of advantages: they do not involve pre-selection according to rigid criteria, so that buildings not designed for industrial activity, but nevertheless used for it, might be included; buildings where industrial use had not left any overt trace (the anonymous shed) may be identified; buildings of minor industries as well as major ones may be recorded; pre-industrial buildings of industry may be included; sites and structures can be set in their context, linked to interrelated industries, transport networks, settlement and community. Relationships between industrial and non-industrial economies, and the emergence and development of industrialisation can also be identified. The inclusive approach avoids argument about what constitutes industrial; it means that there need be no primary selection by type of industry or type of structure; it enables industrial buildings to be considered in their spatial and social/economic context (Binel 1986: 99–103).

On the other hand, unless this inclusive inventory can bring together the work of a range of different experts, all these things may not be correctly identified and understood. The information gathered may be of value in a historical context but may not itself advance the ability to make good planning decisions. There is still a great need for better knowledge of particular building types, so that comparative evaluations within general categories and over wide geographical areas can be made in the context of planning work.

It is for these reasons that other surveys have focused on the buildings and sites of particular industries. The Swedish Central Board of Antiquities, for example, has sponsored a series of inventories assessing the sites of various industries including brewing, brick making, iron production and paper making (Nilsson 1983, for example). In France, the Inventaire Général has also sponsored thematic surveys of particular industrial building types in additional to wider-ranging regional surveys (Belhoste, Cartier and Smith 1987: 150–7).

Some surveys have undertaken to investigate building types more narrowly defined, such as the Yorkshire mills survey of the Royal Commission on Historical Monuments (Falconer 1987: 162–3); English Heritage is commissioning typological surveys of specific industrial building types to enable adequate comparative evaluation in conservation decisions; in Britain, the Scottish Development Department has led the field in typological inventory of industrial sites and structures. Surveys of the buildings and sites of particular industries may yield valuable information about that industry, but will not necessarily significantly add to the understanding of a particular landscape. Complementary study considering the local context of the industry will enable these detailed investigations to contribute more to an understanding of the development of the industry and its impact on landscape and culture, and it is important to be aware of what the survey may leave out. For example, the exclusive study of textile mills may overlook the local role of domestic production and workshops (Binel 1986: 99–103); the study of coal-mining sites may not register the traces of coal-using industries.

Practical questions regarding the allocation of resources may necessitate studying only the buildings of a particular period. But this restricts the possibility of understanding things in the context of their development: the vernacular origins of a particular building type, the pre-history of an industry, may be overlooked. It may contribute to a tendency to isolate things in the past. Failure to adequately consider recent history may weaken long-term heritage management, a factor which is now being addressed in a growing number of contemporary documentation projects (see below).

However the subject is selected, and in whatever context the information derived is to be used, it remains important to ensure that the geographical boundaries and theme are not anachronistic and that typologies adequately relate to the development of an area or an industry.

Method of study and types of knowledge

The adequacy with which these themes can be addressed depends on the academic basis of the survey. The need for disciplines of study which are particularly designed to deal with industrial culture has already been demonstrated. Industrial archaeology provides one such tool for the evaluation of buildings and sites, drawing heavily on the methods of traditional archaeology. It looks at buildings in operation, and as they change through time. It attempts to turn away from preconceptions and iconic images of industry, its technology and architecture in favour of a wider historical approach which analyses the site or building as a functioning artefact, and considers the pre-history of sites as well as their continuing history, to help explain their development. The detailed archaeological analysis of a building or a site enables a history of industrial change and development at the micro-level, while consideration from the point of view of process provides a more comprehensive evaluation. It is necessary to retain from architectural history some awareness of the role of design, to avoid subordinating all to a narrow definition of function (Buchanan 1980; Cossons 1975; Stratton 1990).

The inventory of buildings carried out at Le Creusot, for example, developed a typological approach which closely related the development of local building design traditions to changes in the organisation of an industrialising society. By paying the kind of close attention to local building types which has more often characterised studies of vernacular building, allied to analysis of documentary material, the inventory was able to suggest ways in which at least the domestic architecture of an industrial community was the product of particular economic and social relationships (De Villiers and Huet 1981).

The architectural, archaeological and technological features that comprise the industrial landscape are capable of study and interpretation from a range of different perspectives and the social historian, economic historian, historical geographer or sociologist will have something to add to the ideas of the industrial archaeologist. Typically in Britain, it is the archaeological and architectural disciplines which have a primary role in the evaluation of buildings and sites. Without diminishing the importance of these disciplines, the approach more often taken in Sweden would stress the value of multi-disciplinary study at the outset. Where possible, inventories also consider technology and work processes, the social frame-work and the network of other local activities. This approach recognises a hierarchy of qualities corresponding to degrees of context-dependence in a building or site – while aspects of design, construction and function may be readily discernible from studies of surviving fabric, the experience of work, work conditions and organisation will only be partially visible, but may nevertheless constitute a vital part of the site history. Understanding and interpretation of sites and buildings will be enhanced by study on as many of these levels as possible (Berckmans 1990; Bursell 1975: 214–17; Nisser 1986: 35–46).

If, as we advocate, the subject is taken to be a historical or cultural landscape (a place and its people), different research strategies must be adopted. In this case, it will not simply be surviving material resources that will be evaluated. One might consider buildings which no longer survive, but also ways of life, cultural attitudes and memories. Innovative studies of this sort have been undertaken in France and Sweden, com-bining an open-ended understanding of landscape resources with a commitment to interdisciplinary investigation.

In Le Creusot, the Ecomuseum commissioned wide-ranging inventories which dealt with sites and buildings, but also with objects and archival material. It aimed to bring together as many resources as possible in the exposition of local histories, doing so not purely as a scientific investigation, but as a collaborative project requiring the involvement of local people. This approach remains exceptional in the scope of its definition of resources (de Varine-Bohan 1973; Scalbert Bellaigue 1981).

Four Swedish researchers have taken two industrial com-munities, Hälefors and Munkfors, as the focus for intensive investigation. The subject of study is the transformation of traditionally constituted industrial communities under the impact of the specialisation and rationalisation of industry and the growth of municipal government. The researchers look at economic history, the transformation of the environ-ment, the effects of change on people and their ways of life, and the geographical changes in the landscape and its population. It is hoped that this knowledge can be fed back into future development strategies and conservation in the two areas that are the subject of the study. The integration of these understandings into local policy will present a challenge to depart from conventional physical resource assessment, but how this might be achieved is yet to be determined, as the parameters of the study are strongly academic (Bursell, Morger and Nisser 1990).

Form and uses of result

Most systematic inventories relate to physical landscape resources. Many have been commissioned only in the process of defining conservation criteria and priorities. This has its effect on the comprehensiveness of the survey, but also influences the form of the results. Records which were designed purely for administrative purposes remain limited in their use. Britain's Listing record, for example, is at present largely designed for administrative purposes, and gives information primarily for identification. Concern to extend the usefulness of the Lists lies behind the introduction of indexed output, while attempts to ensure that the Lists are more responsive to local historical development and its characteristics may also extend their relevance.

Survey work carried out with a research-oriented remit may be of greater general use. The Royal Commissions for England, Wales and Scotland have been actively engaged in recording industrial sites since 1979 (for example, Falconer 1986: 27–36; Hay and Stell 1986). At present there is a poorly developed relationship between the recording work of the commissions and the compilation of the Statutory Lists. The detailed and much admired work of the Commissioners is time consuming, slow and expensive, and protection decisions cannot afford to wait. The architectural bias of the Commissions has not always been sympathetic to culturally focused study, but the surveys constitute an important academic resource. Indeed, these records may form an impressive documentation for buildings which no longer survive – the Commissions' remit covers the recording of buildings in advance of demolition.

The Historical American Engineering Record (HAER) also carries out inventories with a brief that is not solely drawn up in relation to conservation decisions. HAER was established in 1969 as part of the documentation carried out by the National Park Service. Preservation societies and State Historical Commissions have sponsored these inventories of industrial sites, and have been able to use the results in adding buildings to the National Register of Historic Places. But the inventories are not intended solely for this purpose, and the brief established by the National Park Service was intended to provide a record of the physical evidence of the national industrial history. In this instance, recording and identification of buildings for protection spring from the same process (Malone 1986: 47–53; Delony 1990).

In Sweden there is also a commitment to recording which goes beyond simply registering buildings to be protected. Local authorities are encouraged to carry out inventories of their historical landscape resources, using these to identify specific sites for conservation, but also to establish and define local character as a context for general planning. The comprehensive inventories commissioned by the Belgian government under legislation of 1976 intended to study and evaluate sites for protection, but also to stimulate interest in and concern for the built environment (Van Aerschot 1986: 69–79).

Surveys intended for planning purposes are capable of wider use, but if they are to enable a wider understanding and appreciation of resources, close attention must be given to ways of publicising the information which they contain. Most of the HAER inventories have been published, and although HAER itself preferred to limit the background information on the area of study, and did not automatically analyse the information assembled on separate sites, the directors of the inventories themselves often introduced historical essays outlining broad themes of historical development, providing a context for the evaluation of individual items (Malone 1986: 47–53; Kulik and Bonham 1978). Inventories which remain only as gazetteers of sites without any contextual discussion will be of more limited use. The Swedish system of inventories serves as a series of local guides, offering an introduction to landscape history as well as a resource assessment for use in local planning (see, for example, Stockholm's Stadsmuseum 1984 and Upplandsmuseet 1984a, b).

Studies of buildings, sites or landscapes offer an important potential resource, in both planning and interpretation for heritage. The information that can be derived from these studies is necessarily assembled from specialist disciplines and modes of enquiry. This resource assessment is the first step in a programme of heritage management which also requires processes of analysis and communication: what to do with the information gained, and how to use it. While conservation decisions may require close study of intrinsic qualities of sites and buildings, drawing largely on architectural, archaeological and engineering expertise, in the *interpretation* of landscape resources there is a need for further levels of interdisciplinary study enabling different dimensions of historical significance to be drawn out.

Landscape resources: systems of protection

Any system of conservation and protection requires a system of resource assessment or inventorisation as discussed above. But in making use of this information, the management of a system of protection has a series of other issues to negotiate. It must make choices about how the protection system is to be organised, the criteria for selection and the kinds and degrees of protection afforded. The discussion in chapter 1 has shown that most existing frameworks for protection were not designed specifically for industrial heritage, and fitting industrial heritage in poses general problems which must be resolved in the context of the existing protection system.

Institutional context and organisation

In Britain and France all evaluation for the statutory protection of sites and buildings is handled through national bodies, and decision-making is not delegated. Criteria for conservation are also nationally determined. Sites and buildings are subject to rigorous scrutiny before being accepted for protection. A national context of decision-making emphasises certain things at the expense of others, but does aspire to comparability and comprehensibility. A nationally constituted body may be able to mobilise professional resources not available at a local level. Identification of a limited stock of assets may actually facilitate their management: too many resources may mean too little attention paid to anything. For industrial heritage, a national framework may be apt in providing a comparative framework for the evaluation of development which took place in a national context, and it may be appropriate where the scale and extent of industrial sites and buildings may require the input of national resources to ensure conservation.

In Sweden and the Netherlands there is a local system of selection with only minimal guidance from the central government. In both countries, this is a relatively new introduction, and is therefore largely untested. The system will only be as good as the commitment and knowledge of the local governments concerned. This is a particular issue in the Netherlands where local authorities vary enormously in size, and some do not have any paid officers. Such a devolved system will not facilitate comparability and comprehensibility but, where there is sufficient local commitment, does have the potential for enabling a wider range of buildings to be conserved, and for reflecting a more specifically local history and interest (Riksantikvärieambetet 1989; Nijhof 1990a).

In the Netherlands, a national inventory project carried out by the county governments is considering the whole built environment, 1850–1940. The results of this inventory are published, and are made available to local authorities, but decisions about new nominations to the register of protected buildings will be taken at the local level. County administration will monitor the effectiveness of this system in an attempt to ensure that important buildings are not left off the register, but the aim is to encourage local commitment to conservation (Nijhof 1990a). The attempt to marry awareness of local interest with recognition of nationally significant buildings could provide a valuable framework for a more comprehensive conservation system than that which is currently available either under a nationally-oriented, or under an exclusively local system.

Itemisation and classes of protection

In Britain there are three classes of protection: Ancient Monuments, Listed Buildings and Conservation Areas. Each category arises from a different legislative base. Ancient Monuments and Listed Buildings are designated through the agency of central government, while the designation of Conservation Areas is largely a local matter. The survey work which underpins each type of protection is carried out separately, and it is not always easy to achieve the co-ordinated protection of complex sites which cannot be simply classified as either building, monument or site (Suddards 1988).

While criteria and procedures for selecting buildings and sites for protection are clearly defined, criteria for selecting areas are much more poorly developed. Designation of Conservation Areas is a local responsibility and there is no real framework to ensure adequacy either of designation or of management. Existing boundaries are rarely based on awareness of morphology for example, much more often on immediate visual stimuli or on contemporary property boundaries. There is often a poor commitment to the management of Conservation Areas.

Similar divisions are maintained elsewhere, but the distinction between item and area status is not always as sharp as it is in Britain: in France, for example, powers in relation to Listing extend to the surrounding area to create a heritage zone or 'eco-protection' (Leniaud 1985; Vincent 1987: 104–7). The survey work which identifies resources is not always itself divided according to the same categories. In Sweden, the state county administration can designate buildings for protection, indicate the way in which the building is to be cared for, and make regulatory provisions governing the surrounding area (Riksantikvärieambetet 1989). Such provisions may have a special relevance for industrial buildings and monuments which formed part of a functional system.

Evaluative criteria

The English conservation system has relied heavily on visual, architectural–aesthetic considerations, although more recognition is now being given to the historical qualities of a place. This acknowledgement of the importance of historical criteria may be of particular relevance to the protection of industrial heritage, and is accompanied by a commitment to a programme of research which will identify the principal characteristics and lines of development in the buildings and sites of key industries (White 1990).

In the Netherlands, too, evaluative criteria have been reinterpreted to allow more recognition to historical rather than purely aesthetic qualities. Scientific importance and social significance, mentioned in the Monuments and Historic Buildings Act of 1961, but rarely taken seriously at first, are now accorded more weight (Ten Hallers 1985).

Sweden provides a contrasting set of criteria for the evaluation of buildings using historical significance or presence in a settlement of historical interest to determine value. Outstanding architectural merit in itself will not make a building eligible for protection, but only in so far as it represents part of the cultural context of the building (Riksantikvärieambetet 1989).

In the state of Massachusetts, survey for protection has been revised to move away from dependence only on aesthetic or visual criteria, embracing social science in giving recognition to function, process and vernacular design. It considers historical context and works with reference to the landscape as a whole rather than to individual properties within it (Weslowski 1984: 90–5).

In France, the Historic Monuments Act of 1913 lays down historical and artistic criteria for conservation. The wide scope of the historical criteria enables the classification of industrial monuments as part of the heritage. Scientific criteria are specified in an act of 1930 concerning the conservation of sites (Leniaud 1985; Vincent 1987: 104–7).

The Industrial Heritage

Although there are clearly problems with criteria heavily organised around architectural history, historical criteria alone may not deliver an appropriate register. Where the aim is the *physical* protection of items of special interest, it is important that the historical criteria selected are appropriate in a planning system concerned with environmental design, and that physical protection is the most apt response to the historical interest identified. For example, is building conservation an appropriate way to memorialise a famous person or famous invention? It is the typological development of industrial buildings and sites which can most aptly be registered through conservation policies, and it is important that research underpinning conservation criteria is focused on the buildings and sites themselves.

Protection

Countries vary in the degree of active protection provided by registration. In Britain, the presumption is in favour of conservation, and powers exist for this to be enforced. While the necessity for some change is admitted, it is also assumed that a building will not be substantially altered, and guidelines governing permissible change are drawn up (Suddards 1988). Local authorities have leeway in the determination of degrees of permissible change, but may lack the expertise and information base to make choices which fully reflect the particular character and interest of the individual buildings.

The system of control is less comprehensive elsewhere. In Sweden, regulations governing the care of designated buildings are intended to be framed if possible in agreement with the owner, and they lay down the minimum standards consistent with the maintenance of the historic interest of the building. Sweden has very few statutorily protected buildings – 953 in April 1989 – and relies heavily on local ordnances to put teeth into a conservation policy (Riksantikvärieambetet 1989). By contrast, Britain has some 400,000 Listed Buildings, and it would not be possible to draw up individual schedules for the management of each.

In France, the system of control is also flexible. Under the 1913 act, protection is intended to be complete, and is even deemed to involve restoration to original condition. On the other hand, the 1930 sites legislation is more general, and buildings within a classified site may be altered if the general character of the site is respected. If a building is deemed to merit protection in every detail, it will be classified as a historic monument, but if an industrial complex is considered interesting for its general lay-out and for the presence of non-architectural elements, then it can be protected as a site. This flexibility will only be successful if there is a good body of knowledge for the evaluation of items and their importance, and a clear understanding and specification of what aspects of an item should be preserved. Like the Swedish system, it is possible to set out conservation intentions for each site.

The French system also draws distinctions between the type of protection appropriate for a site which is no longer in use, and one which is still used and therefore still subject to change. The designation permitting flexible conservation standards may be more appropriate for an industrial site which is still in use, and control over architectural quality may be of less relevance to industrial structures than control over the general disposition of the site. Cases would have to be assessed on their merits. The operation of a flexible system necessitates the establishment of an adequate base-line and clear criteria in order to ensure that the right degree of protection is applied to the right components of the site. It therefore requires a more rigorous site-appraisal if it is to be an effective tool (Leniaud 1985; Vincent 1987: 104–7). However, with adequate resources for assessment and administration, such a flexible system of control may ensure a management programme responsive to the particular character and interest of industrial buildings.

Landscapes, sites and buildings: resource management

The management of heritage resources in the sphere of buildings and landscapes uses the conservation criteria and processes outlined above as its first tool. But the effective use of conservation in an integrated heritage management strategy requires a more detailed process of evaluation to determine uses and interpretive agenda.

The need for detailed appraisal may be particularly acute in the case of industrial sites or buildings where value and interest may go beyond the immediate architectural components of the site, and which may face particular challenges regarding future viability. Industrial buildings are often in areas threatened by redevelopment through high land values or urban decay. Their significance may not be widely known or appreciated. Dereliction or decay, unfavourable siting in relation to land-use zoning, vulnerability to changes in function or process are typical of the problems faced in the management of the industrial heritage.

Industrial buildings may not be recognised as of importance until their primary use is threatened: any form of re-use is likely to involve fundamental change to the building and be destructive of traces of its history. Effective conservation strategy may therefore have to establish appropriate new uses while recognising the limitations of preservation through new use. The latter may suggest the importance of recording and documentation programmes; the former suggests the necessity for an integrated approach which sets conservation firmly in the context of economic development.

But in the first place there is clearly a need for survey methodologies which are specifically designed for industrial buildings, sites and landscapes and can give a detailed schedule of individual components and their interrelationships in defining exactly what elements require what degree of protection.

Determination of realistic conservation objectives depends in the first place on a detailed assessment of resources and a clear understanding of exactly why and in what context the site is deemed of value. There is scope for establishing grades of significance which will guide planning authorities in how to manage heritage resources in future. The issue is not simply whether to conserve but how to do so. The particular reasons why the resource is valued must be specified: is it important for technical, architectural or other reasons, for social and economic history, as a local landmark, etc.? Is it the building that is important, or the process, or its cultural context? This evaluation requires a comparative framework: is the site of international, national, or local value? (See, for example, Lindsley 1980.)

Questions like these form an important component of the Monuments Protection Programme which is being carried out for Scheduled Ancient Monuments in Britain. This programme aims to identify monuments of national importance, but also acknowledges that there may be more appropriate alternatives to Scheduling. It gathers information on condition of monuments so that priorities for preservation and resource allocation can be established. It notes that preservation might be motivated by potential information gain or educational value as well as by landscape importance. Criteria for protection include assessments of state and extent of survival, rarity and period representation. The programme includes industrial sites in its remit, although it was designed to be applicable to all types of field monument.

Similar management appraisal criteria form part of the cultural resources survey programme for the state of Massachusetts introduced in 1979. Here, in addition to historical and contextual information, consideration is also given to extent of knowledge, agents of destruction or attrition and constituents of protection (Weslowski 1984: 90–5).

Specialist inventory work can establish detailed criteria for conservation, and the kind of flexible approach to conservation characteristic of the French system can translate this into an appropriate degree of protection. English Heritage is working to encourage locally focused heritage audits which would be able to evaluate groups of buildings and different classes of site simultaneously (Butt 1989: 38–42). The Borough of Calderdale has set the pace in Britain for showing what can be achieved when conservation is not simply treated as an add-on, but is fully integrated with economic planning (see chapter 2).

In order to make such integration a viable proposition, there is scope for the development of techniques of appraisal which bring together historical evaluation with assessment of economic viability – matching resources to uses (see, for example Eley and Worthington 1984; Reichen 1985). Various methodologies for a local area study which would attempt to match resources to uses have been proposed, although constraints of cost have limited implementation. In Washington DC, Partners for Livable Places work with an amenity strategy which is primarily concerned with economic regeneration and the creation of new jobs: a heritage plan takes culture in general as its subject, and includes the natural environment, recreation and leisure and urban design (McNulty 1989: 21–5).

A recent Civic Trust appraisal of Burslem in the potteries contrasts a face-lift scheme of thirty years ago with awareness now that regeneration depends not just on the proper care of the urban fabric, but on an understanding of the economic fabric of the area, and a willingness to work with local people. The survey that follows studies retailing patterns, employment patterns, vacant floor space surveys, tourism potential, traffic, as well as heritage resources. It uses a townscape analysis which delineates spaces and landmark buildings, and also surveys of available organisational resources for regeneration. It does not have a very tight conservation component at all, but does provide the basis for analysis of economic context and policy framework (Civic Trust Regeneration Unit 1989).

In framing an environmental management strategy, it is not sufficient to be able to demonstrate the worth of a particular building or site – a viable and compatible future for the building must also be assured. But the acceptance that heritage can play a part in urban regeneration should not obscure the fact that the interests of *industrial heritage management* will not necessarily be best served by the retention of facades as townscape components. There may be a case for more far-reaching and literal conservation to protect certain sites and buildings in their integrity. There will certainly be a case for programmes of interpretation, dealing with those aspects of a history which are not carried forward through simple retention of the fabric.

Conservation planning has played an influential part in setting an agenda for inventorising resources around particular uses (the formulation of protection policies). From the perspective of cultural resources management, the different techniques that have been applied to the inventorising of resources for conservation have different strengths and weaknesses. Inventories are generally organised around classes of things which may be seen in an area context, but which do not necessarily elucidate the area as an entity, or consider the territory itself as a resource. Even the best-designed and best-intentioned conservation policy will have limitations from the point of view of cultural resources management: there will still be areas where historical resources are spread too thinly or where there simply isn't enough that has physically survived to benefit from a conservation policy.

Statutory conservation is inevitably concerned with the fabric, not the use, and while integration with economic planning and development may go some way towards tackling this problem, conservation alone is rarely in the business of sustaining activities which are no longer viable. An area-based heritage programme with its remit defined either as regeneration, or as interpretation and the cultural agenda, could not rely only on a conservation policy to frame a detailed strategy for the local area.

The dominance of conservation planning in establishing public definitions of heritage has sometimes meant that too much is expected of it. At a local level, there is often interest in the micro-history of the area, to a depth which would be inappropriate as the basis for a conservation strategy: it would mean keeping everything. Conservation may not always be the most appropriate way to register a local history.

A cultural resources management programme with a wider brief would provide a context for conservation policy, but would not solely rely on it. It would also require economic support to sustain existing uses, and the development of complementary conservation, recording and interpretation programmes. It would require a rigorous conservation programme with good specialist input into designation and flexible management options clearly reflecting reasons for interest. But a broader-based heritage strategy would also recognise other kinds of resource: ways of life and work, memories, etc. This broad approach to the definition of heritage resources would need to be balanced by an equally broad approach to the possible uses of heritage resources, in which conservation would be one option alongside interpretation and recording.

Museums and sites: conservation and collecting

Traditionally, museums have been the custodians of artefacts classed as heritage resources, and have collected to conserve and to study. Collection has certain characteristics: it involves removal from context and display according to some principle; it often involves a change in ownership. It may involve the immediate commitment of resources, and certainly assumption of responsibility.

In 'old' heritage, artefacts from an industrial culture were likely to be seen in certain clear-cut ways. They may have been viewed as art objects; they may have been viewed as technological innovations, or as symbols of local development. These points of view provided a way of making sense of objects removed from context and arranged serially, but are less satisfactory from the perspective of industrial culture, which is more concerned with production and use in context and with understanding sequences of innovation and change.

Industrial culture is a challenge to museological conventions of collection and interpretation because it embraces the technical and the commonplace, the means and mode of making as well as the product, includes large structures, mass-produced artefacts and concepts and customs tangible only through a dispersed set of evidences. It provides a challenge at root and branch – to the content and context of collecting.

Although museums have moved away from their origins in taxonomy and classification to embrace a cultural focus, there is as yet little evidence of strategic thinking concerning the assessment of the resources of material culture and their appropriate treatment in a museum context (see, for example, Hindle 1978; Jenkinson 1989: 119–24). There has been no systematic inventorisation of these resources, and no single system of responsibility laying down standards of care or criteria for conservation. These resources are not by nature part of the public domain in the way that buildings and landscapes are, and therefore have no part in the system of planning control which has provided a framework for the evaluation and itemisation of cultural landscape resources (although some classes of artefact which have a very definite relationship with a structure also receive some degree of formal protection). They are therefore outside statutory regulation.

In the absence of systematic inventories, and even of general agreement over what constitute heritage resources in this field, the potentially enormous resource pool of material culture is tapped by museums according to their own programmes and following their own principles. Documentation systems adopted in common by museums working in similar fields of enquiry may begin to constitute inventories of what has already been collected; the potential use of such a system as a means of structuring information about the wider resource pool of material culture has been suggested as a development of the classification devised for pre-industrial culture by the Musée des Arts et Traditions Populaires in Paris, and some of the documentation systems established for industrial collections discussed below would be capable of structuring wider-ranging research programmes (de Virvelle 1977).

But all too often museums are collecting according to extremely general criteria which may at worst be passive collecting arising from donations or from what happens to be available. Poorly structured collecting policies impose severe limits on the interpretive agenda which museums can develop; this agenda may also be seriously constrained by inadequate appreciation of the relationship between artefacts in the museum, their contexts of making and use, and their place in the whole output of material culture. The development of adequate systems of documentation is therefore a vital prerequisite in the management and use of collections.

Collection and documentation

Documentation work carried out by museums divides into two overlapping areas: it may be a process of gathering information about objects, but it may also be the recording of other things such as working practices. It must serve the purposes of collections management and facilitate the role of the museum in interpretation, research and resource management, both within the confines of the museum and in its relationship to a wider cultural field. In order to achieve this, the scope of documentation must embrace objects in the collection, but also held elsewhere, and must be able to include in the same register documents, books, people, places as well as objects. It requires recording and research as adjuncts to collection (Museums Documentation Association 1981).

Documentation of objects is an important aspect of collections management. It provides a tool in the establishment of a collecting policy and lays the basis for the interpretation of artefacts in the museum. It may do this by organising information on existing holdings enabling strengths or weaknesses to be identified, or by establishing a database relating to thematic contexts. For example, the Museum of Rural Life in Wales carried out a detailed programme of research on rural smithing which involved oral history, photography and collecting (Williams-Davies 1990). Documentation may also help to define parameters for what should be collected. For example, SAMDOK in Sweden uses documentation to establish representativeness as a criterion for collection.

Documentation provides an annotated register of collection, in the first place as basic record of acquisition. It must enable objects to be identified and retrieved, so must provide some form of representation (for instance photographic). It must provide detailed information on provenance and permit cross-referencing to other objects with related provenance (for example from a workshop or belonging to the same business or household). It must include conservation notes, recording analysis of the state of the artefact, and a record of work done.

The categories of recorded information must permit the fullest possible use of artefacts in interpretation, ranging over their physical properties and the contexts of production and use. It is therefore important that information on provenance can be expanded to include documentation on the context of use of either the object in particular or the type of which it is an example. This is likely to involve cross-references to other series of information, for example oral history records, archival or bibliographical cross-references. To enhance the value of its collection the museum should have or should acquire this type of information, working in contexts where a rich network of cross-references can be built up.

It is important to recognise a multiplicity of contexts in which objects have existed and may be interpreted. This needs to be born in mind in any system of classification used to help organise documentation or related research and collection. Such a system must enable access to different contexts and the relationships between them which can inform interpretation and research.

A documentation system adequate to the needs of industrial cultural material must register the primacy of cultural significance – accepting that objects have meaning only in context. It must also recognise a wide range of classes of evidence: sound, images, archival material as well as objects. Documentation systems drawn up in response to the needs of industrial collecting have sought to address these issues.

In Britain, the Social History and Industrial Classification (SHIC) deploys four classifying categories – personal life, domestic and family life, community life, and working life. These categories were devised to deal as well with abstract concepts as with precisely defined artefacts. The system recognises that all objects exist in the context of a use, along with other objects, and it takes spheres of activity, rather than generic types, as its organising principal (SHIC 1983).

The system has been criticised for failing to pay adequate attention either to production or to the possibility of multiple uses (Porter 1988). Its logical mistake is to use categories to give a more or less exclusive referencing system (cross-referencing is not encouraged) because the history of objects may be impoverished if they are classified in categories in which they may not have been exclusively situated. It may not be well able to take account of the historically variable relationships of these categories. Using categories heuristically is valuable, but classifying knowledge according to these categories may be restrictive.

In Sweden, SAMDOK recognises the value of analysis from different perspectives, and the dependence of this in the museum context on good documentation. Like SHIC, it attaches primary significance to objects in contexts, and also uses the notion of milieu (home, work, public, commercial) while acknowledging that these may overlap (Nystrom and Cedrenius 1982; Rosander 1980).

Both the SHIC and SAMDOK classification systems work on the principle that objects can be sited largely in a single category, but recent trends in cultural studies would emphasise the importance of plural histories which the operation of these systems at present only inadequately acknowledges. In particular, it now seems important to recognise the relevance of production as well as use, especially in relation to industrial culture; the possibility of multiple contexts of use, especially when extended to include meaning and value as well as intended and actual function (Fägeborg 1984a); the necessity to account for the specific history of individual items as well as the general relationships within classes of object (Porter 1988: 114).

In order to address these issues, there is a need to develop flexible indexing and cross-referencing systems, establishing matrices which give equal importance to the many characteristics an object may have as evidence of cultural histories. Such an approach is permissible with computerised systems, though not so easy without them. It must also be underpinned by thorough processes of research and recording, enabling specific provenance to be detailed wherever possible (Porter 1988: 114). It requires co-ordination between all departments in a museum system.

As research and recording, documentation may take place alongside collecting and sometimes instead of it, for example in relation to certain kinds of artefact or experience which cannot simply be represented through artefacts. In this sense, documentation enables the museum to extend its range, for example including contemporary experience, comparing local and distant experience and undertaking the interpretation of more abstract phenomena such as work, labour history or social life. The extent and penetration of industrial culture means that a museum collection can only ever be concerned with the fringes of the whole phenomenon – documentation provides a way of extending its reach.

Documentation is of critical importance where collection is not viable. This is likely to be a particular problem in relation to certain aspects of industrial heritage, where artefacts may be too big to be literally collected, or may exist in such quantity as to preclude collection of anything other than a very small sample. It may also be relevant where artefacts are still in use.

Whereas in relation to past societies the ability of museums to present multi-dimensional interpretations may be severely limited by restrictions on past collecting policies, inadequacy of existing documentation, the poor relationship between artefacts collected and total material culture output, the often poor coverage of contemporary industry in museums may partly be a function of the dominant place accorded to artefact collection, together with the restricted availability of artefacts to collect in relation to continuing practices. Some of these problems can be overcome through coherent and systematic programmes which bring documentation and collection together. The successful interpretation of contemporary society depends on a continuum between artefact collecting and documentation – instead of seeing documentation as something which is done to artefacts, museums must see documentation as in some respects itself a type of collecting (for discussions of contemporary collecting and documentation, see Bott 1985–6: 12–14; Cedrenius 1987; Davies 1985; Green 1985; Kavanagh 1983, 1987; King 1987; O'Neill 1987).

The extensive inventorisation programme carried out by the ecomuseum of the community Le Creusot-Montceau-Les-Mines, discussed in more detail below, is based on such a definition of museum functions, and specifically addresses the relationship between what is directly collectable by the museum and what is not. In carrying out this documentation, the museum was able to record the existence of resources, and use them for specific purposes as required, without literally becoming their owner or custodian. This programme demonstrates that knowing where resources are located may be as important as actual care or ownership.

SAMDOK also co-ordinates a programme of documentation related to active collecting. It does this through the establishment of pools or teams of museums working to record and collect in each of the milieus defined as the basis of its classification. At its best, this approach enables co-ordinated and systematic coverage; it provides good supporting contextual research to define parameters of collecting in areas where collecting would otherwise be problematic. However, in practice the centrality of artefact collecting in SAMDOK's perception of museum work has possibly limited the attention paid to certain cultural phenomena which do not have an extension into artefacts. Social practices, for example the changing relationships of men and women at work and in the home, may be overlooked in recording programmes largely devised around artefact collection, though would be more amenable to recording visually or orally. Working on a much smaller scale, a co-ordinated recording programme established by a group of museums in Scotland has its object in photographic and oral material, permitting flexibility in the choice of annual thematic agenda.

Oral history serves as a particular example of the potential of non-artefactual resources for the museum. Often treated as an adjunct to the serious business of collecting, it is increasingly recognised as a valid and enriching activity in its own right, helping not only in the interpretation of collections, but also in defining new roles for museums and creating new constituencies of involvement. Oral history provides a means for museums to work with those areas of experience which are not rich in artefacts, enabling them to consolidate understandings of the local cultural nexus, compensate for bias in artefact collections and validate histories otherwise invisible (Aérospatiale 1985; Brecher et al. 1982; Davies 1984; Hudson 1980; Jones and Major 1986; Mullins 1985; O'Neill 1990; Whincop 1986).

Redefining the relationship between collection and documentation may also open out new possibilities for the reappraisal of past societies and established collections. It may enable museums to reconsider the techniques which they use for interpretation by giving serious consideration to written sources, for example (Burton 1989). The reputation of museums can depend on archival resources as much as on collections, and while these may establish and sustain their authority as centres of research they are rarely integrated directly in interpretation.

Organising for documentation

The extensive (and expensive) documentation programmes necessary to represent the complexity of industrial culture are out of the reach of individual museums. Working within carefully delineated boundaries, such museums may be able to contribute to the understanding and interpretation of defined specialisms. But the opportunity for systematic recording and documentation held out by the accessibility of recent or contemporary history can best be met by collaborative work.

The SAMDOK programme in Sweden aims to establish a pool of resources providing information which is available to all collaborating museums. Central to this is its definition of the country's museums as a coherent overall resource, in which national, regional and local museums all have a clearly defined place. Responsibility for collecting and documenting is divided according to certain agreed themes, with the intention of enabling participant museums to consolidate their own specialisms, while ensuring that effort is not duplicated, and attempting to provide a comprehensive and representative coverage of contemporary industrial society in Sweden (Cedrenius 1987; Nystrom and Cedrenius 1982; Rosander 1980).

The SAMDOK scheme depends for its success on a formal structure of co-operation sustaining a tightly defined agenda for participant museums. Such a scheme may not always be viable, and risks overlooking the spectrum of local experience by asserting the importance of the typical and representative according to nationally agreed criteria. Other collaborations organised on a more informal basis have been concerned to sample diversity rather than attempt systematic, 'representative' coverage. The programme organised by Scottish museums comes into this category, and the Household Choices project established by the Victoria and Albert Museum and Middlesex Polytechnic to document the ways in which people arrange their homes aims to exploit diverse interpretations of the same subject carried out under the auspices of different institutions across Britain.

The richness of experience represented in this project owes much to its encouragement of self-documentation as well as professional observation. Oral history work goes some way towards creating involvement in the documentation work carried out by museums, but museums could also establish for themselves a role as enabler in participant observation and self-documentation. Although the involvement of non-professionals in the documentation process may necessitate departure from the objective record-making encouraged by SAMDOK, it offers immediacy of experience, and may be the best way to extend the reach of museums working with limited resources.

Documentation is therefore one of the crucial functions of a museum. Those interpretation centres which do not carry out any form of documentation perforce operate on a very limited agenda since documentation provides a means to establish a resource base for the future development of interpretive themes and the management of collections. As numerous oral history projects have shown, it may also have a role in creating and sustaining certain constituencies for the museum.

Collecting policies

At present, the use of systematic documentation programmes to inform and guide collecting policy is poorly developed: documentation is led by collection more often than it leads it. However passive it may appear, collecting is a dynamic process – the first and critical stage in the interpretation of particular histories by the museum. A clearly articulated policy is therefore crucial, and must stem from a clear understanding of the relationship between the artefact (including images, oral evidence, even structures) and its context. In the discussion which follows, we consider ways in which collecting policies can limit or extend the scope of the museum.

Collecting for conservation

Motivated by the desire to conserve obsolete or threatened items, many museums would rank conservation or preservation as their prime *raison d'être*. Examples abound of the rescue of obsolete machinery, for example, and museums have been able to fulfil an important role in salvaging things which might otherwise have been lost, since *in situ* conservation is not always an option. But acting in response to threat may skew the collection towards the obsolete, and provides a slanted interpretation of actual industrial history. The basis of the collection for a proposed new museum in Hanover appears to be a miscellaneous series of machinery, available to local enthusiast groups simply because no longer in use. While it may not be possible to guarantee a collection of 'best examples' or coherent series, either through inadequate knowledge, or through the vagaries of availability, collecting in response to threat is likely to be an ad hoc process which necessitates a strong supporting interpretive programme.

Whereas, thirty years ago, it was considered possible to serve the purposes of conservation by removal of machinery *ex situ,* the growing awareness of the significance of context in enabling a fuller understanding of the ramifications of technological systems and the circumstances of their use has produced greater stress on conservation *in situ,* leading to a new kind of museum – the interpreted site (Lindsley and Smith 1973: 55–68).

Conservation through the literal saving of a whole site or complex inevitably involves a massive commitment of resources and therefore a detailed audit to establish viability, which might focus on representativeness, comprehensibility and integrity. Whether the resource is a certain type of machinery, or a complete iron-working site, its conservation needs clear motivation, and should not simply be reactive. It is important that saving can be justified according to clearly stated criteria. This may be difficult without an adequate research base and resource assessment, including reference to other surviving examples. Conservation also needs a clearly structured relationship with interpretation: how can the site be understood, and what can be learned from it? (See chapter 5 below.)

Collection for education

Museums have also assembled collections for education. Many important national science and technology collections originated to provide a resource for engineering training, their contents only gradually becoming reinterpreted as heritage (see, for example, Desvallées 1985). Museums continue to establish study collections in the older traditions of taxonomy and classification. The Museum of American Textile History has a large reserve collection which is rarely seen by the public but which provides an impressive cross-section of textile working machinery. The value of this collection has been enhanced by the rigorous application of collecting criteria, based on a detailed knowledge of the relationship between what is in the museum and what is not (Museum of American Textile History 1984). By contrast, the study collection at the recently opened Design Museum in London does not aspire to be comprehensive – there is no clearly defined basis for collecting and no attempt to relate the collection to the total possible output. These factors impose severe limitations on the use of the collection.

Study collections are assembled on the principle that more or less coherent series of objects are capable of study in their own right. In displaying collections to a wider public, museums are now more likely to structure the educational potential of their collections through an explicit programme of interpretation. While this may enable the general cultural context of artefacts to be explored, the inadequacy of much object-based study in museums and a lack of confidence in its value has limited their educational potential. Display risks over-interpretation, subordinating possible significations to a dominant theme. Choice of theme should be generated by rigorous, multi-disciplinary study of the artefacts themselves. The educational value of a collection depends on its coherence and the adequacy of its documentation.

Collection and classification

The adequacy of conservation, educational and interpretive strategies depends on a clear appraisal of a unity to study, protect or collect. Museums determine their remits according to particular agenda: in relation to industrial heritage, museums have traditionally taken either a thematic approach – museums of particular industries, processes or products – or a local or regional approach – the industrial history of a region. They may have approached industry through science and technology, or through social and economic history. They may separate industry from general cultural history, or they may include it. They may deal with historical industries but not contemporary ones. Their scope may be local or national. They may be concerned with particular classes of artefact, with particular themes (industrialisation, work, etc.), or with a cultural landscape.

Geographical and historical scope

The tradition of national museums of science and technology, together with the influence of academic history on interpretations of national industrial development, have encouraged museums to polarise on a national/regional or local axis. There are important differences in emphasis between national and local foci. A national or international frame of reference may require a level of abstraction and generality which leaves much local texture to one side. On the other hand, a local emphasis may not be responsive to the greater linkages which are a hall-mark of industrialisation.

The differences can be graphically illustrated by a comparison of The Museum of Time, La Chaux de Fonds, Switzerland, with the nearby ethnographic museum of the watch-making craft. The former deals in concepts, design and invention allied to a reverence for the artistry of its collection, and the local history of clock and watch making is a minor detail in the abstracted story of time. The latter provides a highly specific account of the local industry by showing its context as seasonal by-employment in upland farms. The changing history of production – the development of the factory, for example – falls outside the remit of both museums, but, for all its home-spun localism, it is the ethnographic museum which best conveys a sense of historical contingency and human agency.

Criteria for determining the geographical remit (the location of the museum and the scope of its collection) must be based on a thorough evaluation of the resource, and the historical context of the phenomenon. Did it remain strictly local (craft-based industries), or was it national or even international in impact (major steel works or ore mines, for example)? Assessment of the remit should take account of local specialisms of a wider industry – for instance in the textile and iron industries, service industries and food production.

Confusing these levels risks anachronism, where for example major industries are represented through minor craft-based localisms. A small blacksmith's forge in a disused steel works at Charleroi, Belgium, may be the beginnings of a more ambitious project, but does little to interpret its surroundings; the museum at Hastra, the electricity supply company for Hanover, emphasises *consumption* at the point of *production*;

Pilkington Glass Museum in St Helens, Lancashire, aims to tell the story of glass in general and its collection is largely based on broad sampling of decorative categories of glass and some relationship to processes. The museum is on the main factory site, but there is no history of the company, the family, the place, the workforce, and its collecting policy concentrates exclusively on products.

Where the extent and dispersal of an industry or phenomenon do not have a peculiarly local character, such as the applied sciences and technology, or where it is an integrated and interdependent phenomenon, there may be justification for a national focus enabling the industry or phenomenon to be investigated and understood as a subject in its own right. National museums of science and technology can provide such a function, but are themselves open to the criticism that they may ignore the international stage (Moreton 1988: 132–3).

Nationally focused collections may be able to dramatise relationships with modern industry which may not be in the same place as the historical industry. There is also some sense in having national museums of certain industries forming study collections which can clearly show comparative and typological development of process or technique, and the contribution of particular industries to a national economy. But a museum that aspires to represent an industry or phenomenon nationally must have the resources to match its ambition. The Museum of American Textile History in Massachusetts began as the Merrimack Valley Museum and extended its scope only as it developed opportunities to collect over a much larger field. It will shortly be moving from purpose-built premises to the storehouse of a former woollen mill, but otherwise makes small concession to the detail of the local history with which it began.

While industries may have a national significance, they will also have had a specifically regional concentration and impact, and it is important to remember that a comparative overview necessarily abstracts from many relationships which can best be conveyed in local museums or interpreted sites. The museum must be able to dramatise the relationship between the national and the regional or local. This might be in regional variations of national technological developments, or it might be in local work practices and social organisation. Siting of museums of industry should be determined in relation to the industry itself rather than simply by reference to perceived available markets. This has the benefit of enabling local and national interpretation to be brought

together, and it also enables connections with the wider industrial landscape and culture to be drawn out by the museum
(Raistrick 1972: 267–82).

The physical scale of *industrial remains* may be such that no
private project could support their conservation and interpretation, and in this case there is some justification for rigorous
selection to ensure viability through national support. It may
simply not be practical to have more than one example of a
conserved large-scale rolling mill or steel works, and the
ability of museums to collect so as to represent such large-
scale operations will be severely limited (Bowditch 1988).

Similarly, certain sites or types of industry may be of such
importance to the national economy, or be so typical of
certain stages in economic development, that some kind of
national support should be forthcoming. Organisation on a
national level gives a potential concentration of specialist
knowledge and resources which may be vital to the success
of certain types of project. In Sweden, for example, the oil
refinery at Engelsberg in Bergslagen is a rare survivor which
requires specialised technical expertise and resources which
are not available at the local level. At Gnosjö, a rare survivor
of a once typical regional industry received state support in
the creation of an interpreted site. The problems involved in
the conservation of the Rammelsberg ore mine site at Goslar,
Lower Saxony, are beyond the means of the local area, and
national support is appropriate without necessarily implying
that the site should become a national museum of the iron
industry.

Certain types of industrial activity were not regionally specialised but might have been found anywhere. In Belgium, the
dispersal of the brewing industry, and its recent concentration,
have resulted in large numbers of breweries now falling out
of use, but often with enthusiastic local support for re-use as
a museum. It would be inappropriate to centralise resources
and have one museum of the brewing industry, but equally
unsustainable to have hundreds of small local museums all
doing the same thing. Co-ordination of interpretation can
ensure that a number of museums with the same general
subject in fact present different and complementary aspects
of its history, and the Flemish Association of Industrial
Archaeology (VVIA) aims to foster informal co-operation to
achieve such co-ordination.

A further problem relates to the collection of artefacts which
are literally found everywhere – mass-produced items for
instance (see, for example, Bott 1985–6: 12–14; Desvallées

1985; Green 1985). Nationally organised specialisms designed either to represent major national industries or to deal with the problem of ubiquitous mass-produced goods have been advocated but could overlook local interpretations, and obstruct the understanding of regional and local histories. One approach to this problem is the co-ordination of regional and local levels of organisation such as is being developed in Darlanas county in Sweden. A regional cultural heritage is interpreted through themed museums based on local histories. There are fifteen communities and it is intended that each should have its own theme, getting ideas and advice, specific exhibitions, inventories and publications from the county museum.

Handling the national/regional relationship and the inter-connectedness of advanced industrial economies therefore necessitates not only broadly based interpretive programmes but also collaborative organisational arrangements. The Dar-lanas approach seeks co-ordination within a single museum system, while in Catalonia a decentralised structure for the Science and Technical Museum of Catalonia sustains special-ist industrial museums in different regions (Casanelles 1987: 212–14; Casanelles 1990).

An alternative approach in the absence of a structured museum system is the creation of networks of association. In Sweden, SAMDOK advocates co-operative approaches to specialisation of collection. This voluntary association of Swedish museums of cultural history, launched in 1973 to address the problems of duplication and gaps in passive col-lecting, has succeeded in reorienting collection on a broad, nation-wide basis by dividing responsibility between different museums, and co-ordinating loans (Cedrenius 1987: 15–19; Nystrom and Cedrenius 1982). The association of CCSTIs in France undertakes similar co-operation. In Scotland, where an informal association of industrial museums has already undertaken joint documentation programmes, the Scottish Museums Council is considering commissioning a feasibility study for a network of industrial museums (see chapter 3). Such a network would provide improved co-ordination for industrial collection, documentation, conservation and interpretation and could enable the substantial achievements of independent museums in this area to be consolidated and sustained. Integration of interpreted sites with agenda-based museums may enhance the possible understandings of both.

These issues arise principally when the resource is selected according to historical or thematic criteria, as type of industry, activity or artefact. Where the subject of the museum is taken to be a landscape, and therefore local by nature, the issues in determining the agenda are rather different.

Ecomuseums in France and Sweden have taken a territorial approach to the determination of a remit, basing their thinking on an industrial ecology or cultural landscape – the territory of a people. 'Territory' is populist in tone and implies not just an archaeological or aesthetic landscape (which is likely to be the English approach) but the people making the landscape – its subjects and possessors. While such a concept risks reduction to an idealised folk notion, it does highlight the creative impact of culture on the environment and brings together ideas about the resource and who it is for. But if the subject is the people, how are they given a voice – how treated as a resource?

The Ecomuseum of the community Le Creusot-Montceau-Les-Mines has been one of the few institutions to attempt the systematic inventorisation and documentation of the cultural resources of its territory. In its early years, it made inventories of handicraft works, of machinery and of archival material as well as of sites, monuments and buildings, and also organised a programme of research using specialists from various different disciplines. It took a radical approach to collection, asserting that all objects, whether movable or immovable, in the community are in effect part of the museum. It was able to do so by distinguishing legal from cultural property.

The museum intended to acquire things which did not have an owner, which were under threat and which had no current use-value. While this accorded with traditional thinking about the curatorial purpose of a museum, conservation was no longer seen as the primary goal of the museum since it was intended that, where possible, continuing usage would be the best guarantee of conservation (and the museum was prepared to accept the risk of alteration or destruction). It was felt that strict curatorial conservation should apply to only a fraction of the reserve collections.

The museum's interpretive responsibilities extended beyond the bounds of its own property, and it distinguished between a collection *in general*, left in the hands of its several owners, and a *reserve collection* which the museum would actually hold. It proposed that all objects which keep for their owner a value, whether functional or affective, should remain with their owners and form part of the general collection. They would be represented in the museum only in the form of an inventory card and might be borrowed for specific projects. Objects which had lost their primary value but which were an important source of evidence for the community, its history and environment, would go into the museum's reserve collection for conservation and use in interpretation (de Varine-Bohan 1973; Evrard 1977: 6–9).

Although such a scheme could not form a practical basis for museum work in most cases, it at least acknowledged a problem which many museums are wary of addressing: that is, the relationship between what is in the museum and what is outside it. It acknowledged that the object is only one element in the whole social, cultural and natural ensemble. It hoped that the museum would be able to help shape the attitudes of owners in giving recognition of cultural value. The museum's responsibility was defined as the identification of resources, encouraging their dispersed care, and mobilising them for particular uses (de Varine-Bohan 1973).

The approach taken at Le Creusot contrasts with the strategies for resource evaluation undertaken elsewhere. In Sweden, the Ecomuseum Bergslagen attempts to cover a much greater territory and therefore has to take a far more selective approach to the identification of resources. The area is so large that it is not easy to see in what sense the landscape makes sense as an economic and cultural territory with a real historical integration. Its resources are defined primarily as the archaeological traces of former activities.

In the United Kingdom, the Ironbridge Gorge Museum began with aspirations to be a total environment museum but its role has reduced to extend directly to a number of discrete sites. It has carried out a number of detailed inventories of resources, but these have all had an archaeological bias – there is for example no serious attempt to integrate the Friends' oral history recording project into the mainstream of the museum.

Collecting strategies: themes vs artefacts

Running through all the various determinations of scope, a fundamental distinction remains between those museums whose parameters are defined in direct relation to a set of objects, and those where they are defined more in relation to an idea or concept (industrial history or work, for example). The role of collecting in relation to the work of the museum must be differently defined in each case.

If the museum defines its scope in relation to a particular class of artefact, it is important that there is an explicit understanding of the relationship between collecting and interpretation. The context of collection must be appropriate to the cultural significance of the object – whereas, in the past, the basis of collecting may have been age, rarity, integrity or happenstance, there is a need for rigour in defining the basis of the collection, and awareness of the limitations of what can be achieved simply through objects (see below, chapter 5).

Object-centred collection must recognise the limitations of collection, taking account of survival rates which may be poor where things were badly made, perishable, or used to destruction; it must recognise that certain classes of object may be unavailable because still in use or too expensive, or incapable of being moved. While objects are capable of interpretation from diverse perspectives, there are aspects even of their own histories which cannot be dramatised without detailed complementary collection and documentation. The histories of making and use will not necessarily be given directly. Other histories will have such a peripheral relationship with objects that they will be left out altogether.

Museums which are organised around an idea face the problem of matching things to concepts. What basis does the idea have in material culture, and how adequately can it be dealt with in the limited parameters of museum work? The translation of concepts such as 'work' or 'social history' to a museum context risks over-simplification or setting up icons which illustrate but do not challenge (Jordanova 1989: 21–6). Themes and ideas may be ephemeral: how can changes in perspective be accommodated in determining breadth of collection?

Museums which begin with an idea must subordinate a collections policy to an overall interpretive plan. Interpretation which tells a particular story or attempts to reconstruct a context requires appropriate collecting policies in order to be effective. The ability to do this may depend on the resources which the museum can mobilise. Convincing context reconstruction of workshop or domestic environments especially needs to be an explicit object of collection and research, perhaps using the experience of those involved to make representations of themselves. At Grangesburg, part of the Ecomuseum Bergslagen, workers' apartments of the 1930s and 1950s were re-created using local memories and donations to sustain authenticity.

Museums which seek to represent a particular industry must ask how readily the industry can be represented through collectable artefacts, and what aspects of its history can most aptly be dramatised through them. Museums taking as their subject a regional industrial history must consider how definitions of industrial are arrived at and what they may leave out. There is a tendency to mis-recognise small-scale production, to overlook home-based work, or to concentrate on production at the expense of reproduction or consumption. Collecting policy can profoundly influence the way in which industrial history is represented – as technical process, as enterprise, as art, as way of life. Museums may also draw their chronological boundaries so tightly as to exclude recent and contemporary industrial history: where this is included, it may suggest a very different structure for collecting, and a different balance between collection and documentation (King 1987: 20–7; O'Neill 1987: 28–32).

Collecting in practice

The case studies which follow show the value of tightly defined policy in enabling multiple readings, and demonstrate the necessity of adequate background research drawing on different disciplines and experience. They show the importance of siting collections in relation to other programmes – documentation, interpretation and research – and suggest that collecting policy must be based on full resource assessment.

The Museum of American Textile History, North Andover, Massachusetts, began as a collection formed by a local historical society. There has been a gradual extension of collecting from the founding concern with machinery and textiles from the local woollen industry, adding in stages machinery from cotton, silk and linen industries, and shifting from a local focus to a national collection with collection boundaries redefined to include man-made and contemporary materials in 1984. It was only with the appointment of curatorial staff that any consistency was applied to collecting policy: in the sphere of pre-industrial collecting, for example, policies were adopted concentrating on type, chronologies and geographical areas to try to achieve representativeness. An 'imagined perfect collection' was taken as the yardstick against which to measure the existing collection and compensate for its shortcomings (Museum of American Textile History 1984).

In the area of industrial collecting, a similar appraisal in 1984 admitted that at first there had been a 'collecting mania' with no clear guidance, and that a policy emerged only gradually to produce an emphasis on change over time rather than

20 (a) & (b) Workers' apartments of the 1930s and 1950s in Grangesburg, Sweden, have been re-created drawing on local memory and donations

simply focusing on early mechanisation. The collection began
as a record of technology and came to serve for research
and interpretation of the role of textile workers, managers,
builders, etc. The collection was put together according to
academic priorities, and interpretation was seen as elucidating
it rather than influencing its orientation (Museum of American Textile History 1984).

Collection policy at the Museum of American Textile History
has been adapted to suit changing academic preoccupations,
and, whereas the original emphasis was on explaining the
technology, current thinking emphasises the relationship
between technology and labour. This has meant extending the
collection to include artefacts, photographs and documents;
factory paraphernalia are being collected now to enable the
working environment to be understood and re-created. But
there are limitations to the flexibility of collecting in what
started out as a technology museum, although new ways of
interpreting can also help to redefine the purpose of the
collection and extend its value into new fields.

Plans for a new museum at Hanover in Germany have a local
or regional frame of reference, and are not tied to a particular
industry. In the disused buildings of an engineering works,
Hanomag, it is intended to establish an industrial museum
for the region. The society behind the proposal came together
from two collectors' clubs, one concerned with steam engines,
the other with cars and tractors, to form a museum which
hopes eventually to become a company. The aim is to make
a museum which will essentially present the industrial history
of Hanover, showing the main industries of the city and its
region. The society is acquiring material to this end wherever
it can, and has a large newspaper press, a group of late
nineteenth-century machine tools, a large locomotive and
various cars.

The attempts to establish this museum highlight the fact that
it is very difficult to adequately collect to represent 'industrial
history': there are problems over the availability of items to
be collected, amply demonstrated by the patchy collection in
the making at Hanomag, which begins to skew the emphasis
in this case towards the older rather than the more recent
industries. The Museum of American Textile History encoun-
ters a similar problem in seeking to represent recent industrial
change. There are also issues concerning the adequacy of
representing industries through their movables. Without
careful consideration of interpretive agendas there is a risk
that the object becomes an icon for the industry, and is likely
to be a static and pictorial representation of history. There

21 (a) & (b) Hanomag,
Hanover: the beginnings of an
industrial museum?

are also problems with defining exactly what is meant by industry in this context: is it technology, is it products, is it production, is it work, is it culture?

To date, collecting at Hanomag is seriously constrained by the history of the project: the incipient museum gives space to collecting and restoration projects conducted by volunteers, beginning from quite narrowly defined interests. At Summerlee, by contrast, there is a broader basis of support for the new museum project, and this can sustain a more ambitious programme of collecting, which takes as its subject not just the particular industries of its area, but the varieties of experience and modes of life to be found there. Summerlee has used loans and documentation to extend the range of its collection, and is sustained not only by strong local support, but also by its connections with an informal network of museums of social and industrial history. From the beginning, it has also recognised that 'collecting' industrial material inevitably involves substantial restoration and care, and has given a high priority both to backstage working space, but also to showing this restoration work as a dimension of its public programmes.

Making a museum simply with what's collectable has its limitations. The American Precision Museum at Windsor, Vermont, has what is probably the fullest collection of machine tools anywhere in the United States, but they have not been assembled according to consistent criteria, limiting the value of the collection even to show the development of the machine tools themselves. Its use in the interpretation of other histories is at present severely constrained.

Hastra, the electricity supply company for Hanover, has a small museum founded in 1979 to mark the fiftieth anniversary of the company which was re-opened in new premises in 1985–6. The museum is organised round the distribution and use of electricity, with a large collection of objects ranging from domestic and office equipment to technical equipment relating the the supply of electricity. The emphasis is on older things, although there are a few new products on display. It does not document the work of the company, nor does it relate to the company and its demonstration rooms for new products. Things seem to have been collected because they were about to be scrapped and concentration on small and collectable domestic products seems to be a rather easy way out of a problem. If the industry and the company itself had been defined as the resource, the results might have been rather different.

22 Summerlee, Coatbridge: an industrial museum in the making
(a) machines being brought in prior to laying out displays
(b) restoration in progress
(Photo: Summerlee Heritage Trust)

172

By contrast, at Norberg, within the Ecomuseum Bergslagen, survival of a brass foundry exactly as left on its last working day is so complete that it merits every effort taken to secure a future, and holds out the possibility of interpreting not just a process, but also an entire working environment.

In all these cases, it is the potential for making connections which should help to determine collecting policy – there should, in other words, be an understanding at the outset of what the relationship between collection and interpretation can be. There is a need for clear articulation of the themes for collecting and interpretation, and this is as relevant for a museum devoted to a single idea as it is to one devoted to an encyclopaedic collection. This has implications for the organisation of the museum itself and its departmental structure.

Because collecting is an activity which takes things out of context, it is important that museums are able to account for the relationship between what is in their possession and the total possible resource pool. This goes beyond documenting the individual objects with their provenance to having some awareness of where they fit in to the total possible stock, and understanding the context for the classification itself. Collecting must therefore be related to programmes of research relating to context, to inventorisation and to the objects themselves.

Making connections from a collection requires a broad-based and flexible collecting policy. Artefacts require contexts in order to be meaningful, and drawing out their relative meaning requires support from oral record, images and words (Conradson 1984: 57–9). To enable machinery to say something not only about process and technique but also about working life, for example, collection from factories could include personal equipment, work stations and examples of 'vernacular innovations' showing how machinery was actually used (Fägeborg 1984a: 60–3; 1987: 214–16). Collecting in the Nordiska museum has been reorganised to make this possible. When a tapestry works in Birkenhead closed down in 1970 the Williamson Museum and Art Gallery collected not only examples of product and machinery but also archives, and, together with the Merseyside Community History project, undertook a programme of oral history and photographic recording, creating a valuable interpretive and research resource (Johnson and Moore n.d.).

But museums are also coming to recognise that collection may not be the best or most practical way to represent or deal

23 The Machine Hall at the American Precision Museum, Windsor, Vermont

24 (a) & (b) Brass foundry, Norberg, Sweden, as it survives from its last working day

with certain kinds of history, or even with certain kinds of object; very large objects out of context might possibly be best recorded rather than literally physically displayed. Continuing industry need not be disbarred from the museum simply because it is in current operation. Museums in Sweden have led the way in documentation programmes dealing with contemporary industry, and similar work is undertaken elsewhere, issuing in exhibitions where literal collecting is not an option.

The community museum at Springburn in Glasgow exists in an area which was once the largest locomotive building area in Europe, entering massive decline from the 1960s. Academic resource assessment might have said that the most appropriate theme for a museum in this area would be the history of the locomotive works, but this would be to ignore more recent histories which might also be part of the heritage – in this case the history of de-industrialisation. As a community museum, the project wanted to deal with the relationship between the local character and tradition, and adaptation to change, and structural changes in industries. It therefore makes exhibitions which all deal with the present as well as the recent past. Their proclaimed purpose is the validation of a recent past which had been more or less obliterated, giving witness to the present rather than making a record for the future. The museum mounts issue-based exhibitions, and ephemeral displays of community work (O'Neill 1987: 28–32). A documentation project on women's experience of child-rearing, for example, resulted in an exhibition 'Springburn Mothers' (cf. Brecher 1982 on working lives).

The Museum of Work that is planned for Norrköping in Sweden also proposes to dispense with the traditional role of collecting. The proposals here stem both from a particular and innovative institutional base which exists outside conventional museum practice, and partly from the interpretation of a concept – work. It is intended to be an innovative and co-operative agency bringing together various types of communication, documentation and research to look at work both over time and globally. It is therefore intended to be an international museum, acting as a contact point between a diverse range of organisations and institutions, and its ideas depart from conventional representations of heritage – the aim is not to show the experience of work in the past, or to show machines and artefacts, but to explore the meaning of work and associated political, cultural, economic and social issues. It will not have a collection of its own, and will rely heavily on images and interpretive technology.

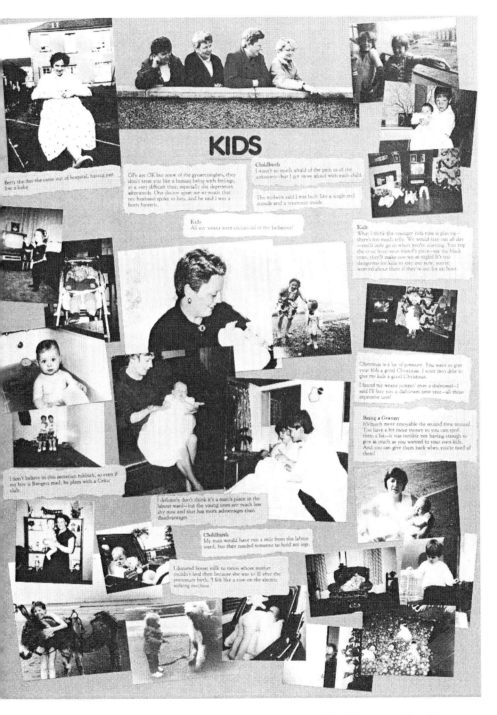

5 At Springburn Community Museum, Glasgow, documentation projects bring history up to date (Photo: Springburn Community Museum)

Conclusions

An emphasis on industrial heritage has helped to change the boundaries of museums and the balance of their activities and even objectives. In the context of industrial heritage, it is not acceptable to say that museums are essentially concerned with collections. The relationship between recording and collecting has long been an issue, but for industrial heritage most museums have not yet realised that what they are trying to do depends on changing the balance between these two functions. Removing the obstacles to success depends heavily on the implementation of successful documentation and recording programmes. Management of industrial heritage cannot contemplate comprehensive collection – its typical artefacts are awkward, expensive, extensive, and cannot be representative of the wider scope of industrial culture. To maximise the interpretive agenda, strategic collection requires systematic coverage. In the first place this calls for inventorisation, and it also involves studying the relationships between artefacts. Many different types of documentation are needed to permit connections to be made, including records from business history and work history, for example. Exploiting these rich resources to the full requires collaboration and interdisciplinary study. Collecting policy must be situated in relation to inventorisation and supported by documentation and scholarship, with strategic objectives drawn up in relation to interpretation and shared responsibility for preserving different kinds of resources.

Museums using documentation to good effect include the Museum of American Textile History, which has good library and archive material, and puts great stress on research time for curatorial staff. Many museums are not in a position to do this themselves, but could extend their links and liaison with other groups, for example with industrial archaeological societies like the VVIA, which works closely with museums in Flanders, or with colleges, schools and government institutes. Links with other museums may enable the shared use of scarce resources, and permit complementary approaches to interpretation.

Bringing different groups of artefacts together may have a relevance for study purposes, but there is no real necessity for all the artefacts to be physically in one place. What is important, though, is to know where they are. There is a need for consolidated registers of collection. SAMDOK provides such a register for contemporary collecting, but the concept does not embrace all historical resources.

Museums must distinguish between stock and flow: a 'stock' is the collection conceived as a final resting place for things that are rare and precious. In industrial heritage, the rarity of things may not be known, and for certain types of artefact may not be an issue. Museums should be receptive to ideas about flow in which they would collect, assess their collections, record and compare them and evaluate them for use. Artefacts could then be routed for conservation, interpretation or even disposal. The Ecomuseum of Le Creusot provides a good example of flow where the emphasis is on recording and knowledge but siting is a secondary consideration, subordinate to knowledge and understanding.

The effective management of industrial heritage may need either different types of museum, or different types of institution altogether. It certainly needs a more structured and co-ordinated approach – the management and interpretation of cultural resources is too important, too complex and too wide ranging to be left to an ad hoc dispersal of resources. There is a need for criteria which can define and compare different models of organisation relating identification, care and use of resources.

Interpretation: linking resources and uses

5

Interpretation can be seen as a considered process of con-
structing and testing understandings, and as the communication of significance and value. But its communicative
function is inseparable from a process of giving meaning and
value which involves not only detailed historical knowledge,
but also ways of working that themselves foster shared commitment to the heritage resource. Interpretation is founded
on thorough evaluation of the resource, its connections and
ramifications and the contexts of its making and use. It comp-
lements collection and conservation, not only in drawing out
the significance and meaning of resources and their contexts,
but also in compensating for absences. Its scope is also defined
by the nature of the organisation, the objectives and construction of its communicative function.

Interpretation is therefore an integral part of the balance of
resources and uses which is central to any heritage project.
Separation of interpretation from other curatorial functions,
which is inherent in the use of 'professional' interpretive
agencies, may undermine the long-term strength and viability
of heritage projects. If interpretation is seen simply as a communicative process, then there is a danger of short-term assessment and the quick identification of themes. Such a view
may under-value the heritage assets themselves, taking little
account of changing and developing attitudes to the constitution of resources in an area. The interpretive agenda will
be constrained unless it is situated in a dynamic relationship
with collection and/or documentation, and unless it is able to
be responsive to changing patterns of use.

Interpretation necessarily involves a selective focus, though
there is a variety of focal planes. The discussion in this chapter
goes from landscape, to site, to collection, but could as well
have taken any other route through these different focal
planes. Choice of route is itself an important aspect of inter-

pretive strategy, but all projects should think about all the planes identified here, and how they can be brought into an interpretive scheme which will necessarily be focused on one level more than on another.

The interpreted landscape

The over-arching objective of any interpretive programme should be to enhance understandings of the landscape and to encourage its care, whether the context is tourism development, environmental regeneration or the fostering of a local sense of place. To these ends, interpretation may aim to give information, or to cultivate ways of viewing and understanding. Industrial landscapes are often poorly appreciated and understood, and interpretation may help to foster awareness of what industrial heritage can be, or it may be able to provide more detailed understandings of certain aspects of industrial heritage or of a particular industrial landscape.

Most interpretive planning begins with an assessment of the physical resources of a landscape and its characteristics, and may go on from that assessment to think about the histories for which those resources stand as evidence. While landscape is generally understood as a contiguous geographical entity, or as a view, industrial landscapes may not respect such boundaries, or may constitute new ones. They cannot necessarily be understood from what is presented in the view or mapping.

Industrial activity may be extensive in its effects on the landscape of a particular place. Occasionally this forms a coherence of the kind which characterises planned settlements such as the Swedish Bruks, New Lanark in Scotland, or the Grand Hornu in Belgium. Sometimes a single industry may generate a simple settlement or co-exist with older patterns of land-organisation. Particular patterns of activity may reorganise space through functional interrelationships – in the proliferation of transport systems, or the transformation of a landscape through mining, for example.

More often the industrial landscape is far from coherent: it may be an extensive urban environment resulting from complex patterns of development and successive modifications, a highly differentiated assemblage of apparently unconnected components. Development processes may have been poorly controlled and unevenly distributed, pollution and decay may have taken their toll (Harvey 1990; Trinder 1981: 367–77).

The Industrial Heritage

When defined as a geographical entity, any industrial landscape is likely to embody a continuous history of use and
change, and complex interrelationships of components as
more or less coherent networks. Particular landscape boundaries are determined in relation to the surviving features of
patterns of interrelated human activity, but the landscape is
formed as a spatial and temporal continuum. Thus, landscape
interpretation has to deal not only with complex spatial and
functional interrelationships established and activated at any
one time, but with the modification of these patterns over
time.

But a physical landscape can also be represented as a place of
living and working, shaped and apprehended through different patterns of use. It may be said to include other material
cultural resources, as the Ecomuseum of the community Le
Creusot-Montceau-Les-Mines attempted to embrace any
aspect of material culture in the territory which it defined; it
may include memories and slight traces of use which have no
physical component.

Industrial culture also establishes relationships through patterns of activity which may transcend the limits of the local
area. The histories of local industries may be shaped by
decisions taken elsewhere, and changing populations may
bring their own histories from outside the local area.
Interpreters must take decisions about what to frame as industrial landscape and how to reach outside this frame to those
other things necessary to understand it.

Landscape interpretation has been poorly developed as an
aspect of heritage management: managers of heritage
resources have often been concerned not with the whole
but with specific sites in it, and have rarely developed the
connections to redress this selectivity. On the other hand,
while interpretation of whole landscapes does have a literature, this has often neglected the historical dimension to concentrate on immediate visual qualities (Tuan 1977). However,
following the work of Kevin Lynch, there is now a growing
literature which attempts to work with the landscape in its
integrity, constituted as an open-ended phenomenon (Lynch
1972; Gold and Burgess 1982; Lewis 1979). To the different
disciplines that have been concerned with reading the landscape, this literature would add the importance of an affective
dimension – the current meanings which landscapes hold as
places in which to live and work. Others have countered a
physical emphasis with the recognition of populations rather
than topography as a way of defining a landscape. For heritage
interpretation, these debates interpose important issues: land-

scapes constituted as heritage may still be places to live and work, and interpretation must address the place of heritage and its relationship with the lives and landscapes which survive.

Responding to the complexity of landscape resources necessitates the application of a range of disciplines. Many interpreters of heritage resources choose to be guided by historical study, adopting its narrative technique, and preferring to present evidence when it has already been synthesised as a theme. But historians are not very well able to handle spatially dispersed and complex processes of change, and, when the resources of a landscape are subordinated to a story, there is a risk of over-simplification.

As a science of enquiry, archaeology offers an approach to the interpretation of landscapes which could be of particular value for its ability to deal with synchronic and diachronic patterns. Historical geography and urban morphological study provide a similar framework for handling spatial relationships as they develop over time. Ethnography provides ways of thinking about how landscapes are shaped through use, and how meaning and value may be encoded in them.

A landscape may be understood through detailed academic study; it may also be validated through less structured celebration of a sense of place. The practice and activity of interpretation in making records, developing skills and investigating evidence may sometimes be as important as the results. Local amenity societies and industrial archaeology groups have been able to achieve high standards of documentation and research through participation. In addition, the closeness of many of these groups to the local area has enabled them to give space to the detailed texture of recent social history often overlooked in other contexts. In the tradition of 'Dig Where You Stand' (Rehnberg and Sörenson 1987: 69–71; Lindqvist 1981), encouragement has also been given to workers' self-documentation. Participation may be a means of drawing in different histories through experience, complementing and extending the range of academic enquiry.

In order to realise the rich potential of landscape as a resource, its interpretation must bring together different hierarchies of value, varieties of understanding and degrees of knowledge. Interdisciplinary study, inter-agency co-operation and involvement can extend understandings of landscape through different contexts and levels of meaning.

Although landscape selection by museums and other agencies

for direct *management* necessitates the imposition of boundaries, the unit to *interpret* does not have to follow such strict criteria, and can provide a way of reconnecting separate subjects and themes. Interpretation can respond to and develop historical resources in a way which literal collection and conservation cannot – a museum does not have to own what it interprets. Neither does interpretation have to follow the same strictures as planning, but can act as a complement to conservation policy, compensating for its limitations as well as providing a basis for greater understanding.

The landscape therefore constitutes an open-ended resource which can be accessed by different agencies through different modes of knowledge and experience. There are now many organisations involved in the preparation of material relating to landscape interpretation ranging from specialist groups like Pennine Heritage Network in England, to agencies with a wider remit such as the Italian Automobile Association, in conjunction with tourism development or as a process of enhancing local interest.

The discussion which follows dramatises thematic issues in landscape interpretation, and the implications they hold for the organisation and management of resources. While recognising the considerable work carried out in this area by other agencies, it does so by considering the role played by museums, both in the provision of readings of landscape, and in the mobilisation of constituencies of interest and involvement.

The foundation of all interpretation should be the open-ended assessment of resources. Beyond this, museums have two compelling advantages: they may directly manage a landscape, and they may also collect and display resources for understanding it. In practice, the management function has often acted as a serious constraint on the assessment of resources – museums have been unwilling to engage with those aspects of landscape over which they have no direct control.

Industrial history has shaped particular kinds of landscape, which may be reconstituted through the interpretive agenda of museums defining a landscape as their subject. The Ecomuseum Bergslagen presents an extensive landscape of interrelated mining and iron-working sites which developed in parallel with agriculture in a rural context rarely becoming either fully industrialised or urbanised. Fourmies-Trelon interprets a small industrialising region in which small-scale agriculture and large estates have both been closely related to the establishment of factories and limited urban development.

At Fourmies-Trelon and at Bergslagen, the extent and diversity of the territory covered by the ecomuseums have issued in particular types of organisation. At Fourmies, the museum organisation has a centralised administrative structure, but is also committed to being dispersed across a series of sites which represent a wide range of local landscape types, and are intended to reveal stages in the history of the area, as well as its contemporary variety. The museum is seeking to establish collaboration with other projects in the area, bringing a number of practical benefits, but also enabling the culture of the region to be demonstrated much more fully.

The Ecomuseum relies on the variety of local landscape types and the interpretive work carried out on each site to create a sense of the spatial diversity of the region, and uses this diversity to suggest the way the area has developed over time. But Fourmies-Trelon does not attempt to provide direct interpretation of links between landscape types – its central base is itself concerned with one particular site and one particular history, and there is actually very little material to relate this to the urban environment outside. It has successfully introduced landscape interpretation as one component in its system with the 'Sentiers d'observation' trails at Wignehies (see below), but has not yet extended this principle to a more thoroughly urban environment.

The Ecomuseum Bergslagen in Sweden is a network of small museums and local historical associations loosely grouped as an integrated concern, but as yet without a strong central organisation. It seeks to validate its claim to be a 'total environment museum' by encompassing a comprehensive collection of sites classified thematically and intends to dramatise the formation of a landscape through human intervention and has chosen to do this through a number of discrete themes – colonisation, mining, transport, fuel extraction and the formation of communities (Rehnberg and Sörenson 1987; Sörenson 1987).

There is a good basis of research behind this selection of themes, but, perhaps more importantly, the Ecomuseum is primarily a federation of existing projects and associations, and as yet has no plans to initiate new site-based projects of its own. By providing a framework (with resources) for the existing projects, it provides the possibility to develop understandings of interrelationships which would not have been visible in a non-federated system.

In both cases, the networked organisation facilitates the interpretation of a wide range of themes, and has the potential to illustrate the interrelationship of components in the formation of a cultural landscape. But simply being able to draw on a range of different sites does not necessarily itself permit the representation of those relationships which make sense of the landscape as an entity: this problem is particularly acute at Bergslagen where the Ecomuseum draws together existing museums and associations each with their own concerns, and does so over a vast territory.

There is a danger that the museum will simply remain a series of separate sites, with mines in one area, foundries in another, estates in yet another. Geographical and chronological relationships in the landscape are not always easy to identify: the landscape does not organise itself into coherent narratives and the demonstration of processes of change and inter-relationship may best be served by criteria which are not the same as those for the conservation and even interpretation of individual sites. Some of the areas incorporated in the museum already have rich and varied programmes of conservation and interpretation, dealing with a wide range of types of site and sustained by a range of types of project, but elsewhere industrial remains are isolated and long removed from any obvious connections with other than a natural landscape.

If the Ecomuseum is to attain a real role as a 'total environment museum', it will need to develop an off-site interpretation or publication programme which can provide a framework holding together the various elements of the regional industrial story. The creation of a centralised organisation for the Ecomuseum could provide an important means of holding together the disparate elements of the area, reinforcing connections between the different parts and demonstrating the cultural integrity of the region as a whole.

At the moment, the variety of modes of working encompassed by the different organisations federated to the Ecomuseum Bergslagen enables a multi-focused understanding of the industrial past, both historical and recent. The ecomuseum, however, is largely constituted as an agency of tourism promotion in the context of economic regeneration, and there is a danger that the desire for a unified regional strategy will discourage full consideration of local variations. The museum does not have the commitment to the human resources of its area which has characterised the French Ecomuseum movement and the relationship between professionals and amateur enthusiasts has not always been easy. But it will be important to sustain the vitality of local museums, and to encourage and guide them, rather than impose academic programmes. Local places and people are a resource and not just a medium for getting things done, and the different approaches which they can bring may help extend the interpretive range available to the Ecomuseum, combining the validation of local identities with the creation of a viable tourism initiative.

In the Ironbridge Gorge, the landscape was devoted to industry from an early date. Characterised by a high degree of specialisation its range of interrelated activities came to support a small-scale integrated urban landscape. It was a scenically spectacular, intensely exploited component of a larger industrial region, the east Shropshire coalfield. The Ironbridge Gorge Museum is a single, centralised organisation which is also concerned primarily with tourism. Conceived as a 'total environment museum', it now concentrates less on the interpretation of landscape resources than on interpreting aspects of local history in dispersed sites, retaining a significant role in the local management of the wider landscape through involvement in the planning process.

While this site-based strategy enables the museum to manage the local history through a series of coherent narratives which bring out its national significance, it leaves a lot of hostages to fortune. Site boundaries have been defined in a way that interrupts the functional integrity of landscape features, and there have been severe problems with differential care of different classes of monument. Certain aspects of the landscape and its history become hard to see – the museum has little to say about local housing, for example – and certain of its historical industries are poorly represented – coal mining, quarrying, boat-building, are represented only iconically in the open-air museum, which cannot do justice to their duration and significance. Having no central interpretive facility, the museum is unable to dramatise the interrelationships between its sites and cannot adequately contextualise them, either in the Gorge itself or in the wider region. The ramifications of local technological achievement in national and even international industrial development cannot be explored.

These museums, and others like them, were established with a specific remit to work within the wider landscape. With the possible exception of the French ecomuseums, they have defined their resource base primarily with reference to specific archaeological and historical sites, and have often failed to look beyond the immediate boundaries of site ownership. In areas with a high concentration of industrial sites, or with site types which survive in large numbers, it is unlikely to be viable to conserve and directly manage as heritage more than a small proportion of the whole. Whereas criteria for direct management may be based on selection of best examples, the possibility of understanding either the fuller scope of site types or their articulation in a particular industrial landscape will be severely curtailed unless consideration is also given to the interpretation of resources which are not directly managed. Documentation and research programmes will both identify appropriate sites for museum use, and also provide contextual information (see the discussion in chapter 4 above, and also Mende 1987: 91–8).

Museums have approached interpretation primarily through coherent stories, dependent on particular monuments, sites and buildings. Discrete site emphasis is relatively easy to do, whereas engaging with spatial relationships and change over time demands a different, multi-disciplined knowledge base, which challenges the narrative approach that is often preferred. As a result, museums have tended to be highly selective about their landscape interpretation, whether on or off site, filtering out the landscape by subordinating its totality to a particular theme or period.

Museums have also attempted to make landscapes into museums, or make museums of landscapes in a more literal sense, imposing a boundary as an open-air museum, or reconstructing a past landscape. The possible benefits of this in reconstructive archaeology for individual sites and structures have been amply demonstrated in open-air museums interpreting pre-industrial societies, and the reconstruction of particular industrial sites has sometimes facilitated the understanding of the technological problems involved. Environments constituted by the more fragile archaeological remains of industry may benefit from the enhanced protection which this treatment may assure: the Töllstorps Industrial Museum at Gnosjö in Sweden, for example, has achieved the protection of a small industrial landscape composed of a series of water-power sites, which it has enhanced by the introduction of other relocated structures.

More usually, the requirements of conservation are met by a mixed management strategy: the Swannington project hoped to achieve a degree of special protection for its rich industrial landscape remains through a mixture of special planning control and direct ownership (see above, chapter 1). Conversely, most open air museums may have few on-site remains to protect, and will more typically work through the re-location or re-creation of structures from elsewhere.

The reconstruction of entire environments as undertaken at the Black Country Museum, Blists Hill and Beamish in the UK goes beyond the requirements of conservation and the interpretation of particular components as an exercise in social history interpretation, attempting to show the way things were and recovering coherence from the shattered fragments of blighted industrial areas. The popularity of these sites attests to their undoubted success, but there are dangers in their approach unless it is thorough in its research and rigorous in implementation. It risks creating a synthetic experience which does not enhance an understanding of the wider environment outside the museum, and which may be unable to demonstrate interrelationships and change over time. Blists Hill, which has come to interpret a narrowly defined period, now briefs its demonstrators to provide the missing depth in time. Beamish adopted a looser chronology which enables it to provide a comparative dimension. But, by assembling components from dispersed geographical areas, both preclude a detailed understanding of the make-up of local vernacular landscapes.

Museums have therefore defined a limited remit in relation to landscape interpretation, often confining themselves to immediate spheres of influence, and taking as a starting point a historical theme rather than the landscape itself. But it is not just the constraints of direct management which have limited the vision for the interpretation of industrial landscapes. Ideas about historical landscapes do not always fully exploit the actual resources that survive and may miss opportunities by drawing plans which simply aim to use the landscape to illustrate a history derived from other sources rather than fully registering the history which the landscape itself reveals.

Many agencies may attempt to represent a place as entirely characteristic of a particular period. In Ironbridge, for example, twentieth-century history is largely overlooked, and visitors are encouraged to see an eighteenth- and nineteenth-century landscape. Interpretive plans have involved the restoration of buildings to an earlier state by stripping away later alterations to recover the original designed appearance. While this creates a visually coherent environment, and a resource for the interpretation of eighteenth- or nineteenth-century history, it is a poor use of actual environmental resources, which graphically illustrate one of the characteristics of this industrial area – the rapidity of change and adaptation.

At Lowell in Massachusetts, the establishment of the state Heritage State Park and heritage centre in the context of urban regeneration has ensured a commitment to environmental interpretation from the beginning, using exhibition and video to introduce the history and development of the town from its beginnings to very good effect. There is also a programme of guided walks which aim to take this history out into the surviving landscape of the town. However, this has been done by devising tightly controlled themes which do not all have an equally strong relationship with what does survive. As a result, large parts of the urban fabric remain uninterpreted. The themes selected are not clearly related to surviving features and are derived not from resource assessment, but from general historical narratives.

On the other hand, the landscape that survives, especially in industrialised areas which have been subject to waves of clearance and redevelopment, may not have coherent visible histories. The physical evidence may be biased towards the most recent phases of use; there may be extensive or piecemeal alteration, adaptation, rebuilding, as layers of different uses are superimposed on each other; dereliction and decay may also take their toll on the coherence and legibility of the landscape, restricting what can be achieved through literal on-site interpretation. Ability to dramatise interrelationships in a highly fragmented surviving landscape, and drawing out the significance of landscape features anywhere, requires good off-site interpretation. Using their ability to collect, document and display, museums and heritage centres could play an important role in this area.

The heritage of industry is as likely to constitute cleared sites with no visible history. The Ecomuseum of Le Creusot-Montceau-Les-Mines has shown how museums can fill gaps like this by offering interpretation using other sources to show how areas of the city have changed over time. Chapter 1 discussed the series of exhibitions and publications which have used maps and photographs to show the cycles of development and redevelopment which have been a characteristic of the industrial history of the area (Clement n.d.). On a smaller scale, the museum at Market Harborough, UK, used an archive of photographs from the 1930s alongside an oral history project to re-animate in an exhibition the urban backlands lost to slum clearance (Mullins 1986–7: 20–2).

Examples like these admirably exploit the resource material available to museums in the form of documentation and archival material, and their ability to marshal this material through display. There are histories from landscape which the physical environment itself cannot reveal, and museums are well placed to act as resource centres for these contextual histories. Some museums have assumed this role in collecting material culture or oral histories from a territory; the Ecomuseums of Le Creusot and Fourmies-Trelon provide the clearest commitment to a definition of landscape as cultural territory (see above, chapter 4).

Linkages in landscape interpretation

The selection of sites for direct management is itself a process of interpretation, and museums have been slow to develop responsibilities for the landscape beyond their boundaries. In addition to the development of interpretive material for this wider landscape, much could be done through collaborative work. There have been various strategies for enabling this: museums may have their own departmental resources to draw on, they may draw in academics working in various fields, they may collaborate with other museums, or with other agencies, including contemporary industry, in order to extend the field of interpretive opportunity. The ecomuseum of the region Fourmies-Trelon has an academic advisory committee, and, in addition to its own establishment as a museum system, is also concerned to collaborate with other agencies in its area. Bergslagen is looking for opportunities to work alongside existing industries in its area, including them in the range of sites laid before its visitors.

Landscape interpreters may choose to emphasise **connections** made through the functional or typological links between different areas and sites. They may prefer to focus on **texture**, suggested through the juxtapositions and relationships between sometimes contradictory elements in a topographically defined area. By virtue of the range of sites within their remit and their organisation as networks, some museums may be able to suggest definitions of landscapes through connecting together different components.

Exhibition could do the same in the presentation of histories which are not immediately visible, opening out landscapes which radiate away from the local. It may also address those aspects of the landscape that fall between specific sites, and in doing so may convey something of the texture of a particular landscape, an aspect unlikely to be presented through the management and interpretation of sites separately or in series. Publications may also address both elements, and the trail guide provides a case study of a type of publication which aims to do exactly that.

A number of agencies have established trails, either to encourage close observation of a particular place, or to suggest the thematic interconnections between different places. The trail is an apt device for the representation of the interrelationships which characterise any industrial landscape. Local trails (especially if designed for walking) can present more of the texture of a topographically defined landscape – engaging with the interconnections of industries with each other and with settlement, with the immediate spatial organisation of industry and with its effects. They can contribute to understanding how a particular landscape works, and the interrelationship of its elements (Percival 1978).

The community of Norberg, within the Ecomuseum Bergslagen, has a strong commitment to the conservation and care of its industrial landscape. Linking an impressive range of conserved and interpreted sites, it has developed a series of trails to introduce the visitor to its very rich industrial heritage. These trails establish links between different sites of a common industry, but they also permit investigation of the intensive physical transformations wrought by industrial activity in a closely bounded environment. Published leaflets and guides are sometimes supported by information panels on site.

Working with the municipality of Wignehies, the Ecomuseum of the Fourmies-Trélon region developed a series of *sentiers d'observation* at Wignehies. The footpaths were a feature of the area, as routes connecting the town to the fields and factories, and have been conserved and restored for active use. This has provided an opportunity to interpret something of the landscape texture of a village which became a town with the industrial revolution. It presents a complex settlement with a rural landscape and farmsteads on the village fringe related to an urban morphology of factory, tenements and terraced housing. Well-signed routes are supplemented by a guidebook and interpretive panels, and are increasingly well used (Bonnet and Cortois n.d.; Goujard 1988).

The Ecomuseum has begun to develop a similar trail in the small town of Trelon, but the urban industrial trails devised by the Ecomuseum at Le Creusot have set the standard for the interpretation of more complex townscapes. Here there is no on-site interpretation and the visitor relies on a detailed guidebook. The book is underpinned by a good body of research, and the routes take in cross-sections of the townscape ranging sufficiently to draw out the spatial relationships between different areas of settlement, concentrated industrial and commercial land-use. It permits close inspection of many significant features of a local industrial landscape.

The region of Le Creusot is too extensive to be covered purely

26 (a) & (b) A mining landscape in Norberg, Sweden: pithead tower from the 1930s, and collapsed workings at Klackberg

27 Rural and urban
landscapes discovered on a trail
at Wignehies:
(a)–(c) 'Fermettes'; workers'
and employers' housing

(d)–(f) weaving sheds in use; and a brewery

by a series of walking trails: the scale and extent of industrial activity here were such as to have created a region with highly differentiated development, and vast areas given over to specialist manufacture. To enable some of the complexity of the region to be presented, the ecomuseum has also developed a series of extensive trails. These are organised thematically, tracing communication routes, or linking mining, iron-working or ceramic manufacturing sites (François 1982).

Trails that cover a large geographical area may take a thematic approach like this, giving an indication of specialist regional production and organisation and providing a comparative dimension to the understanding of different sites of a common industry. This approach provides an opportunity to connect sites in the mind and re-create historical connections (such as links of supply, manufacture and market, or sites on a common power source, etc.). It may also be appropriate to indicate the general diversity of what industrial heritage can be in a region, providing an introduction to regional resources, and some trails have been prepared to introduce regional industrial heritage without thematic selection. In either case, the value of such an introduction will be enhanced if supported by the opportunity for the visitor to find out more through detailed interpretation in a museum. Comparative thematic or regional trails must mirror historical inter-connections and relationships if the whole is to be greater than the sum of the parts, and if they are to act as more than a simple gazetteer of separate sites.

In Franche Comté, the regional government and the Société des Arts et Traditions Populaires have collaborated to produce a compact guide to the industrial heritage of the region. The leaflet serves as publicity for, and an introduction to, a series of museums and major sites offering more detailed interpretation, but also includes sites which are not specifically interpreted, or which are still in use. The guide presents a series of interrelated sites over a wide area, giving a sense of the diversity of regional industry and showing patterns of activity which in some cases still continue.

At their best, on-site interpretation and trails serve as a valuable stage in the identification of landscape resources and, if well designed, may be able to enhance understandings of landscapes of industry, whether constituted as a close-textured local environment or as the looser association of sites across a region. Both must begin with surviving features of the landscape and their central concern should be with looking. Neither can deal effectively with what is not immediately visible.

An industrial guide to the Franche Comté includes historic sites and working factories

But the ramifications of a landscape may take in social and cultural histories, aspects of economic organisation, national or international links. These histories may be reflected in the physical properties of a landscape, but are given more fully only through other sources of evidence. A publications programme may enable these further connections to be dramatised, relating physical resources to other material, or a locality to more distant places. Exhibition is another means of presenting these other histories, also relating different classes of evidence. Both must be underpinned by a programme of interdisciplinary study and documentation. It is in this field that museums have the opportunity to develop techniques of study and presentation which use the range of resources at their disposal.

The interpreted site

Industrial archaeology has promoted the study and conservation of sites and this has given rise to a whole new category of heritage interpretation. It is commonly assumed that the integrity and authenticity of the site should be allowed to speak for themselves and the object of interpretation should be to make this possible. However, in reality sites do not speak for themselves, and interpretations have always to be constructed. There is as much artifice in the interpreted site as there is in the presentation of a museum collection.

It is important that the different functions of conservation and interpretation are clearly recognised, since conservation is not sufficient in itself as an interpretive device and re-presentation of a site may offer too narrow an interpretive agenda. Conservation may be implemented at various levels of exactitude – it may be largely concerned with the fabric, it may extend to the immovable contents of a building, it may extend as far as the more ephemeral evidence of daily use. The extent and focus of conservation may shape an interpretive agenda, but as the validation and explanation of meaning and value, interpretation will not be served by conservation alone. This is as true for sites which survive in a good state of survival and repair as it is for ruins.

Perceived physical integrity may in fact be illusory. What survives or is in direct care as heritage may be only a fragment of a greater complex. But even on sites which have retained their integrity, physical boundaries can be pushed out through extensive transport or power networks, and individual sites may make best sense in a wider geographical or historical context – textile mills in their relationship with domestic production, settlement, power and transport networks; mining sites in their relationship with processing, distribution and use.

A single site has a context in relation to other sites of the same or similar type, dramatising rarity or typicality. It is also at once a technological or engineering achievement, a centre of production (and hence also for distribution), and a place of work. Interpretive strategies need to develop detailed analysis not only of the resource itself, but also of the possible contexts in which it can be understood (see for example Berckmans 1990; Bursell 1987: 216–19; Victor 1981).

Whether simple workshop or major industrial plant, all sites exist in complex systems and not even the simplest can be fully understood in isolation. Industrial sites are often characterised by complex sequences of change over time – in response either to wear and tear, or to updating with new technology, or to complete reinvestment in another type of operation. In sites which are no longer in use, the state of survival and visibility of purpose are important issues in establishing a remit for interpretation.

Assessing communicative potential

Interpretation needs to be informed by a comprehensive resource assessment, analysing the site and its contexts. This assessment will consider the histories which an industrial site best reveals, and identify those aspects of industrial culture which are not easily visible through site-based programmes. It will ask what needs to be done to draw out the different possible histories of a site. Interpretation may be concerned with explaining what's there; it may also be about filling in the gaps – compensating for what isn't there (see also the discussion in chapter 4 above).

Interpretive planning should take supporting resources into account, and should make use of an audit of them. These resources might include archaeological evidence, documentary material, oral testimony or other surviving examples of similar type. A decision to focus on the interpretation of recent history may be taken where there is likely to be adequate record and good memories. Thorough documentation may enable reconstruction. The Museum of Rural Life at Saint Fagans in Wales carried out its oral history study on rural blacksmithing to underpin its reconstruction of a forge (Williams-Davies 1990: 68–9). The skill and experience of local people may also be a resource, for instance permitting the re-working of machinery and the demonstration of processes. Archaeological evidence may be able to contribute not just to knowledge of structures and their lay-outs, but also through analysis of artefacts and deposits may add information about what was made, and in what way. In Lowell, for example, detailed research using documentary, oral and archaeological evidence was able to make a decisive contribution to the interpretation of social history in the town (Beaudry and Mrozowski 1988: 1–22).

Perceived importance of the site must also enter the calculation of how to interpret. The only surviving site of its kind may require different treatment from one of many. Complete conservation might be the best option for a rare survivor of a once widespread industry, or for the most complete survivor. Conversely, it might be better to invest in complementary interpretation on sites of a type which survives in large numbers. Heritage managers must ask whether it is a good idea to have yet another conserved brewery, railway or steam engine, or whether more could be contributed from a more lateral interpretive agenda (Robbins 1988: 81–8).

Historical relationships with other industries, or with markets, companies, a labour force and a locale, and the relationship with contemporary industry, may also generate interpretive themes. At the glass museum at Trelon, for example, the main focus is a workshop demonstrating craft production, but this has recently been effectively complemented with an exhibition of images and artefacts which discusses the changing technology and applications of glass production up to the present. The small forge at Nans sous Sainte Anne adds labour history to its site interpretation (see below).

Interpretation should also complement the work carried out by other museums and agencies. This is especially an issue for industrial heritage where sites may be costly to conserve and interpret, where certain types of site may survive in great numbers, and where industries may have been closely related with each other. In Flanders, the VVIA aims to encourage informal collaboration to ensure a good distribution of themes and resources. It has, for example, set up a study group in the flax region of Kortrijk to co-ordinate local initiatives with the aim of establishing an ecomuseum. It is, of course, a similar co-ordination between hitherto separate initiatives that is a major function of the Ecomuseum Bergslagen at present.

The House Mill project in the London Borough of Newham (see chapter 6) plans to restore its late eighteenth-century tide mill as a working industrial monument, but this is not to involve literal restoration as a working flour mill. Instead, it is proposed to take the tide mill power technology used locally by a variety of industries as a theme capable of linking on-site interpretation with its local context. Viability of any heritage project in this particular area is dependent on a strategy which can make connections beyond telling the history of one particular site, and the project also plans exhibition space and services in a reconstruction of the adjacent mill-owner's house. It hopes to encourage the development of other attractions to form a network of related projects throughout the area.

Certain histories will remain literally invisible without detailed research, including those of the people associated with a site, its products and their uses. Interpretation can be a form of compensation for what is not actually visible on the site itself. In order to exploit this potential, it is important to involve different kinds of research and therefore different disciplines (for example ethnography, sociology, social history), as well as different source material in animating the site. Analysis of buildings, sites and machines may be able to provide evidence for the organisation of work as well as process (Victor 1981); oral testimony may add a dimension of experience to structural analysis or documentary research. Video and film of industrial or craft processes may supplement oral record, providing a resource invaluable in the replication of working environments, but also a possible substitute for it.

Site-based resource assessment will permit many different stories to be told, and in fact drawing out more than one story should be the object of a good interpretive plan. Such a plan will provide points of orientation which might take the form of a narrative, or a classificatory scheme, chart chronological relationships or map geographical connections. But these points of orientation should foster awareness of the full richness of the resource, evoking rather than concealing the range of its histories.

Where the interpretive scheme is not founded on detailed evaluation of resources, it may even conflict with the conservation, care and appreciation of existing assets. On its Blists Hill site, for example, the Ironbridge Gorge Museum has the ruins of a nineteenth-century iron furnace with associated transport, preparation, processing and working areas which are not interpreted at all because these ruins do not fit with the overall scheme for the open-air site. The open-air museum is a highly popular operation, but relates uneasily to the actual resources of its site.

Site interpretation as subsidiary activity

What status should the site itself have in an interpretive scheme? Interpreting the site by restoring it to its original form is not always a viable option. Extent of survival or availability for direct management may rule out interpretation through the literal representation of former use. It may be too expensive or too limiting, or there may be insufficient evidence to support it. Calculations of investment in relation to uses and understandings may suggest that a wider-ranging approach would be of greater benefit. There might be a need for greater emphasis on context rather than the literal re-presentation of the site – for example where existing general industrial heritage interpretation is poor, or where the site was a highly specialised component of a stratified production process making little sense on its own. Co-ordination with other, similar or related sites might suggest a more structured and analytical approach to exploit the many possible narratives concerning a particular industry or theme.

Redundant industrial buildings or derelict sites may be appropriately re-used to house regional industrial history collections with scant reference to the particular history of the site, but the site itself constitutes a resource, even if it is not to be directly re-presented or literally conserved. Summerlee Heritage Trust at Coatbridge in Scotland is a museum of local industrial history and working life, established on the site of an iron-works and using the buildings of a crane shop from the 1960s. The surviving archaeology of the iron works has been investigated and is displayed, and the museum building is sited to take advantage of these ruins, for which it can act as a viewing platform. Scale models have also provided a reconstruction of the site as it was derived from the archaeological evidence. The crane shop is a single undifferentiated space with little specific functional character. It houses reconstructed workshops with operating machinery which suggest a partial ambience, but also provides the museum with a very flexible general-purpose space. The museum is not just concerned with the history of its own site: its remit is the wider industrial history and culture of its region. The presence of heavy industrial relics and the infrastructure of an intensively exploited landscape have possibly encouraged a bias towards engineering and factory work in the representation of regional history, but the museum is working with, rather than against, its immediate physical resources.

29 (a) & (b) At Summerlee, the excavations of the iron-works form an important part of the site; inside, a large-scale model helps visitors interpret what they see

A similar decision to depart from strict replication lies behind the museum at Fourmies, part of the Ecomuseum of the Fourmies-Trélon region (Camusat 1987: 101–6). Here, the weaving sheds from a textile works have been adapted as a museum which, like Summerlee, takes as its theme the industrial and social history of its area. Its collection of machinery is displayed in a production series, but is designed to demonstrate not only stages in a process, but the changing technology over time. The rest of the space is devoted to a series of domestic and workshop interiors, exhibition panels and displays.

At Fourmies the subject of the museum is industrial life and culture rather than any particular industry – the museum uses a range of interpretive techniques to richly evoke this history. The principal focus is on textile production, as the major local industry and original user of the building, although the particular history of the building itself and its operating company is rather overlooked. However, the museum integrates its account of the major industry with that of the less specialised local economy with some success.

At the Hanomag site in Hanover, the proposed industrial museum occupies one building in a series of abandoned premises, which themselves form only a small part of a whole complex much of which is still in use. The building is seen merely as a house for general industrial collections, and the history of the premises may form only a small part of the whole scheme. As a fractional element of a larger site, representation in its former use would be inappropriate. Arguably, there is a need for a general industrial museum in the city, which might attract more interest and support than one which is company-specific, but the intention to conserve the buildings of the site would be enhanced by an interpretive scheme discussing their history developed in parallel to the main strategy.

A particular industrial history can be told appropriately on the site itself without necessarily implying its literal re-presentation. At Røros in Norway, the copper smelting house, a prominent local landmark (and major structural survivor of the copper industry), was destroyed by fire, twice in the 1950s and 1970s. Reconstruction using archival sources in 1986 made it possible retain the appearance of the original, and it now serves primarily as a monumental symbol housing a museum of the industry.

Inside, partial representation of the structure as it might have been originally is supplemented by a series of devices

(c) The Hydroon Crane Works provides a flexible exhibition hall for displays on social and industrial history (Photos: Summerlee Heritage Trust)

employed to symbolise the history of the site: the use of black paint symbolises the smelting hut. Parts of the operating system have been rebuilt, including part of the filter system which is intended to show the environmental problems of the industry, tying in with other exhibitions about pollution. But, in addition to partial representation as smelt-hut, the building has also been designed to include exhibition space. Themes for exhibition consider the relationship between natural and cultural histories, and will set the copper-works in its local context looking at administration, health, welfare and government. A magnificent series of working models has been constructed to show the operation of copper mining and smelting and it is proposed that these will eventually form part of a representation of the entire town based on pictorial evidence. Information boards will take up the story by showing the history of the site up to the present, as well as explaining techniques.

Site interpretation as primary activity

Complete surviving complexes ranging in scale from the small metal-working shop at Gnosjö to the ore mine and crushing plant at Goslar pose their own problems of interpretation. Complete survival offers opportunities to present a precise working context, showing it in working order or even (especially on smaller sites) actually working. Process and technique and working environment can be demonstrated on an intact site, which may also evidence the organisation of the company as well as of production. But working conditions can only be hinted at and the composition of the labour force, the products with their markets and uses, will be only poorly visible if at all. Sites which ostensibly survive intact have in fact already lost certain crucial aspects of their history by virtue of the fact that they are no longer in primary production, and it is important that interpretive planning recognises and compensates for this loss. Maintenance of a redundant industrial site as heritage provides the chance to conserve and explain aspects of an industrial history, but risks overlooking the critical history of change and supercession – why the site is no longer in its primary use – if it stops short at conservation.

Surviving industrial sites with a highly specialised function may not be very easy to understand in isolation and need the context of their relationship to other industries or to their users. An example might be the machine tool industry, which is often presented simply through the machines themselves

30 The industrial landscape of Røros is to be interpreted in the reconstructed smelting hut

31 (a) & (b) The Ecomuseum Bergslagen has commissioned an artist to prepare reconstructive drawings displayed on site; Klenshyttan charcoal iron furnace

Klenshyttan 1918

with scant consideration of their application. Large integrated sites like the ore crushing plant at Goslar in Lower Saxony which carried out a complex operation may also not be readily comprehensible. Industrial processes are often literally invisible – the generation of electricity is an example. Sites like these will require intervention or accompanying material to enhance their communicative potential.

The history of the site will also shape and constrain interpretive possibilities: many industrial sites have survived only by virtue of successive adaptation. Within a single type of use, buildings will have been expanded or contracted, new machinery introduced, new working practices adopted. Many sites have gone through complex histories of different uses – the bridge house of Moira furnace, Leicestershire, UK, for example, was re-used as housing during the nineteenth century, and the Bedlam blast furnace complex in the Iron-bridge Gorge became a brick-works for a time. These histories may be a resource for interpretation, but they may also obscure the communicative potential of the site. The period and time span of use are also important: a site in recent use will offer different resources in terms of both literal survivals and supporting documentation from one which went out of use a long time ago.

Re-presentation of a site as it was at a single period has the benefit of clarity, but may be felt to leave too much out. A number of strategies have been used in presenting change over time. At the Abbeydale Industrial Hamlet in Sheffield, for example, different parts of the site have been interpreted to show different periods of its development, spanning its history up to closure in 1933 (Peatman 1989). This is a well-tried strategy which acknowledges historicity, but selective reconstruction risks dissecting the site into a series of tableaux without seriously addressing their relationships and the ways in which successive generations may have modified the site. Phased drawings or models which represent the whole site at different periods of its use may be a way of coherently showing change over time while also respecting relationships between components in use at any one time.

Industrial remains may also survive only as ruins or archaeological traces. Incomplete survival necessitates interpretation to compensate. It might exceptionally be by physical reconstruction (see below), more often through on-site panels or published material illustrating the form and operation of the site. The Ecomuseum Bergslagen has employed an artist to create reconstructive drawings which show sites as they might have been when in operation. Placed on boards at the site itself, the drawings are an effective way of illustrating context. Other museums have used scale models to suggest original structure and appearance.

Archaeological investigation coupled with other research may be able to recover a sense of the integrity of the site, and this can be presented graphically. But the contribution which archaeology as a science of enquiry itself makes to this understanding is rarely presented. Visitors are more often encouraged to begin with an image of the site in its original integrity, than they are invited to share the archaeologists' investigative assemblage of evidence from fragmentary survivals.

Conservation-led site interpretation

Management of industrial sites as heritage must involve a commitment to conservation, but the degree of conservation, and its relationship with interpretation, may vary. There is a growing tendency to use a very direct relationship between the two, relying on literal conservation and leaving things (or reinstating them) as they are or were.

Since the early days of an industrial heritage movement, there has been an emphasis on conservation *in situ*, and interpretive ideas have developed in relation to this. Such an emphasis reflects a growing conservation consciousness, together with awareness of the importance of maximising research potential by minimising interference. However, strict conservation may sometimes be at odds with enhanced comprehension: conservation of monuments as ruins may be justified on archaeological grounds, but the base of a steam engine may seem almost meaningless to the non-archaeologist. Conservation of this kind necessitates further interpretation to suggest what the structure was and how it worked, how it became ruined and what is now missing. Even conservation of recently working sites is not sufficient in itself – industrial processes are rarely self-explanatory, and the ramifications of a single site are unlikely to be visible.

Conservation is often itself interventionist, and involves such decisions as what period to conserve to, and in what state the site should be represented. Decisions on the period to represent should be based on assessment of the intelligibility of the site, the significance of the various phases of its use, and the extent and interest of later alterations. While it may sometimes be appropriate to strip away to an earlier integrity in the interests of clarity, curatorship must recognise that a history has been removed and could itself provide material for supporting interpretation.

Moira furnace in Leicestershire was built in 1804. Of idiosyncratic design, it ran only for two periods of ten months between 1806–7 and 1810–11. By the middle of the nineteenth century, the bridge house and engine house had been adapted as housing, and it continued in domestic occupation until the 1970s. North West Leicestershire district council has carried out a partial reconstruction, restoring the bridge house and furnace, though not the casting shed or engine house.

The short history of the site's use as a furnace, and its much longer use as housing, might have suggested other strategies than reinstatement for the interpretation of the site. Partial restoration risks over-emphasising the most spectacular component of the site; nevertheless, the relative simplicity of the structure, enhanced by the fact that it was not in long use, enables a clear understanding of the operation of the furnace itself. The later history, and the ancillary buildings and features of the site, are dependent on complementary interpretation, which has been implemented through exhibition, trail guides and interpretive panels (Cranstone 1985).

Increasingly, museums are taking a further step to suggest interpretation 'as if'. This arises largely from the extent of survival of industrial sites which have been in relatively recent use and which may therefore survive intact. It may involve conservation not just of the fabric and machinery, but of the whole working environment. Conservation to this degree of exactitude is expensive, and needs rigorous guidelines to justify it. These should come from critical assessment of the resource and its context: is it a good example of its type; is it intact; what can be learned from it; what resources are available for its interpretation?

How far can interpretation 'as if' be taken? Options range from the technical display of process to the complete presentation of a working environment, or the re-presentation of a site in real or simulated operation. A site can be interpreted literally as if still in use – or it may just be displayed intact. Sites which have not worked for a very long time, and which do not have skill and experience and everyday clutter behind them may not be amenable to presentation 'as if' without extensive investment in reconstruction and context recreation. Resources may not be available to do this with conviction.

Where re-presentation is not taken this far, it is important to be clear about what is being left out: interpretation must be honest about its own limitations and must clearly distinguish between display intact and display as if in use. It is not adequate to present a machine hall as if in its original condition of use if it is merely a collection of working machinery. Reconstructed sites may not mirror precisely the scale and nature of the original operation on which they are based; while the viability of reconstruction may depend on such changes in scale, it is important that these are indicated if the site is to serve as more than an illustration of technical process.

The differences between showing how a site worked, and showing what it might have been like to work there are not always adequately understood and signalled. Whereas plant and machinery can be reinstated to operate using archaeological survey techniques and engineering skills, the re-creation of working practices involves research into the organisation of labour, and the recovery of skills, which may not always be a realistic option. The re-creation of a convincing working environment needs to be an explicit object of collection and research – the necessary detail may only be available for sites in use sufficiently recently to be able to draw on the experiences of those involved.

Although interpretation 'as if' may apparently supply a sense of context (by showing machinery in its setting, for example), it also has serious limitations. One of these is that it may fail to address later history – why the site survives as it does and why it is no longer in use. Fixing the interpretation to the point of closure also precludes the earlier history and development of the site; growth and change cannot easily be seen. There are dangers of mystification, even romanticisation. Wider contexts may be overlooked – relationship with other sites, sources of supply, markets, labour force; 'as if' interpretation can make a superficial gesture towards social history but cannot really replicate working conditions and culture. In order to compensate for these inadequacies, there is a need to develop wider strategies of interpretation.

Literal interpretation 'as if' makes best sense where there is good survival of the whole ambience of the works rather than simply the machinery. It is likely to make best sense for recent survivals which are well documented, although may have a role in reconstructive interpretation (see below). In spite of its apparent offering of a totality, this kind of interpretation still leaves gaps which must be filled through complementary programmes.

The J. E. Hyltens metal works at Gnosjö in Sweden survives and is interpreted as a complete metalworking workshop last used in 1974. The works was established in 1874 and moved to its present site in 1914. When it closed in 1974, it was the largest and oldest of a network of small workshop industries in its region. The town council purchased the building in 1978 with financial assistance from the state on condition that everything in the building was kept intact. Established as a factory museum, the aim is to show the site as it had been on the last day of its working life, without intruding any direct interpretation, and relying on guides as animateurs to bring it to life and meaning for its visitors.

Interpretation concentrates on demonstrating aspects of machinery and finishing processes, typical products and equipment, but, because the focus is limited to what is actually visible on site, it is not possible to understand how this fits into its local history, and, because only certain processes are demonstrated, it is not easy to understand technical flow, and the organisation of work within the site.

Machinery on the site actually operates to produce hand-bells and other small artefacts which are sold to visitors. Although these products are based on models made at the works at some time in its history, they are certainly not typical of production in the years before closure. The warehouse provides a display of the more recent output: valves and spigots for fire extinguishers, etc. The slight inconsistency between the period represented in the general ambience of the site and the products currently produced may serve to emphasise craft rather than the capitalist organisation of production, and risks misrepresenting the history of the company. Hand-bells can be made by a single operative, and this risks simplifying the historical division of labour on the site: while production of small saleable goods is justifiable on economic grounds, and does enable aspects of production to be understood, the limitations of this practice must be addressed and compensated in other interpretive material.

There are sharp local divisions about how industrial history at Gnosjö should be understood: the 'Gnosjö spirit' of entrepreneurship and hard work at whatever price has been held up as a model of economic regeneration on the one hand and castigated as an employers' mythology on the other. By default, the strongest identification on the site is with the

32 (a)–(d) Aspects of interpretation 'as if': patterns, and machine shop showing turning and polishing at J. E. Hyltens brass works

entrepreneurs, although this is implicit and the balance could easily be altered.

The manager's office survives complete with coats and hats hanging behind the door, but on the work-floor there are no traces of the workers. Commitment to literal conservation has precluded any representations of the workforce in the factory itself, but the illusion 'as if' is perforce incomplete, and requires rethinking if some of the hidden history of the site is to be reinstated. It would not necessarily disrupt the integrity of the site to introduce interpretive material to fill some of the gaps.

Sometimes simple visual devices which would serve as reminders of what is not actually visible on the site could be employed without interrupting coherence. In another context, the Workers' Museum in Copenhagen symbolised the invisibility of women to the working environments it re-created by the use of clear silhouettes. The intrusion of such an unrealistic symbol into what was otherwise a carefully crafted re-creation was an effective and powerful reminder of histories which are not always visible. This technique could perhaps be employed successfully elsewhere.

Some of the limitations of conservation-led interpretation are being addressed by the Gnosjö town council and the association which runs the museum: plans are taking shape to develop an ecomuseum for the region making use of the nearby open-air site at Töllstorps. This site aims to show the relationship of agriculture and industry in the region and already includes a collection of small water-powered metal workshops (either collected or surviving *in situ*). It provides a historical perspective for the metal works, though does not give its contemporary context. The association also aims to complement the site itself by collecting archives, machines and artefacts from factories in the area, and seeks to protect other related buildings and the water power system. It hopes to open another museum for the display of machinery, to develop access to the archive and to establish a visitor centre which would aim to show some of the relationships with contemporary industry.

On a similar scale, at Nans sous Sainte Anne, Doubs, France, a small family forge has been preserved as it was when last in use, and is managed by the Association des Arts et Traditions Populaires Comtoises. Tours of the forge as it was left provide a sense of historical contingency and an anecdotal element, with interpretation dependent on demonstration. The site operates but is not actually in production, so interpretation

can dissect how it functioned in some detail. The Association has documented the history of the forge, drawing on oral evidence and the examination of artefacts as well as business and public records. A storeroom houses a supporting exhibition which underlines connections between the changing composition of the workforce, work practices and skills, designs of products and market destinations as the firm developed a specialism in scythes and sickles and then succumbed to corporate concentration (Brelot and Mayaud 1982).

These two sites, and others like them, are rare survivors, and their interpretive agenda has been shaped by the requirements of conservation. In both cases, some of the shortcomings of literal conservation are being addressed through supporting interpretive schemes, helped by good documentary and other material.

Both these sites have adopted an interpretive strategy that depends on personal guiding. This strategy enables an atmosphere of authenticity to be maintained, and permits minimal interference with the site, either by introduction of interpretive material for self-guiding, or by the more stringent protective measures which would be necessary without supervision. Guides can provide detailed social history and contextual information if properly briefed. But the use of operators as guides may not always be a practical option, and it may be hard to find training in the appropriate skills to demonstrate techniques which have been superseded.

Interpretation in conserved sites like these relies for much of its effect on the ability to demonstrate machinery. In doing so, is it technical process or skill or labour or conditions which is being demonstrated? Various factors will constrain the possibilities: the machinery may work but not perform its original function; it may have been adapted to run on a different power source; organisation of labour is likely to depart from the original, while meeting modern standards of health and safety is likely to involve changes in operational practice. Demonstration of technique requires skills which may no longer be readily available, and the intensive staffing required to carry out re-enactment may impose limits on access and use of the site. It is unlikely that interpretation can really demonstrate conditions and experience of work or the social relations of production, although these may be implicit in the organisation of the site. With thorough research, documentation and training, it may be possible to interpret skill through operating machinery, but there will be aspects of factory organisation which will still remain invisible (Hills

(c)–(e) demonstrating with the water-power system; forging with trip hammers; and showing tools and products

1977: 157–68; Victor 1981). Representation 'as if' may leave a number of questions unanswered, requiring further interpretation to provide context.

An operating site poses particular problems of interpretation: how is it to be interpreted when it is working, and what happens when it is not? Small, craft-based industries can sometimes be successfully interpreted by the operatives themselves, and this has worked well in some of the workshops at Ironbridge and the machine shop at Hagley, Delaware, for example. At Slater Mill, Rhode Island, ex-operatives interpret both the process and the conditions, talking about what it was like to do this sort of work. But this strategy is not an option on larger, more complex sites like the wrought iron works at Ironbridge, where visitors must keep their distance, where heat, noise and the necessary speed of work preclude direct communication. There is a risk that the museum will simply re-run the site, failing to interpret it at all, relying largely on visual spectacle.

Small-scale industrial workshops based on manufacture have a chance of working again, and use as museum may possibly be able to sustain their operation. Much of this is at the level of craft, and intervention in the revival of larger-scale production is unlikely to be viable without major injections of capital or liaison with agencies of economic renewal. However, some museums have undertaken more ambitious projects to reinstate elements of intermediate scale productions (for example the Blists Hill wrought iron works), and intervene in continuing practice (Fourmies and the Walsall Leather Centre, see above chapter 2).

A number of heritage-related projects have tried to establish themselves as repositories of skill: Brighton's Engineerium used its machinery and model conservation workshop as a basis for training programmes, and ten years ago the French government supported the creation of centres for the conservation and demonstration of redundant tools, machinery and techniques by skilled workers. But the network of Centres of Scientific, Technical and Industrial Culture, which was intended to sustain practical technical culture and act as a springboard for economic regeneration, was largely displaced by the technological orientation of La Villette (see above chapter 2, and Desvallées 1985; Templeton 1981: 39–43).

The extension of literal conservation into demonstration of working processes may not always be viable, either within the limits of local economic and human resources, for health and safety reasons, or because machinery is too vulnerable to permit continued use. At Klevfos, in Norway, some of these issues have been addressed in devising an imaginative programme of complementary interpretation. When the paper mill closed in 1976, local people and former employees at first talked in terms of a traditional-style museum. But their ideas eventually took shape as a project to preserve the factory with its machinery, using the experience and enthusiasm of local people with some technical back-up from the local museum, and government schemes providing some labour and funding.

Work is all done in-house and, as the foreman and manager (the only permanent staff) had both worked for twenty-five years in the industry, can be done quite cheaply. But the project is heavily dependent on local resources which cannot at present sustain the operation of machinery on the site, which would be both expensive and dangerous. For the time being, efforts are concentrated on keeping the factory dry and protecting the machinery.

Nevertheless, the museum plans to show how the factory was when it was running, but has chosen to emphasise the social rather than the technical, working primarily with local constituencies. They have initiated some innovative interpretive projects, including a cabaret based on interviews with former workers using a trade union choir of local amateurs. Written by a seconded teacher, it was performed on sixteen evenings, way in excess of estimates, and was also televised. The songs relate to different parts of the factory – the song of the paper mill workers, the song of the soda burner – and are based on oral history research. Pre-school children have also visited the museum, making pictures, and former workers have also been involved, through the singing but also through other projects such as making a traditional workers' felt coat. These are small-scale projects, but encouraging use of the site as a venue of exhibition and events has helped to create interest in the work of the museum. Interpretation through these collaborative projects may be ephemeral, but provides a celebration of shared histories which has been of great local value.

Associated with the factory itself, a series of apartments have also been restored to represent local conditions in the 1920s and 1950s. These have been put together by a student using local knowledge and donations to create convincing reconstructions of domestic environments, as supporting social historical material for the factory complex itself. Other supporting programmes are being inaugurated, with funding from a trade union providing for a documentation centre which will address both history and present management issues.

The project demonstrates what can be achieved with limited local resources. But this kind of interpretation demands a steady input from local people which will not always be forthcoming. At the moment, there is a large body of local expertise and memory concerning the factory in operation: this will not always be the case. The museum needs to develop a documentation programme to record this local lore and knowledge: it also needs to develop a more permanent programme to interpret the complex operations that took place on the site.

Operation and re-use are never likely to be an option for interpretation on conserved sites of large-scale manufacture, processing or production. At Goslar, the Rammelsberg ore mine operated until summer 1988, the end of a history of exploitation that began in at least the third or fourth century. Above ground, there survives a landscape of mining that includes traces going back to medieval times, including slag heaps, a water reservoir and the passes along which the ore was transported. Below ground, there are also substantial remains of the medieval mining activity, as well as a late eighteenth-century system of adits and water power. But the most spectacular above-ground remains are those of the ore-dressing plant. Designed by a leading industrial architect in the 1930s, it survives as it was left on its last working day in 1988, with all machinery intact.

Original plans for the re-use of the site recommended gutting the ore-crushing buildings and redeveloping them as a mixed-use tourism centre with a swimming pool. Interpretation as heritage was to be confined to some exhibitions about later mining, and the retention of the eighteenth-century and medieval shafts. However, largely owing to the dedicated persistence of the curator and Reinhard Roseneck from the Lower Saxony Heritage Institute, the intention now is to conserve the whole site as it was left, though of course without actually reinstating production. This will involve expensive decontamination of the crushing plant, but will enable visitors to follow the complete processing operation and witness the scale and organisation of a major company. Processing, management and work routines all have a clear spatial dimension on the site. Given the spectacular and historically important nature of the site and buildings, and good connections with existing local tourist attractions, this scheme has the potential to attract large numbers of people if backed by sufficient investment.

34 Klevfos, Norway:
(a) a cabaret brings history
back to life

(b) & (c) temporary art
exhibitions attract attention to
the disused paper mill

(d)–(f) workers' apartments
furnished to illustrate life in
the 1920s and 1950s

The Rammelsburg site dramatises some important issues: what to do with the extensive, complex sites of near-contemporary industry; different ideas about what to conserve, and what to include, and what it is economically feasible to conserve. Interpretive choices could have emphasised the baroque heroism of pure technology, the architectural unity of the site, or its socio-economic aspects. Visitors will follow the route taken by raw materials through the site, which will be displayed more or less intact, though it is proposed to take apart some of the machinery, the better to display its mechanism, and to remove some to install exhibition space, though without interfering with the general atmosphere of the site.

The expense of the project requires underpinning from state and federal governments and must hope to attract a large through-put of visitors, casting itself as a national or even international monument. Nevertheless, spectacular though the site is, it is also an important local resource. As the visitor follows the route taken by the ore, the operation of the machinery can be explained in technical terms, but the site can also be animated by an account of the work required in the operation: how many people worked in the plant, where were their stations, what it was like to work there. Since the plant closed down so recently, there are good local resources to make this possible. Inclusion of space for exhibitions creates the potential to broaden out the themes which can be covered on the site: for example, the recent history which culminated in its closure.

Retaining a redundant power plant at Zwevegem, Flanders, as a conserved monument also highlights the problems of using conservation as a substitute for interpretation: how can interpretive material be introduced, how avoid simply mystifying with the sheer scale of the plant and the invisibility of the process itself? There are serious limits on what literal conservation can achieve and it is important that it is balanced by off-site contextualising material. While there may be no adequate substitute for the site itself to dramatise the scale and nature of production, it is important that conservation is linked with a good interpretive strategy to explain the working of the site. Unlike manufacture, pure production is less amenable either to demonstration, or to verbal explanation. There must be more stress on the interpretive material on the site and it is important to draw out the ramifications of the site – which might in this case lead towards discussion of the use of electricity for example. This means a complementary programme of interpretation off-site.

35 The monumental ore-crushing plant, pithead and miners' baths at Goslar

36 Reconstructed power transmission, Polhem's Wheel, Norberg, Sweden

In many cases it will simply not be practical to literally conserve major industrial monuments, and consideration will need to be given to the development of techniques of recording which can provide an adequate substitute for preservation. It may be that the interests of interpretation as explaining the operation and significance of a site may be better served by good documentation than by conservation.

Reinstatement, reconstruction and operation

Literal conservation is never sufficient as an interpretive strategy, and there may be times when it is not appropriate. Where a site is inadequately intelligible as it survives, there may be a role for reinstatement or reconstruction to facilitate interpretation.

But reconstruction is not a substitute for conservation, there is a risk that the resource itself will be diminished if reconstruction conflicts with what survives. It can only be justified in so far as it enhances the understanding of a site: it may be a way of de-mystifying a ruin, and restoring visual coherence to a site; the **process** of reconstruction itself may also be a way of learning more about a process or technique, and the organisation of labour which sustained it. In each case it can only be carried through with good supporting material (e.g. documentation or oral evidence) and careful research (e.g. archaeological enquiry). Too often, reconstruction is used in illustration or to evoke an experience rather than to satisfy historical enquiry.

Interpretive programmes depend on detailed research already carried out, but do not necessarily simply illustrate information derived from other sources. Interpretation through reconstruction can itself be a research process, but this will only be the case if there are clearly defined problems needing to be solved, and if these problems can only or best be solved through reconstruction. For example, reconstructing a blast furnace without running it may answer some questions about design, the technology of construction and the science of engineering, but can say very little about the relationship between design and use. The same questions about design could possibly have been answered by the construction of scale models or drawn reconstruction or the application of computer programmes. It may be that archaeological investigation and analysis – deconstruction rather than reconstruction – are of more use academically, and reconstruction may simply be a way of applying knowledge derived from archaeological enquiry.

Although reconstruction simply to show what something looked like is a dramatic communicative tool, it is limited in its academic value. But reconstruction can make a decisive contribution to knowledge if it is oriented around problem solving, adequately researched and carried out according to procedures which avoid anachronism. Experimental reconstructions of smelting furnaces to demonstrate casting operations, for example, have been able to challenge assumptions about the operation derived from metallurgical analysis, and make suggestions about operating practices (Coles 1973; Kruse, Smith and Starling 1988; Bamberger 1984).

The same commitment to experiment characterises the reconstruction of machinery or equipment. The Science Museum in London is assembling Charles Babbage's Difference Engine Number Two. The reconstruction is intended to make a decisive contribution to the debate about whether the failure of his calculating engines was owing to the limitations of nineteenth-century machine tool technology or to managerial problems – disputes with his engineer and inadequate support. In setting out to enter this debate, the project is committed to as high a degree of historical exactitude as possible, and has had to find ways of compensating for the sketchy detail supplied in Babbage's own surviving drawings. Modern techniques are being used, but to a precision appropriate for the nineteenth century (Swade 1990). Reconstruction helps explain a partially surviving power transmission system at Norberg, Sweden, and enables the ambition and sophistication of the eighteenth-century technology to be appreciated more fully.

Reconstruction involves major investment which is of necessity concerned directly with only one aspect or phase of the history of a site. It will therefore not always be the aptest way of interpreting a site, and an audit of archaeological and historical resources should be used to determine both whether and how to reconstruct, and how to balance this with other interpretive material.

How extensive should reconstruction be? Is it the entire site or a limited part of the operation? Should the water-power system and the blowing mechanism for an iron furnace be reconstructed? If they are not, their absence requires interpreting, but understanding of the site will inevitably be dominated by one component. Partial reconstruction is likely to deliver only partial information.

What should be the relationship between the reconstruction and the original? If a surviving monument is itself reconstructed, there is a risk of damage (especially if the site is actually going to re-run) which may destroy archaeological information. If on the other hand it is reconstructed elsewhere, there may be serious limits to how far the context of the original can be replicated, affecting the validity of the reconstruction. The moving and re-erection of industrial structures pose particular problems in the destruction of archaeological layers and loss of context, and are generally no longer encouraged except in exceptional circumstances and with detailed investigation and recording (Lindsley and Smith 1973: 55–68).

Should reconstruction be based on new build or the salvaging and rebuilding of old? Small-scale building reconstruction at open-air museum sites has established methodologies for both, and the use of full-scale models as at once applied archaeological research and interpretive strategy has been tried with some success at the Archaeodrome, Beaune, France. Strategy is likely to be dictated by state of survival and by assessment of the value of the site for preservation. Industrial sites which have been out of use for some time may be supporting a significant ecology: assessment should take this into account when determining the extent of intervention.

Construction of a replica may be an alternative which can sustain the preservation of original remains where present-day building requirements would involve excessive or destructive intervention (for instance concealing or damaging archaeological levels), but replicas will not always be appropriate and are limited in what they can achieve – there are serious limitations with replica coal-mines which may provide a partial spatial experience but will not in themselves add significantly to either the understanding of the industry or its conditions of operation. The illusion of authenticity may not accommodate the very different cultural assumptions which present-day visitors will bring to a site.

Smaller manufacturing sites may be amenable to reconstruction to permit operation. The relative ease with which this can be done for craft-based production has spawned many model smiths', carpenters' or wheelwrights' shops.

For some, Colonial Williamsburg, the restored eighteenth-century capital of colonial Virginia, with its lavish financial and intellectual resources, represents best practice. Craft processes and products play a key role in the interpretation of the tidewater colonial town, and the museum has reconstructed a very extensive range of craft workshops in which work with patterns and processes characteristic of the period is dem-

onstrated and completed for sale or commission. A programme of local historical archaeology and documentary
research has informed the choice of objects and techniques
for reproduction, and has also been utilised in a series of
printed interpretive guides.

The success of animated reconstructions in the more folkic
context of open-air museums like Sturbridge Village, Massachusetts, or Skansen, Stockholm, and the ambitious total
environment recreation at Williamsburg, has helped to inspire
the development of operational reconstruction in industrial-
processing contexts. Scale of investment and difficulty of
recovering appropriate skill rule this out in most circumstances, but the most ambitious project at Ironbridge Gorge
Museum to date has been the re-creation of a wrought iron
works using machinery from the Atlas Ironworks in Bolton
in a building from the Woolwich dockyard (Smith and Gale
1987).

Reconstruction to standards sufficient to permit operation
may necessitate compromise. Changes in operational practice
may have to be made – for example a new power source may
have to be introduced. In re-erecting the wrought iron works,
Ironbridge Gorge Museum is in fact only re-creating a fraction
of the original, but representing it as a coherent working unit.
These changes are justified if they enhance the clarity of the
site and its operation, and if they do not misrepresent the
scope and the competence of the original operation, but are
themselves a resource for interpretation: modern interventions
must be identified.

Reconstruction may be justified where it contributes to
problem solving in an academic agenda, but will never be
sufficient as an interpretive device. While it may be a valuable
tool in enhancing understanding of a site, it has its limitations.
It may marginalise the evidence and history of change; it
creates an illusion of integrity which may overlook less favoured components of the site where physical reconstruction
is partial, and which risks misrepresenting the context of
operation.

Like conserved working sites, reconstruction must clearly
distinguish between technicist interpretation and the fuller
historical context which might embrace social, economic and
cultural histories. Verisimilitude risks obscuring as much as
it reveals if these distinctions are not made clear. For example,
interpretation of the crafts at Williamsburg makes a thorough
and accomplished exposition of technique using appropriate
tools to produce appropriate products. But what this cannot

itself reveal is the economy, society and culture of the town which sustained these crafts and made sense of them in their original context. Product design, the organisation of enterprises, with their labour and the markets they served, conditions and organisation of work are not directly visible in a technically focused interpretation; lacking that primary cultural ambience, the visitor sees only technique, but is not necessarily aware of what has been left out.

Since interpretation is not simply a matter of communicating and creating an experience, but is also a process of coming to understand, museums should say something about their own processes of enquiry: it is helpful to know what research has been carried out, what compromises have been made, how far what is done now differs from original practice. Answering these questions should be part of the documentation process – but museums do not always document their own interventions, let alone consider this suitable material for public exhibition. Examples of best practice come from museums working in other contexts – industrial heritage examples are hard to find, though Summerlee demonstrates its commitment to documentation by employing its own photographer, and has mounted an exhibition of portraits of staff, and, in the presentation of museological sciences, the Americans lead the field. Visitors to the reconstructed Plymouth Plantation, Plymouth, Massachusetts, must first pass through an exhibition showing representations of the pilgrims and presenting a historiographical problem. This is followed up by an exhibition showing the techniques of historical and archaeological enquiry which contributed to the reconstruction itself (see also Saumerez Smith 1989).

Reconstruction and re-working are themselves resources requiring further interpretation. Lessons drawn from the process of reconstruction (or deconstruction in the case of archaeological stripping back) are themselves an important resource and could be presented. The work of reconstruction should be treated as an archaeological exercise, recorded at every stage. There are some precedents for using the process of reconstruction as interpretive material in its own right in open-air folk museums (Norsk Folkmuseum, Oslo, and Sturbridge Village, Massachusetts, for example). The Science Museum in London is carrying out its construction of Babbage's Difference Machine in public.

There is a vital need for complementary interpretive material to fill the gaps left by conservation and reconstruction since both can represent only part of the whole history of a site – that they are themselves a part of that history is often overlooked. Some of the gaps in a conservation or reconstruction scheme can be filled by complementary collection and documentation. This might take the site itself as a starting point and go on to trace its linkages in a wider context, both physical and cultural.

The interpretation of historical sites which are no longer in primary use raises issues which may also be encountered in the interpretation of industries which are still in operation. One critical question concerns the sufficiency of the site itself to tell a history. Where they are practicable, factory tours may enable visitors to witness production, but cannot provide a historical perspective, explain processes and working conditions, or set the site in context. Where more detailed interpretation is carried out, working industrial sites understandably often opt for design- and production-oriented themes. Museums may have a complementary role in the documentation of contemporary industry, recording details of experience as well as processes within the factory, and a recent collaborative project carried out by a group of Scotland's industrial museums aimed to do this, presenting its results in a small travelling exhibition.

The interpretive agenda for sites suggests a general line of development for projects engaged in site-based work: the ability to draw out historical potential accessible for diverse uses requires particular patterns of organisation and must draw on programmes of collecting and documentation.

Interpreting collections

Interpretation in the museum, as on a site, is not just a process of communication to the visitor or the display of a collection – it is part of the way that the museum itself evaluates and understands its material in its relationship to a culture. It is not just about making exhibitions but forms part of the whole programme of the museum. Interpretation can therefore be construed as a process either of telling, or of asking, challenging and questioning. The museum must ask how the visitor is to be engaged in the interpretive process – as viewer, as participator or as scholar.

Sites and landscapes are arranged as they were, and interpretation is concerned to elucidate them through its balance of research and presentation. While complementary interpretation can set sites in context, many of the broader themes of industrialisation rest poorly visible. Best use of resources on a site must begin an interpretive plan with what is there, and go out from that assessment to consider ramifications. Widening economic contexts or changes in the organisation of labour can possibly be shown as they relate to that site, but not all industries or aspects of industrial culture have a physical extension into sites, and site survival and availability will rarely be representative. Home-based work, patterns of education, health care and child-rearing, for example, will not be visible. Transformations in economic organisation and social and cultural experience cannot easily be shown through the agency of a single site.

There are therefore many aspects of industrial heritage which cannot be told through site or landscape interpretation alone. Agenda-based museums lack many of the constraints of sites, and even a collection established already, possibly in another context, can still be treated with some flexibility in the representation of industrial culture.

Museums have been object-oriented in the past, collecting first, and then interpreting. Some did not start out that way, and many technical museums, for example, had collections formed in the service of a precise educational agenda. But, with the loss of this original rationale, many found themselves left just holding the objects. Current critical theory suggests that museums should now be looking inward from general historical themes, rather than outward from a collection (Jenkinson 1989: 139–47). Others have considered that, in doing this, the museum risks becoming a textbook on the wall, its artefacts relegated to an illustrative role (Hindle 1978: 5–20; Vergo 1989: 51). While this debate has unseated the object from its central position, and encouraged a redefinition of what can constitute an object in a museum – extending definitions to include images, sound and written sources as well as artefacts – collection and exhibition remain important.

But although concerned with collecting material evidence of human activities, museum programmes are not limited to subjects which are in their entirety collectable, nor are they necessarily limited to things which are their immediate property. The programme of activities defined by a museum might include the acquisition and care of material evidences, but a related objective should be to increase the depth and breadth of understanding and care for cultural resources which are not the property of the museum, extending an umbrella of commitment over the variable contexts of collections as well as the artefacts themselves.

No class of evidence speaks for itself, and it is the function of interpretation to make histories out of fragments of material evidence, or to use histories to make sense of an evidence. In both senses, it is the relationship established between the fragments of evidence and a set of suppositions and concepts which is critical. The remit for interpretation is therefore given in a relationship between what survives or can be found and the histories which are possible. It is therefore not a passive process of explaining intrinsic meanings, but an open-ended agenda of choices of use and contextualisation. This is as true for collection-based as for thematic or concept-based interpretation, though the typical patterns of resulting stories may be different. Collection-based interpretation is not necessarily simpler or closer to the evidence, because making an interpretation even of simple classes of artefact requires many kinds of evidence.

But the history of museums has not favoured such open-ended interpretation of industrial culture. Museums have collected particular categories of artefact which they have interpreted according to certain paradigms and, even where these have specifically related to industrial histories, they have often been highly limiting; museums have attempted to replicate specific contexts, in order to show examples of workshop or domestic interiors, but often this has been the outcome of a generalised research process; museums have adopted a narrative role, and subordinated the complexity of experience to the relative simplicity of a closely defined theme; they have limited the communicative potential of interpretation by a commitment to objectivity taken so far as to exclude any evidence of debate or controversy, often ignoring the history of the museum itself, and the problematic relationship between its collections and the culture which produced and used them; departmental divisions within museums and between collection, interpret-ation and documentation have made it hard to offer new understandings by new uses of material or new connections (Burton 1989; Saumerez Smith 1989: 6–21).

Dimensions of knowledge and experience

Interpretive possibilities are bounded by the resource assess-ments which underpin them. The range of material evidences which can be used in a museum include objects (which may not all have been viewed as industrial), but extend beyond the collection itself into experience and memory, images, text and the spoken word. They include the local environment, the greater history of an industry or a culture (local, national, international), the memories, possessions and experience of local people, and the diverse interpretations available through interdisciplinary study. The area the museum serves, the people it seeks to involve, also constitute part of its resource base.

A collection which is not rigidly confined to certain typological categories of object will enable a richer interpretive programme to be presented: at the Museum of American Textile History, the extension of collecting into the daily paraphernalia of a factory has been developed hand-in-hand with an interpretive programme intended to examine the issue of work. Similarly, the more detailed the documentation, the more interpretive possibilities are opened up. Different analytical perspectives on objects themselves may reveal multiple histories, as for example the study of machinery to reveal its vernacular adaptations and, through them, a sense of the relationship between operator and machine (Fägeborg 1984a: 60–1).

Complementary documentation also opens the way for a richer interpretive agenda. In the interpretation of the recent past or contemporary experience, oral history has a pre-eminent part. For example, it provided evidence for the social use of industrial processes at Ramnas Iron-works in Sweden (Bursell 1975; Bursell 1987: 216–19). Oral history was also used extensively in preparing the exhibition 'Furnishing the World' at the Geffrye Museum in London. The museum was concerned to balance its earlier emphasis on a product (furniture) by consideration of its makers and users, and wanted to encourage local people to participate in documenting their own history. In the process, information on aspects of work which were poorly documented in written sources was brought to light, enabling the museum to pay greater attention to the work of women furniture makers for example.

Choice of interpretive themes in the small museum at Springburn in Glasgow has been dictated by sensitivity to the concerns of local people, choosing an emphasis on recent change rather than the representation of the area in its heyday. Oral history provides a vital source of material, and local people are drawn in through their own artefacts, photographs and memories, sometimes themselves working on the design of exhibitions (O'Neill 1990: 21). Determination of period to interpret has also been influenced by the strength of local memory at Fourmies (see below). Domestic interiors at Klevfos and Grangesburg have been set up with similar ideas in mind – they are sufficiently recent to be based on donations and on people remembering how it was.

Museums need a grounding in academic disciplines in both

the understanding of their immediate resources and the recognition of their broader contexts. The presence of a broad and interdisciplinary knowledge base can enable the re-evaluation of existing collections, and encourage a wide-ranging approach to the definition of new programmes. Such interdisciplinary approaches may depend on re-thinking conventional subject divisions within the museum: the Nordiska Museum in Stockholm and the Victoria and Albert Museum in London have both done this. They may also depend on gaining wider constituencies of support and involvement. Museums which aim to represent recent and local histories, or themes based on experience, are likely to do so successfully only if they can rely on extensive participation. In histories where experience and memory are of less value – in early industrial histories, for example – the ability to draw on different areas of expertise may be critical.

Contexts for understanding

Collections of artefacts have their particular contexts of production and use, and the physical extension and life-cycle of an industry constitute an immediate resource. Each could be ramified via linkages to other histories; each must also be placed in a pattern of spatial and chronological relationships, sensitive to human experience, and with an awareness of the inevitable absences from a historical record.

The discussion which follows is intended to serve as a general introduction to the dimensions of imagination which museums, whatever their subject, must address in dealing with representations of culture.

The spatial dimension

Industrial culture embraces a number of different kinds of spatial experience: the territory covered in a journey to work or during the working day, territory covered by materials or products, the territory covered by business organisation, by competing or complementary industries. Space can be experienced symbolically or psychologically – used to define a discipline or reinforce a relationship of authority. Different kinds of space may interconnect – work and domestic, public and private – as separate but overlapping spheres.

Museums have delineated local geographical space by the making and display of maps and plans, and by model making. They have presented images, mock-ups and reconstructions of domestic and workplace space. They have interpreted the view from the window, and provided guides to the landscape outside. Interpretation has also enabled the visitor to experience different spatial organisation directly: the ability to go into a room-set, for example, creates a relationship entirely different from that of onlooker. Taking space seriously requires the maintenance of an appropriate scale in reconstructions – the Workers' Museum in Copenhagen has re-created small and cramped attics as part of its exhibition, 'The First Industrial Workers', and visitors to the Museum of Work in Steyr must be funnelled through a tiny domestic interior.

Many museums working with industrial heritage are still wedded to a local topographical history approach, with convenient categories of home and work which may not adequately reflect the complexities of spatial organisation of a culture. Choice of categories may implicitly undermine commitment to a topographical focus by making it hard to see the full range of local resources. A tendency to concentrate on local or regional specialisms, rather than ranging over the many ways of making a living encompassed in a particular area, may mean that those occupations and industries which are not regionally specialised are rarely given serious treatment.

On the other hand, the selection of topographical boundaries may not be wholly appropriate for the interpretation of industrial heritage. The organisation of space which is not local – for example the journeys of people or of products – may be a critical aspect of industrialisation, but is often overlooked. Designing a project entitled 'Change in the City', the City Museum and Art Gallery in Birmingham sought to register the heterogeneity of its inner-city culture, and did so by taking population, rather than place, as its starting point. It saw the city itself as an entrepôt in a process of cultural exchange as diverse and changing populations accommodated to living in the city. Following out a chosen theme of food and drink, the project workers also followed connections that took them outside the city itself, recognising the relevance of non-local production for patterns of local consumption (Jenkinson 1987: 33–9; Jenkinson 1989: 147–52).

Time and change

Museum collections are often founded on survivals from earlier periods, and the ability to understand change lies at the core of their responsibility. If they are to avoid simply holding up a mirror to 'the way we were', they must be able to show adaptation, alternatives and choices. But how is change over time represented in museums? How much time is covered in the scope of exhibition or documentation programmes? How does the museum respond to recent times, and how can different experiences of time and rhythms of change be dramatised?

An important context for the formation of the Workers' Museum in Copenhagen was the visibility of change, and the museum focuses attention on the 1950s as a decade in which Denmark was perceived to have become an industrial society in order to look back and remember, and also as a point of entry to the presentation of earlier histories from the 1930s and 1870s. The Community Museum at Springburn in Glasgow was established in the wake of devastating change in the local and regional economy, and deals with this explicitly in exhibitions which relate present to past. These exhibitions have been constructed in sufficient detail to identify several phases in change and development, rather than relying on simpler before-and-after comparisons (O'Neill 1987: 28–32).

Many museums offer a rather undifferentiated chronology relying on general contrasts between 'now' and 'then' and passing over less dramatic phases of development and adaptation. The careful re-creation of particular contexts risks representing a snap-shot in time without a history, prompting facile comparisons of then and now. Such contrasts, as representations of memory and change, may have a value in so far as they create an involvement with the visitor, but can only be effective if they avoid stereotyped comparison. An acute sense of contingency has been poignantly captured by precision in the representation of particular histories in the Workers' Museum in Copenhagen: the empty spaces in a room set from the 1930s where the furniture is said to be in pawn reveal a moment with a history which gives the visitor pause. Its exhibition, 'For Life and Bread: The First Industrial Workers' takes as its subject the formation of a new class of industrial workers in the last decades of the nineteenth century and it deliberately contrasts the older ways of craft-based production with the newer forms of factory work (Vasström 1987: 180–8).

Museums have injected a deeper sense of time into their displays by showing objects in series to demonstrate development over time, and have also created contexts in series, for example room sets, to show changes over time. Beamish open-air museum uses its reconstructed terraced housing to compare living styles at different decades, and the same approach has been adopted with paired apartments at Grangesburg and Klevfos. But this serial arrangement risks a simple emphasis on progress and linear change (Moreton 1988: 132–3), and the museum needs to be clear about what exactly is intended to be the subject of these displays – they may simply be showing changes in taste or technical process.

The social impact of technical and economic changes has been explored in an exhibition of a family history at Nans sous Sainte Anne, following the family operating the forge over several generations. The Museum of American Textile History uses the technical progression of its machinery in an exhibition showing changes in the nature of work. It uses reconstructions to dramatise points in a story, not to sustain an illusion of authenticity, and they depend for their effect on a relationship with more traditional modes of address. At the Museum of Work in Steyr, Austria, and Manchester Museum of Science and Industry, a simple series of machine tools are animated by discussion about changing organisation on the factory floor. Dramatisation of routine, and changes in the symbolic measurement of time, have provided themes in the Sogne Folkemuseum, Norway, combining stages of life, seasons of year, time of day in a calendar of activity represented by objects, images and text. Similar integration of a yearly calendar with longer cycles of change could be an effective tool in the interpretation of industrial histories.

The theme of change can be dramatised through complementary material to illustrate earlier or subsequent histories. Many museums have extended their collecting policy sufficiently to include contemporary material, and even where this may fall outside the major interpretive remit, references to contemporary practice can provide valuable accompanying contextual material.

Reflecting diverse experience

Interpretations of industrial heritage risk creating representations of an apparently integrated culture unless they also reflect on absences, tensions and contradictions. What histories fall through the gaps in a collecting policy, or in the representations of work, for example? Where are those who didn't work – the old, the unemployed, the sick, children? How are different experiences of social and cultural position dramatised? How can the museum make connections with the diverse populations who have been drawn into the development of an area, and who may now constitute its audiences?

37 A shadow on the wall is all that is left of furniture now in pawn, in a room set of the 1930s, Workers' Museum, Copenhagen (Photo: Allan Schnipper, Arbejdermuseet)

38 How can a museum show work that is done, but disregarded? A perspex charlady in the Workers' Museum, Copenhagen (Photo: Allan Schnipper, Arbejdermuseet)

Hidden histories can be addressed through strategies of display with concomitant collection and documentation designed to include a broader cross-section of material. Concentration on dominant regional industries has often tended to marginalise certain sectors of the population. To counter this, 'invisible' women (perspex cut-outs) people workplace displays in the Fifties' exhibition at the Workers' Museum in Copenhagen, and displays at Fourmies show domestic as well as factory-based work. Few museums are prepared to take the professional and managerial classes seriously, however, and they do not carry out the kind of detailed social anthropology which could begin to represent social structures and contrasting life chances and experience (Conradson 1984).

Alternatively, different ways of working may reach different constituencies and enable coverage of other themes. Outreach policies have been particularly successful in this respect. The Ecomuseum of the community Le Creusot-Montceau-Les-Mines initiated a local temporary exhibition programme aimed to foster links with its communities and work directly with their senses of historical value. Themes were selected following detailed local inventories, discussed in chapter 4, and exhibitions were assembled around objects brought in by local people, who also contributed their own knowledge of them to the documentation process (Combier 1977; Scalbert Bellaigue 1981; Silvester 1975; de Varine-Bohan 1973). Ironbridge Gorge Museum, hedged in by a tightly defined interpretive agenda on its major sites, is planning a new programme of small community-based exhibitions to encourage people to loan their own objects and treasures for display and to validate something of those local histories which cannot be dealt with elsewhere.

Evaluating its existing twentieth-century decorative arts collections the Victoria and Albert Museum found that documentation was patchy on provenance and had nothing on how things were used, seriously limiting interpretive possibilities. When making room sets for earlier periods, curators had carried out or commissioned specialist research, but the museum wanted to lay down a sounder basis in contemporary documentation for the future while also addressing current debates about consumerism and influences concerning design and the home. It did so by initiating a collaborative project with Middlesex Polytechnic, which enabled it to gain access to a range of experiences the museum couldn't easily reach itself. The project, discussed in chapter 4, works through a mix of self-documentation and professional recording, in a programme which takes place largely outside the museum itself.

An effective interpretive strategy must therefore be under-pinned by close understandings of themes and artefacts with their chosen contexts. It requires sufficient resources and documentation to dramatise different meanings and connotations. It is shaped and constrained by the structure of the organisation and its relationship with its constituencies of support and involvement.

Collection-centred interpretation

Museums have approached the interpretation of industry from two directions: they have taken an objects-oriented focus or a narrative/theme-oriented focus. Taking an objects-centred approach can be valuable, and may be requisite where there is a large existing collection. Objects can be exploited as a rich source of evidence in their own right, but lack of knowledge and research has constrained their potential. The interpretive agenda has been limited on the one hand by an assumption that objects will speak for themselves, and on the other by a fear that they will not speak at all unless firmly contextualised. Taking as its objective the multiple use of a resource, interpretation should avoid over-contextualisation as much as connoisseurship.

But the objects-centred approach has had its limitations: museums tend to approach the establishment of industrial collections according to certain stock themes, and the linkages from the artefacts are not always exploited either in the development of complementary collecting and documentation programmes or in elaborating interpretive material. Industries can only be partially represented through their major artefacts of production, yet it is these artefacts which are often at centre-stage. These limitations are often as much to do with the limited vision in which objects are held as they are to do with actual constraints on the value of objects themselves as evidence.

For example, production machinery is generally interpreted to show process and operation, but is not often linked through to other themes such as sources of materials, markets, users and uses. Process is often exhibited independently of product. Collections of machine tools are rarely discussed in terms of their linkages with other industries, even though machine tool manufacture produced intermediate goods; their role in changing definitions of skill and their conditions of operation are rarely discussed; collections of textile machinery are rarely discussed in conjunction with the types of material they produced, its uses and effects on the clothing industry, and changes in dress and fashion; the whole environment of the factory, with its management and ancillary services, is very rarely considered; power halls often deal exclusively with generation rather than use of power. And how many railway museums deal with the impact of the railway on regional and national economies, and the social history of rail travel? (See, for example, Hudson 1987; Porter 1988: 102–27.)

Objects cannot speak for themselves, and what they offer depends on the ability to read them. Curatorial practice must be supported by multidisciplinary research enabling multiple readings, but interpretation should not simply present the results of research – it should enable participation in the evaluation of resources (see also the discussion in chapter 3). At the least, this might take the form of additional information added as text in counterpoint to the main theme. At the Coalport China Museum at Ironbridge, for example, strands of a social history of work have been added to the basic interpretive text supporting mock-ups arranged to show the sequence of production. A video based on written and oral recollections of working life also supplements the narrowly technical and decorative arts orientation of the museum. However, the different histories are poorly integrated, and the social history is not carried through with conviction into the collection and display.

Other museums have gone further and juxtaposed different kinds of material and different kinds of evidence to suggest new interpretations. This technique was used at the Geffrye Museum's 'Furnishing the World' exhibition, where edited recordings from workplace interviews were played over domestic room sets. By inviting comparison between product and process, this approach enables the visitors to make their own interpretations. In a similar spirit, Fourmies used the juxtaposition of photograph and mock-up to good effect in its representation of a workshop. The Community Museum at Springburn uses a collage of objects, images and oral testimony to articulate recent local history through experience (O'Neill 1987: 28–32). But many museums have been reluctant to encourage visitor involvement in interpretation, preferring to synthesise sources in narrative rather than display and problematise fragments of dispersed evidence (Burton 1989; Jordanova 1989: 22–40; Skramstad 1978; Vergo 1989: 51–4).

Museums have also re-created social contexts for the display of objects, a technique which has found much recent favour. It should by now be clear that such re-creations can only be as good as the resources put into them, and themselves require interpretation (Saumerez Smith 1989: 19–21). Best practice relates such reconstructions to other interpretive material and communicative techniques, since reconstructions do not and cannot speak for themselves. Both at the Museum of American Textile History and at the Workers' Museum in Copenhagen, careful attention has been paid to the relationship between reconstruction and conventional exhibition. A carefully established agenda at Copenhagen defines precisely the points which are to be made in each reconstruction, and these are given further attention in a complementary exhibition which introduces different source-types – photographic and documentary evidence – and provides a concise discussion of issues. In its reconstructions, the museum is not afraid to break the illusion of representation in the interests of dramatising a point, and has done so to good effect to reassert the hidden history of women workers.

Displaying and interpreting objects in a re-created context is obviously a valuable way to demonstrate aspects of their production and use, but its flip side is that it can be inflexible, limiting the use of objects to the illustration of a single story (Hindle 1978). This problem will be compounded where displays are made with heavy investment discouraging change. There is a risk of limiting future options and alternative strategies if museums organise their entire collecting policy around one interpretive theme or context. Objects must be presented in some kind of context, but the possibility of their interpretation in different directions can be retained either by a carefully framed long-term programme of changing display, or by the use of contexts which do not attempt to be literal replications.

All museum collections which are assembled rather than conserved are bedevilled by the 'clean' state of collection in comparison with a recently used machine shop, for example, which might show the alterations and survivals of machines from different periods all in use at once. This is an issue which museum collecting and interpreting needs to take seriously, if replicas are to be developed to show other than simply mechanical process. In reconstructing domestic working environments, Fourmies has tackled this issue by invoking experience and memory to include small incidental detail. A small workshop has been assembled as a mock-up from photographic evidence: juxtaposition of the mock-up with a greatly enlarged photographic image enables the visitor to enter into the interpretive process rather than just seeing the results. Reconstruction to high standards of authenticity makes sense only if there is a collection strong in compatible elements, and where complementary resources – written or oral description, visual images – are good. It is not a useful option if the collection is more diverse, or if available knowledge and resources cannot sustain the high specifications necessary for the illusion of authenticity.

Appeals to wider histories are made from a base line which may be pure technology on the one hand, or pure decorative arts on the other. The following discussion takes collections of machinery as a series of case studies, looking at the way in which existing collections have been redefined, and how interpretive strategies have been devised to deal with the relationship between the object and the greater history. The history to be told must relate to collection and associated resources, and also to the technique to be used.

There are a number of possible points of entry to interpretation for a museum based around a collection of machinery: machinery can be used directly to illustrate the technology of production, but it can also be used in a discussion about skill, the nature of the labour process, and working conditions. It is the social history of work which has more often been appealed to in diversifying possible readings. The context of a wider programme of complementary collecting and documentation is of course a crucial component in developing these linkages.

Compare the following approaches to the interpretation of machine tools. The Museum of Work in Steyr, Austria, has a machine hall interpreted around the theme of working conditions. The collection is not all from a single period, and its presentation makes a compromise between illustrating technical progress and specific context. Although superficially resembling a machine hall, the lay-out follows a rough chronological sequence with little groupings which approximate to particular phases but are not intended to suggest coherent workshops. The machines are contextualised through panels with text discussing the work situation and conditions, sometimes specifically in relation to the machines themselves, sometimes more generally. The machines are used to introduce wider issues like hours of work and occupational hazards, and, in a sense, any sequence of machinery could have done this.

The Greater Manchester Museum of Science and Industry is more concerned to animate the changing technology of the machine tools themselves. It uses interpretation by former machine tool operators to develop ideas about labour and skill, describing how successive modifications in design affected the organisation of the factory floor. Its use of oper-

39 (a) & (b) Workshop reconstruction compared with photographic record, Fourmies

ators to develop these ideas is a simple and appropriate way of linking the artefact to a history.

Slater Mill in Rhode Island and Hagley in Delaware have used their collections to re-assemble a machine hall 'as if'. At Hagley, the machine shop has been reconstructed to circa 1860 but, as there are widely differing dates for some of its machines, its value is limited by a lack of academic rigour in assembling the shop. In this case, choice of a particular historical context does not make the best use of the collection, and relies on superficial visual effects for its success. Academic reconstruction is also reliant on good complementary material, including collections of incidental detail, and detailed documentation.

At Slater Mill, all the machines were collected to a tightly delimited period, and they are all used, though not so much to demonstrate their own processes as to service the textile machinery elsewhere. The machine hall is not maintained as though work was going on there constantly, and is only open for guided visits (Penn 1980).

Interpretation at the American Precision Museum in Vermont is minimal: the collection represents a hall of fame – important examples of inventions and innovations in machine tool design and manufacture – and the static displays are an experts' museum which treat the objects as nearly self-explanatory. The machines are not operated, and there is nothing in the display which relates either to the social history of their use, or their applications in other local industries.

Interpretation here partly reflects the collecting policy, partly the pioneering nature of the project in its early formation. The collection has been assembled on the basis of 'best examples' from the development of a process over time. This is a different objective than that behind a reconstructed machine shop, which could not do justice to its chronological range. Developing an interpretive strategy based on contexts of use for this undoubtedly important collection would require a more extensive collecting policy to develop both a more representative sample of machinery and the complementary material which could animate it.

But even without enhancement, the museum could exploit its potential as a study collection. Its best resource is the knowledge derived from close analysis of the machines. Although its display makes few concessions to context, the museum does in fact have good contextualising material in the form of publications, film and video, but this is not keyed in as a

40 (a) & (b) The American Precision Museum, Windsor, Vermont: heroic machinery?

guide to the machines themselves. Older museums collecting in this area have tried to present insiders' knowledge and connoisseurship to enable understanding of how the machines worked, and the American Precision Museum has the expertise to continue in the same tradition, showing what to look for in a machine tool, and offering detailed analysis of machine design, construction, operation and adaptation.

The perceived pre-eminence of the textile industry in early industrialisation, coupled with the collectability of its machinery and products, has led to the establishment of many museums which take some aspect of the industry as their subject. Most are also starting off with a collection of machinery. Whereas early thinking was concerned simply to display conserved machines with minimal interpretation, this has monumentalised the machinery and limited its educational use. Best practice now acknowledges the importance of contexts either to show linkages between sectors or to dramatise the social history of work.

Some museums have attempted to re-animate their collections to enhance their learning potential. Many rely on being able to operate their machinery to do this. The collection at Slater Mill includes machines representing different processes and periods, overlaying chronological development with technological process. But interpretation is not just about technological change, as demonstrators are able to talk about conditions of work at the same time (Penn 1980).

A collection which is strong in compatible contemporary machines can be assembled to demonstrate a production line or replicate a workshop, if supported by good complementary collecting. Fourmies has opted for the first in interpreting its textile machinery. The major part of the collection is machinery which relates to a sequence of processes in wool spinning with only a narrow chronological range. Display is arranged to show the flow principle and the stages in the processing of the raw material, with some attention paid to comparing the same process at different periods. The machines are demonstrated by ex-operatives who show how the machines work and what each does to the material. At the same time, simply through the deftness with which they work, they are able to convey some sense of skill.

At the Museum of American Textile History, a comprehensive collection of textile machinery across time, place and process had for a long time been interpreted simply as technology. Recent thinking has emphasised the importance of labour as a central theme, and in developing this the museum has been able to take advantage of successive extensions both to the collections and in scholarship available to the museum. Its collections now include artefacts, photographs and documents which relate to life in the mills, factory paraphernalia as well as machines. Research work carried out by the museum staff has concentrated recently on the effects and experience of technology, and has been strongly influenced by recent currents in labour history.

The interpretive scheme proposed for the museum traces development over time from domestic production, via small factories to rationalised industry, making the most of a collecting policy which now has no specific chronological boundaries. Demonstrators are used to carry out the interpretation in a series of mock-ups, which use sound and light to dramatise the changing setting of labour. A series of realistic settings are complemented by the display of other artefacts and photographs which can give a wider context to the specific representations of the mock-ups, and enable them to be peopled. Demonstrators are trained to discuss issues of organisation, skill, control and conditions. The interpretation is heavily dependent on mainstream historical research, underscoring the importance of interdisciplinary study and collaboration as the basis for soundly developed collecting and interpretive strategies. The scheme makes an effective relationship between general cultural history and collection, although its themes have come from academic history, rather than from detailed appraisal of the collection. Possibly the rigorous analysis of particular machines might have added to the stories that can be told (Gross 1984: 63–9).

An interpretive scheme like this relies for much of its effect on the ability to operate machinery. But not all museums have the wherewithal to do this: machinery may be incomplete, too fragile, the skills to do so may not be there, it may be too expensive or even dangerous. In order to demonstrate process and explain the machinery itself if it cannot be made to work, its operation can be simulated, or dissected. Static machinery has been successfully interpreted through the use of models, graphics, or the juxtaposition of different machines and their component products. In the Match Museum, Jönköping, Sweden, diagrams spaced around the machines, some of which are very large, are used to help explain their operation. Other strategies which have been tried elsewhere are the opening up of machines, their slicing or partial dismantling. Working models have been used to good effect at Røros, Falun and Le Creusot, for example. The rolling mill engine at Kelham

Island, Sheffield, only runs occasionally, but a video is used to show it in operation.

Machinery which does not operate may actually make the interpretation of other themes from a cultural history easier, since it enables attention to be focused on other aspects than the moving parts. The mock-up of an engineering shop in the Workers' Museum, Copenhagen, serves primarily to begin a discussion about working lives and conditions: the exact nature of the process is considered to be of secondary importance, and it is in fact a break in the working day which is represented, encouraging reflection about labour and routine.

Discussion of work and working conditions is a commonly practised linkage out from a collection of production machinery to a social history. It is not dependent on the ability to operate machinery, or on the ability to reconstruct convincing contexts, though both may help in its interpretation. It is dependent on adequate complementary resources, and can be introduced either through first-person interpretation or through text, both of which will be based either on first-hand experience or on other sources such as extracts from factory inspectors' reports, diaries, newspaper reports.

Not all industries can be represented by collected machinery or products in museums, and this is especially true of the extractive and large-scale producer industries such as coal mining, or the metal or chemical industries. But even in the absence of the major machinery of production, symbolic objects, for example associated with the discipline of work, or the small hand tools of miners, can help to create a context for the discussion of social histories. The mining museum at Lound Hall in Nottinghamshire, for example, is set out as a conventional glass case museum and treats its tools with an archaeological seriousness and thoroughness. But it also uses documentary material to good effect, dramatising such themes as industrial action and pit accident, and presenting a strong element of social history. Swedish ethnographers have advocated the collection of symbolic objects in interpreting the cultural history of work, so considering the time-clock or the computer console (Fägeborg 1984a: 60–2). The Workers' Museum in Copenhagen completes its '1950s: An Exhibition of the Working Class Family' with a series of symbolic objects – a time-clock, a pressure cooker and a record.

The absence of major artefacts does not disbar museums from the interpretation of industry, although all too often it is

41 Interpretive techniques at Manchester Museum of Science and Industry: (a) & (b) cutting open boilers enables their operation to be demonstrated – but is also destructive

(c) & (d) documentary source material shows paper-making machinery in use

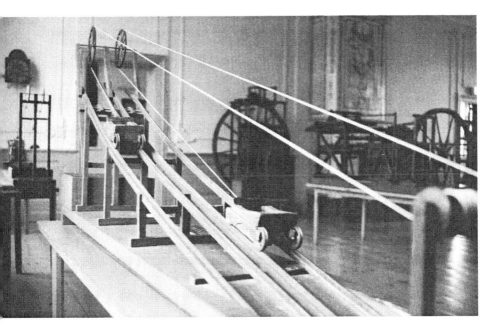

42 (a) & (b) Models in the museum at Stora Kopparberg, Falun, Sweden, illustrate early mining technology

only those industries which have left 'significant' monuments which are given serious treatment in museums. But in interpretation developed around the major collectable monuments of industry, only certain industries can be shown, and then only certain aspects of the industry. For example, this makes it difficult for museums to interpret industries which are still in production.

This issue is tackled to some extent in Sweden through the SAMDOK programme which led to several new exhibitions, and in Scotland through the collaborative documentation programme which produces small exhibitions of photography. At Borås in Sweden, the museum has undertaken a documentation of present production processes, products and working environments, collecting sample books, archival documents and photographs, raw materials and products and only occasionally machines (Larson, Follin and Ganslandt 1987: 132–40). Projects like these illustrate the importance of an integrated strategy of collection, documentation and interpretation founded on a broad assessment of resources which gives the institution the flexibility to respond to a number of different aspects of industrialisation and its culture.

Thematic interpretation

Interpretation centres which do not have collections at all face none of the constraints of accommodating an unwieldy collection to a human story. But where story-telling is the principal component in an interpretive strategy, the difficulty of containing complex histories in the bounds of a coherent scheme often sees resort to generalities. Where there is no clear resource base, the chosen narrative is inevitably derivative, and may have little new to offer in the representation and re-evaluation of local histories.

In the interpretation centre at Fall River, the local textile history is presented by the juxtaposition of enlarged photographs and engravings with text, but the history which is presented is highly generalised and organised into stock categories. The same is true at the Rhondda Heritage Park, where the story of coal is narrated with little chronological depth and little local detail.

Organisations like this have begun with stories and may go on to collect artefacts as illustrations. Neither was intended to work as museums, and the absence of a curatorial agenda has seriously limited their scope. Without a commitment to collection or documentation, and without serious study of local resources, both are dependent on themes derived from general study and have only limited opportunities for re-interpretation based on developing understandings of local resources.

If story-telling is to develop a contribution to the curatorial agenda, it must be used to enhance understandings of particular histories rather than stand as substitutes for them. At the Rhondda the story is all – a spectacular multi-media show which may have something to teach the visitor, but offers little either to an understanding of the site, or to the complex texture of a local history. The major themes of the heritage centre – the story of coal and the choirs – have been chosen for their entertainment value to outsiders who know the area only by its reputation.

The tightly themed programme devised for the Heritage Park has been unable to accept local donations, further constraining its ability to develop a flexible programme of interpretation in the future. Its remit did not include a place for collection or documentation and so it cannot easily accept donations which do not have an immediate role in its chosen theme. It may therefore be denying an opportunity to foster links with its community where donations could have served as a means of coming to terms with its own history. Curatorial input was discouraged on grounds of cost, and although there was for a time a programme of collecting and oral history funded through a job creation scheme it was never a high priority. Without this, the centre is building in inflexibility.

Thematic interpretation works best where there is a clear understanding of how particular resources can contribute to the elucidation of the chosen theme. The Workers' Museum in Copenhagen defines its agenda from a history rather than from a pre-established collection, and launched appeals for donations after themes had already been selected. The mock-ups in its exhibitions of life in the 1870s and 1950s have been rigorously researched and scrupulously presented, supported by detailed collecting. The choice of subject to represent – the paviour's shed of 1952, for example – is made not on the basis of typicality, but in order to dramatise different experiences of work: the shed is there because it represents a complete working unit. There are reminders of people, as individuals or as politically organised labour, in all the interiors, which are all invested with a strong sense of contingency and particularity (Vasström 1987: 180–8).

Building up a collection or interpretive strategy from a general history or theme depends on thorough and detailed resource assessment ensuring the balance of theme to resource; it needs an appropriate use of sources – artefacts, images, documentation – and not simply high-tech narrative technique; the curatorial function is concerned to balance theme to resources in a way which enables a wide base of interpretation and use, ensuring adequate support between the components of the collection on display – relating artefacts to machines, archives to objects, for example. Above all it needs an interdisciplinary approach founded on broad support.

In thematic interpretation, museums have a clear advantage over heritage centres which are not centres of collection and documentation, since their ability to collect and document gives them the scope to present a wider agenda. The Heritage Trust at Summerlee, established in circumstances of local de-industrialisation, has adopted a multi-faceted approach to the representation of local history and has received considerable local support and enthusiasm. High visitor figures are partly sustained by the fact that the museum is a hive of activity and frequent change. It aims to use collected machines and products of the area, objects arranged in mock-ups, oral and photographic archival material, to say something about domestic and working life. By enabling people to visit before the museum was 'finished' it set up a subtly different relationship of involvement with its community, who are therefore not simply an audience. In balancing a varied permanent display with changing exhibitions and a programme of special events, it offers a lot to see and hear and retains a sense of involvement.

Faced with a similar problem of a collapsed industrial base, the Springburn Museum Trust decided not to revert to the heyday of local industry for its interpretation, but to focus instead on recent history in an attempt to understand and accommodate to change. The museum exploits the possibilities of a collage of different sources in articulating qualities of experience, giving a central place to oral history. Springburn does not attach primary importance to collecting, but, in working to establish firm links with the community it serves, it draws in a range of interpretive ideas, loan objects, images and oral histories (O'Neill 1987: 28–32; O'Neill 1990: 21).

The Museum of Work in Norrköping, Sweden, also proposes to be a museum without a collection. Its agenda is given by a theme – work – which it hopes to interpret through exploring its different cultural meanings at different times and in different places. The museum will act through a programme of changing temporary exhibitions, relying on imagery and

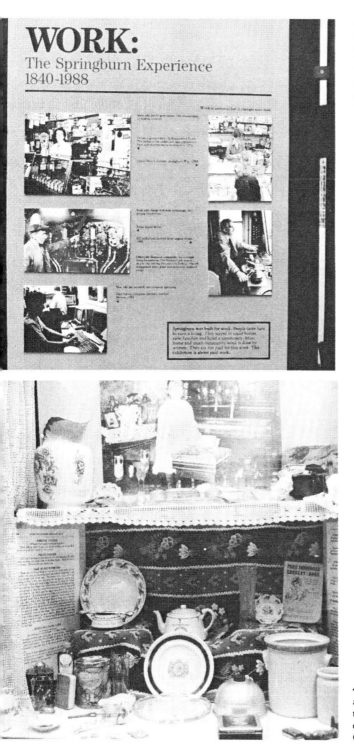

43 Recalling the recent past, recording the present: exhibition panel from 'Work: The Springburn Experience 1840–1988', Springburn Community Museum, Glasgow (Photo: Springburn Community Museum)

44 Recalling the past: images, artefacts and words in 'A Place to Stay 1780–1987', a housing exhibition at Springburn Community Museum

sound rather than objects. It recognises that its subject is too broad to be embraced as an exact science within the bounds of a single institution, and will work collaboratively to document and discuss work as concept and experience. The range and breadth of documentation which the museum is able to command will determine the value of its project.

Project-led exhibitions can play an important part in furthering the knowledge base of the museum, enabling it to develop quickly into new areas, and retain the interest of visitors. Some museums have used temporary exhibition work explicitly to retain flexibility as well as commitment. At Le Creusot, concern to foster the involvement of local communities and maintain relevance lay behind its programme of temporary exhibitions which were the result of collaborative work and were mounted in a number of dispersed locations (Combier 1977; Scalbert Bellaigue 1981; Silvester 1975). A similar concern underpins the exhibitions programme at Springburn, where small project-based exhibitions are within the means of a museum with few resources. The Museum of Work in Norrköping intends to work solely through temporary exhibition, and will keep things only as long as they are perceived to work. In London, the Design Museum maintains a minimal collection, and works largely through temporary exhibition.

The basis of support and the catchment area of involvement are crucial in the determination of an interpretive agenda. The Museum of Work in Norrköping is a foundation jointly established by the Swedish Trade Union Federation, the Central Organisation of Salaried Employees in Sweden, the Co-operative Union and Wholesale Society and the Workers' Education Association. Central to the plan of the museum is its commitment to become an innovative and co-operative agency, which can bring together various types of communication, documentation and research to look at work both over time and globally, exploring its meaning, and the political, cultural, economic and social issues associated with it. Commanding impressive institutional support, the museum can work through and with a network of contacts to make this possible.

In the French ecomuseum movement, two themes have been important: territory and population. The definition of territory as cultural landscape at Fourmies-Trélon has been discussed above. Here, animating the concept of population is taken to imply active participation, working not only through three panels of management, but also in the constitution of the collection which is made up entirely of gifts, and in public involvement in the presentation of objects and documents which they have donated, or in the reconstruction of interiors which they can remember. Attention is therefore focused on the recent memory-based past, and the skills associated with it. In witnessing this basis of experience, the visitor is given a sense of heritage being made, rather than simply being represented (Camusat 1985).

Conclusion

Interpretation is a central function of any heritage project and the whole nature of an organisation helps determine its interpretive possibilities. Interpretation can only be as good as the constituencies and connections a project is able to forge. The way a project is organised vis-à-vis its constituencies will make some things possible and not others; departmental structure in a museum, links made between museums or other institutions, may limit or extend interpretive options.

The cultural agenda of any heritage organisation embraces collection and documentation as well as interpretation. This cultural programme is structured through the relationship between these three functions, underpinned by the balance of resources and uses. Thorough, wide-ranging and imaginative assessment of resources provides the richest scope for developing communicative potential, which in its turn is likely to favour the most sustainable results.

Bringing projects to fruition

6

The majority of today's industrial heritage projects have common roots in a transformation of the industrial structure in the 'advanced' countries which has expanded the scope of heritage and of the heritage movement by displacing both physical and human resources on an unprecedented scale. Successful projects have been able to awaken interest in the cultural potential of this new heritage and its historical antecedents. Most have started as a small initiative, even from individual enthusiasm. They have developed by drawing on different kinds of resources and creating different constituencies, fitted together in a way which gives each project a particular character. They have adapted existing approaches to heritage to form new strategies, extending onto new territory.

The success of projects has depended in large part on addressing the issues discussed in this book: setting aims and objectives in a strategy of resources and uses, evaluating potential resources, creating constituencies and use programmes, devising integrative interpretation, and detailing management of resources for uses. The need to address these issues has not, however, always been apparent in advance. Nor indeed has help always been available on how to address them. The primary lesson of much hand-to-mouth experience has been the importance of anticipating the decisions which must be faced and preparing for them. In this chapter we address choices which arise in project implementation.

Setting objectives

Making objectives explicit at an early stage is important, and failure to do so can have serious consequences; many organisations start with a particular project in mind, which perhaps involves research, rescue or restoration of a specific character, but without a clear sense of for whom this is being done. Statements of objectives should link resources, work and potential uses in a way general enough to make it possible to ask whether the same objective could be achieved differently; or if the incipient group should broaden or narrow its focus. Making objectives clear helps determine appropriate organisational forms and criteria for a range of future activities.

Setting objectives is not a 'theoretical' exercise which is an alternative to doing things. People become involved through practical experiment in some of the alternative ways of defining the project; their enthusiasms can be allied to general objectives, or general objectives tied down to specific interests, which can then form elements to be organised into a development plan. Industrial heritage projects often start on an avocational basis even in existing heritage organisations; prior to a 'feasibility study' or 'development plan', discussion of proposals may run in parallel with urgent attempts to secure the future of threatened resources. Sometimes an exploratory or pilot project, perhaps linked to an exhibition or publication tests out public response.

In clarifying objectives it is important to identify the kind and scope of cultural resources being dealt with, their thematic and geographical and chronological boundaries, and any key or central elements. It is necessary to think about what is to be done with these resources – are they to be studied, collected, conserved, restored, published, exhibited and in what forms? It is also necessary to consider who will be involved in doing this work and for whose benefit it is being carried out: is it for the understanding and pride of local residents or other community in 'their' history, knowledge and skill of industry/practitioners; to increase knowledge and esteem for products, industry, skills, locality; to research and develop particular knowledges, or knowledge capacities; to stimulate historical and technical or entrepreneurial imagination and enthusiasm, to intervene in contemporary industry, area regeneration, etc.?

Statements of objectives which can't be used to say that something will be done with a certain resource by a certain kind of agency to meet certain needs are leaving open questions which must be filled in later. Substantial projects may involve the coming together of several different groups with different agenda and it is important to judge at an early stage to what extent they are compatible: for example, an interest in preserving the 'character' of the local environment may not be congruent with a desire to protect and interpret particular technologies surviving in the area.

Setting over-arching project objectives at the outset and reviewing progress periodically in these terms does not exhaust the setting of objectives in project management. In setting tasks and monitoring results for each area of work, it is advisable to set specific programme objectives (see below).

Choice of organisational form

Some industrial heritage projects and programmes arise in an existing organisation. In this case a question may arise about whether to deal with industrial culture in a separate department, and if so whether on a period or thematic basis. There is something to be said for industrial heritage being covered by an agency which cuts across existing divisions of responsibility and is capable of making links and filling gaps: a matrix approach rather than another parallel department.

For others there is the decision whether to stay as an informal grouping or adopt one of the legally given forms – public agency; company; foundation/trust; society/association; co-operative.

A small group which wishes to restore machinery – or even a building – does not necessarily have to form a society or company or charitable trust; on the other hand it is important to provide for continuing care of any cultural resources, and some form of agreement, trust or covenant – if private – will almost certainly be necessary for small informal organisations undertaking conservation and care responsibilities.

There are certain things that need to be specified in any working agreement at an early stage:

- provisional statement of objectives, which should serve as a point of reference
- name of group or project
- who are its members or constituents
- who holds property on behalf of the group and on what terms
- who has agreed to contribute what income and services, lending of facilities, etc.
- who is responsible for the financial control and monitoring
- who has responsibility for any liabilities
- who is responsible for different activities undertaken

- who has agreed to perform what duties and with what recompense if any
- who is entitled to speak as representing the group
- how policy decisions are taken
- who co-ordinates

Difficulties arise if there is misunderstanding on any of these points. They need not all be in writing, but in a group of volunteers of diverse experience which has not worked together a written point of reference is important. Keeping a group small enough and sympathetic enough of view so that such basic formalisation is unnecessary may be comfortable and guarantee reinforcement by friendships which are necessary to undertake specific sorts of projects such as collaborative research, documentation or publication, or the restoration of particular items, producing a small exhibition, event or newsletter. But this smallness of scale and informality of structure may prove a constraint on what can be attempted.

Any project which takes responsibilities involving different activities, substantial numbers of people or things, which establishes relations with other bodies or intends to continue over time will have to establish governing articles of agreement and also an appropriate legal status and internal structure.

Here it is important to consider whether the project is going to:

- own buildings and land and open them to the public
- collect for posterity
- trade
- receive charitable donations
- publish

Special legal requirements may attach to each of these in certain countries.

Incipient projects must also think about what the adoption of particular structures may help to attain in building up relationships both inside and outside the organisation. For example, if active membership is central to the organisation rather than an adjunct then this should be provided for in its governance. While organisational formalities can intrude on relationships of practical co-operation, there must be provision for continuity beyond particular personal commitments. Societies, co-operatives and company and trust structures all provide for this in different ways – it is important to think about whether the institutional arrangements chosen will be a barrier to or framework for that involvement (Ambrose 1987b; Owen 1987).

Support structure: co-ordinating resources and commitments

Each organisational form implies different ways of valuing and mobilising resources which can have important implications for the development of a project.

In the case of administered agencies, all or most of the resources will be derived from an annual budgetary allocation. Project phases must be related to bids in the resource cycle and depend on external decisions, so planning beyond a year in advance is limited; within the year there may be some cash flow flexibility although public sector managers are becoming more concerned about cash flow; depending on the particular system, there may possibly be inflexibility between budgetary heads and different carry-over provisions between financial years. Public sector budgetary planning is often especially concerned with the level of continuing commitment (such as staffing and maintenance) and it is important in devising implementation plans to prepare development options which can use money that is available on a short term-basis only. A project in the sphere of public administration may have significant amounts of its overheads carried by other budgets, but this may interfere with control over work done.

Voluntary contributions of time or donations can add significantly to resources but contradictions arise if employed staff or budgetary authorities view such contributions as a substitute for rather than a complement or extension of their core commitment; as discussed below it is necessary to plan for the organisation of volunteers in the core staffing – justified as additional expenditure with a multiplier effect. Similar problems exist with the status of revenues earned by the project, such as user charges, sales of publications, etc. Such revenue can be seen as a partial contribution to the administered provision, but if it is to be encouraged to rise then it must be seen to be devoted to a project-related result; this can be achieved through establishing separate trading funds, which are charged with overheads and costs. The question then arises of the source and scale of investment necessary to optimise these operations.

Some of the alleged deficiencies in the public service of public services can be seen to arise from the way they are administered, combined with what is usually a very indirect route of feedback from the public through governmental bodies. This indirectness can be an asset for certain sorts of heritage concerns – guaranteeing continuing responsibility with periodic maintenance, for example – and it is of course necessary for some infrastructure – drawing up inventories for protection, and the implementation of conservation decisions, for example (although there is an alternative self-nomination model).

In a trading company, by contrast, cash flow is dominant and the underlying assumption is that development is financed from revenue earned by the project which is surplus to its immediate operating requirements or from borrowings in anticipation of such profits. Although there is a convention of annual accounting for reporting purposes, more attention must be paid both to short-term cash flow and to medium-term analysis of viability. Instead of budgetary heads, the more significant analysis of operations is by cost centres which have inputs and outputs; the contribution of each to the overall project can be regularly assessed. Budgeting is adjusted on an ongoing basis reflecting overall and sectorial cash flow. These accounting conventions help measure organisational effectiveness – not only operational efficiency and public response but also the appreciation and utilisation of assets. Independence and flexibility in planning is much appreciated by managers. Market orientation concentrates thinking on the value of uses to users.

There are however problems in the company model as a source of support structure and strategy for heritage projects. One is the risk of confusing means and ends. Although objectives may be adopted as a mission statement, the structures and strategies within the model work towards maximising profitability and tend to act over time as a solvent on commitments with which they come into conflict. Members of the public are wary of this possibility and this interferes with the donation of resources of all kinds.

These problems have led to attempts to develop hybrid concerns and also to dividing the activities of projects between different models: trading or property development activities being hived off, for example. Careful thought needs to be given to the range of activities implied in the objectives statement, and how they can be accommodated.

The scale of start-up capital may pose particular problems. Most heritage concerns trading as companies were not started from their own resources, and are therefore owned and controlled in some other interest – for example as part of the public relations of a large corporation. It is now possible however in some places to make a speculative investment in industrial heritage visitor attractions, and it has also been proved that a cultural resources cost centre in a well-established company can be extremely cost effective.

The basic support structure of a society or association recirculates resources from its members to provide designated types of services to them or to collectively achieve certain ends. The development of the society may take place with or through expanding the number of members or the range of services. At one extreme all the exchanges may be in kind or time, and at the other in money, and those concerned with the development of the society have to be mindful of the exchange between them and of the ratio between contributions and satisfactions, offering opportunities for greater involvement. There are differing ethics in running societies between those who see the society as an association of mutual convenience and want to 'get more out of it' and those who value it as opportunity to 'give to greater effect'; as a society grows it is important to provide for differing kinds of involvement, which may be formalised into different kinds of membership.

The management of societies is usually conducted by elected officers with the aid of a committee. The employment of full- or part-time staff by societies has to be carefully handled so as not to squeeze out this second paradigm, as voluntary association is the key to vitality of the society. Planned development in societies is quite delicate for this reason; many societies lack a concept of development except to have more members or perhaps more events. A key element of a support strategy is opening ways for some members to contribute more in time and effort than in monetary investment; raising funds through increases of financial contributions may erode membership breadth, and the consciousness of the society – and perhaps also its articles – may shy away from providing services for non-members, or accepting extensive liabilities. Establishing an endowment for the society can be very important, although if the accumulation of reserves is not seen as furthering the society's programme it can be counter-productive. Nevertheless the society remains the preferred vehicle for knowledge and experience exchange, as well as advocacy, and, where the way has been open for some members to make a greater contribution, many have successfully established and maintained collections and operated visitor attractions either on their own or in partnership with, for example, a local government.

Many organisations of other types have attempted to attach the advantages of a society's support structure to their project through establishing an ancillary membership organisation. This can have a multiplier effect on both organisations, although there can be frictions about the boundary between them – we discuss this below in relation to volunteers and friends organisations.

The foundation or charitable trust has become an increasingly popular vehicle for undertaking heritage projects and programmes of all types because of the suppleness of its support structure. Because the trust is publicly recognised as being established to work towards certain objectives in perpetuity, it is a suitable recipient for all kinds of support, but this makes its administration more complex and places greater importance on determining appropriate structures and strategies. Establishment as a trust is particularly important for projects dependent on the ownership or will of others, as the fate of the Dunlop Archive Project discussed in chapter 2 above reveals. It may be important to protect a collection by vesting it in a separate body for protection purposes as a precaution against liability or bankruptcy. In other circumstances an agreement or partnership between different agencies and bodies may be sufficient, and it may not actually be necessary to create a new legal entity. Such a partnership may, for example, be an agreement between a local society and local government about division of curatorial responsibility or the recognition of a consultative role for local or thematic societies in conservation matters.

In practice there are several different ways of thinking about the administration of a trust. It can be run on a philanthropic model, a kind of private equivalent to public revenue accounting, where the income from an endowment, perhaps supplemented by grants, donations and earned income, makes possible the undertaking of research, conservation work and/or public programmes; such a foundation could result from the settlement of an estate. On the other hand it can be run as a value-based enterprise – a non-profit company with named trustees and specified objectives – which draws both capital and revenue support from different sources, but is otherwise run as any other company. Alternatively it could be an association in being centred round the resources and uses of its members, but having covenanted certain continuing public purposes (Department of the Environment 1988).

Industrial heritage projects have been prominent among recent experiments with the trust form, with mixed results. In many cases the way in which the trust has been run has reflected the assumptions and experience of those who have been dominant in its establishment, rather than a designed support strategy. Those trusts which have been established by government often retain many public administration practices, and fail to take advantage of either earned income opportunities or contributions from the voluntary sector. Others may be so oriented towards voluntary enthusiasm that they are effectively 'out of control', while others compromise their charters for the sake of earned income. To take full advantage of the trust form it is necessary to plan for mobilising grant aid, earned revenue and voluntary effort.

Getting the right support structure is important because it is not easy to change in midstream, as both internal and expectations become entrenched (see the final section below). Projects may have to go through a long gestation period until supports appropriate to the objectives are worked out. A case in point here is that of the House Mill, built on the River Lea near Bow Bridge in 1776, the largest extant tide mill in Britain, and a Grade I Listed Building. Much of its internal workings are intact although decayed along with the building fabric which has been disused through most of this century. The area in which the mill stands, where the major route east from London to Essex and the Suffolk ports crosses the Lea, is arguably the oldest and most important nexus of industry in the London region. Nine mills existed in the locality a thousand years ago and the area has subsequently seen the production of grain, iron castings, porcelain, fireworks, furniture, textiles and beer, as well major sites of Victorian gas, sewage and railway developments. Today the area is a mosaic of 'friches' (industrial wastelands) and functioning firms.

After years of false starts, the House Mill is currently under restoration and is being mooted as the key to an imaginative scheme for heritage-inspired regeneration taking in the whole of this district. Until 1989, the freehold for the mill lay with the Lea Valley Regional Park, a statutory authority embracing the two dozen communities bordering on the 20-mile stretch of this working river from the Thames northwards. The study which guided the creation of the park a quarter of a century ago embodied conceptions of amenity (as open space, 'nature') and leisure (as sport and commodified substitutes) which lacked a cultural dimension and ignored or slighted the industrial heritage. Neither the Park Authority nor the leaseholders of the mill buildings, the Hedges and Butler Division of the brewing and leisure company Bass, saw any value in the mill. Bass had restored the nearby brick-built Clock Mill as its headquarters, closing off part of the stream and increasing pressure on the House Mill structure in the process, but, finding the Three Mills site unpopular and a similar re-use of the House Mill impractical, they had let it decay.

As often happens, this industrial heritage project started as a campaign to save the building. Initially, however, it was appreciated more as an architectural resource than as a technical monument. The then director of the Passmore Edwards Museum envisaged the mill as an extension of the museum service as far back as the early 1970s. Newham Borough Council, which had favoured applying for consent to demolish the building, was persuaded to consider enforcing repairs upon the owners, with the ultimate object of compulsory purchase and grant-aided restoration.

The museum director was more concerned with finding a home for undisplayed collections (some of which related to local industries) rather than with an integrated interpretation of the site. The low esteem of the area and the difficulties of converting the building for alternative use meant that the owners were open to suggestion, but increasing constraints on public finance made it less and less likely that this objective could be realised. When the owners sought permission to demolish in 1976 an opposing study designed to prove the feasibility of restoring the mill confirmed serious technical problems and limited use prospects. Although the council's campaign against demolition was successful in securing short-term consolidation of the building, it failed to raise funding for restoration. Foundations, corporations and private individuals were unenthusiastic about aiding a public authority. The long-term prospects of the House Mill were held in abeyance until an institutional form could be found to mobilise the necessary resources.

Partnership between public, private and voluntary bodies in heritage work has become increasingly important in Britain in recent years. The Passmore Edwards Museum Service had come into existence in 1900 through an agreement between a society, which provided collections and voluntary curatorship, and the local authority, which has provided the main source of funds for conservation and interpretation. Increased local authority funding after 1950 enabled the Museum Service to expand, but in the new situation of the late 1970s it was decided to form a Museum Trust to support its activities and educational work. This has acted primarily as a Friends organisation, but as a registered charity it has been able to obtain grants and other funding not available through a local authority. An extension of the Museum Service into a former railway station on the Thames at North

Woolwich in 1982 was made possible by an agreement between the Trust, which purchased the building from British Rail, the London Docklands Development Corporation, which funded its restoration and conversion, and the Borough of Newham, which covers its running costs.

This experience opened the way to a new approach to the problem of the House Mill. A plan was formed in 1987 by which the property would be passed to a company established by the Museum Trust for restoration. The former leaseholders and freeholders atoned for their former neglect of the building with donations, and English Heritage and other bodies made contributions. The principal donors and contributors joined the Museum Trust and Newham Borough in forming a joint Committee of Management to oversee the restoration pro-gramme. The Museum Trust, which had simply been a conduit for funding in North Woolwich, was now taking on a larger and more uncertain responsibility. Neither the source of funds to complete the conversion of the restored mill as a museum nor who would operate it was certain when the title of the mill passed to the Trust and work began in mid-1989. Partisans of the mill in the local authority and the Museum Trust had finally secured its ownership and support for its conservation without having settled on a strategy or even clear objectives for its use.

Working out a development plan to bring the mill into use has required further innovation, which we discuss in the section concerned with planning.

Governing structure

The choice of form of organisation and the actual governing structure will be influenced by the need to build appropriate external supports. Such supports may be integrated into the organisation through special advisory bodies, through boards of directors, governors or trustees which act as or in an analogous way to shareholder or trustee interests, or in actual committees of management. Irrespective of what form of organisation is chosen there are important choices to be made here: how the represented constituencies should be defined and grouped and what their role should be in the organisation.

Careful construction of such bodies is worth the effort. It is helpful to have reference to the statements about resources and uses in an outline of objectives in order to help define constituencies to be represented.

It is common practice to offer representation to those who command resources – property, political clout, money, knowledge and expertise – likely to be useful to the project. Indeed, it may well be a condition of sponsorship or support to have a representation of some kind in the running of an organisation. It is worth a good deal of persuading to get the commitment of people who occupy key positions in organisations representing different kinds of essential support – this has often proved crucial.

One important external relation is that to governmental authority; is the exercise of governmental authority or the expenditure of public funds necessary or beneficial to the project and how are these to be accommodated? In some situations such support or powers can only be exercised through governmental agencies which can be seen to be controlled by elected authority; in other situations they can be exercised for a trust but not a company or society, etc. Governmental agencies may prefer to pursue certain objectives through involvement in a trust in order to create a superior sense of stability and public purpose, or to promote participation. There may be technicalities to be considered: for example, in Thatcher's Britain local governments were penalised for their involvement in trusts, which meant keeping them at arm's length or creating separate companies to hold assets, but in order to receive European grants local government had to be directly involved in the project.

It is also important to offer to represent other constituencies, sometimes overlooked: the workers of the project itself, those who have been involved in running related kinds of projects whose judgement you respect, and direct representatives of important categories of potential user as defined in your statement of objectives – not only as defined instrumentally, like education for example, but in a broader sense of 'whose heritage' is being conserved and represented; and not necessarily just those who have selected themselves to become the 'friends' of the project. This may lead back to some of the same constituencies which are already represented for other reasons, for instance industry, government, communities, but, because the reasons are different, not necessarily to the same people. This last point is crucial to avoid a pernicious club-like circularity.

This last suggestion may appear controversial. Some would say that it is a mistake to bring these categories, which the organisation deals with in other ways, into its governing or advisory structures; it is to complicate internal politics and also to undermine the responsibility of those who are running the project to learn precisely and professionally how users' needs are being met. Perhaps the representatives are not representative. But we are not talking about enterprises in which the wisdom of being engaged in different projects must continually be judged by the abstract criterion of profitability with all relationships managed to this end. In an institution which undertakes a cultural project it is very important to make sure that the essential parameters and constituencies are built in to any governing or advisory structure that is set up or this imbalance will cause persistent problems and risk distorting the project. Equally, it is important to balance the presence of potentially overweening sponsors and also to achieve the right balance between 'committed insiders' and the 'outsiders' who may well provide perspective and discipline.

Boards may become peopled by too many representatives of the same constituency – too many from the same industry, locality, group of workers, 'friends', nominees of the same governmental agency, and you will find yourself prisoner of a club; a broadly representative sampling of a particular constituency is best established as a special advisory group. There may be good reasons for convening such groups on an ad hoc or regular basis and even of tying them to different parts of the organisation, but their status must be clear and how their advice or decisions are to be input into the organisation must also be clearly defined: they must be channelled in ways that are consistent with the internal structure. There is a real likelihood of specialist constituencies putting forward conflicting lines of thought and there must be a provision as to how these will be handled. Some institutions have quite elaborate hierarchical structures for such groups. It is not generally a good idea to create a situation where discussions are being reformulated and decisions retaken by different levels of groups, as this is more likely to waste time and cause frustration than have the desired effect of thorough consultation. On the other hand, it is important not to set up effective independence for functions that are in practice interdependent; for example, it is not a good idea to have a separate group entrusted with fundraising unless it is clearly subordinate to the overall board.

It is very important to provide for an appropriate means of renewing the board. If the board is purely advisory its succession can be arranged by an informal mixture of its own advice, that of the constituencies it represents and that of the management of the project. If it is a directing or governing body then these arrangements need to be formalised; it should not be wholly self-selecting and self-perpetuating, although members who have retired may be allowed to return after holiday; professional staff or responsible volunteers in the project should be entitled to make nominations if they are not to be represented directly and so should those constituencies which are so organised as to be able to send a representative. Organisations go through cycles and may face continuity problems when the founding generation – particularly the key figures – begin to leave; this can be creative if it provokes a proper organisational re-evaluation rather than an ill-considered lurch to a new set of priorities (Sekers 1987).

The optimal size of such boards is related to the character of their functions: a large body represents perhaps the whole scope of project constituencies but is not able to undertake much work; small groups of less than a dozen are necessary in order to take responsibility and achieve much. There are advantages both ways: as many projects are compromised by board members who do too much as by those who do too little.

Internal lines of communication

The question of internal organisational structure is as important as the type of form. Certain models are presupposed by the types of organisation, but general common-sense principles must be followed rigorously. It is necessary to ensure that everyone involved in the organisation is given information about what is going on overall as well as what is needed in carrying out their own responsibilities, and that they know how they can influence and participate in both decisions and the developing work of the project. This is more difficult when the project involves many different kinds of part-time participants.

People who have worked together closely at the centre of a project may fail to see the need to include others and take appropriate steps or structures. The chaos that ensues may seem an essential part of the project's formative stages and even an integral part of the aura of excitement, but disorganisation of this sort is frustrating, wasteful of energy and conducive to 'burnout' – the atmosphere can suddenly sour. An ominous sign is the emergence of personal polarisations or factions – which often follow or precipitate the creation of different projects within the overall scheme; when this level of complexity is reached it is imperative to clarify roles and structures, but it may be difficult to do so in a tense atmosphere. Better to make it an aim in developing an organisation to work towards a flexible structure and define and adjust roles periodically; in other words make of the structure an embodiment of involvement.

This was done for example at Fourmies where the relationships between professionals and volunteers have been adjusted successively to accommodate the ecomuseum's different projects and their stages of development. Certain volunteers have been picked out as permanently responsible and set alongside paid staff with definite functions (Goujart 1988).

Planning for growth and change

Industrial heritage projects have grown in quite diverse ways; some have had quite a bit of advance planning, others have been carried forward by force of personality or a vivid but vague idea. All have had to reassess their direction at intervals, sometimes because of new opportunities, but often because their initial expectations have not been met (Greene 1987).

Development planning lays out the complex choices which any organisation will have to make in pursuing its objectives. This is done in order to ensure that:

- efforts are directed to series of realisable and compatible goals
- such goals are coherently related to objectives
- goals receive necessary and timely support
- problems and opportunities which arise can be readily assessed, and monitoring has a point of reference
- the feasibility of projects can be demonstrated to potential sponsors and users

Many different kinds of documents have been called 'development plans', ranging from what is really a description of an ideal result, perhaps accompanied by estimates and rudimentary phasing, to detailed schedules of resources and commitments. The kind of plan which is prepared in search of support is really a proposal. It gives a concrete form to general project objectives, and may be supported by estimates for building work, operational overheads, etc., but usually says little about how work is to be defined and carried out. Instead, the emphasis of a proposal document is on proving feasibility, which means showing that, while costs are controllable, the benefits are sufficiently appealing to command widespread support.

The way in which such proposals are prepared depends to a large extent on to whom they are to be shown: they may be tailored to the specific requirements and criteria of particular agencies or grant-aiding bodies, or cast in terms sufficiently general to be shared by, say, all the prospective members of a board of directors. The first test of the effectiveness of such plans is whether they succeed in getting the involvement and support required. As we discussed in chapter 4 above, projects can be held up at this stage because of a failure in preparing their prospectus.

Groups of volunteers can be too involved in certain aspects of what they are doing to take seriously the problems of addressing a wider audience. This may suggest that the process of defining objectives has not been done thoroughly, or simply that the group has not thought sufficiently about how it should address the constituencies from which it now wants support. The support of various institutions and personages cannot be enlisted only as an afterthought. The proposed industrial museum, Hanomag, in Hanover is an example of a project which has not really been able to sell itself and generate support – it has not put its future in a form which can be sold, having been much more internally oriented towards a kind of alliance between mental and manual labour.

Another problem is inappropriate paradigms. When the Wandle Industrial Heritage Groups in East London wanted to go ahead with the creation of a visitor centre in the old William Morris and Company Mills, Wandsworth, they had a feasibility study done by a consultant recommended by the area museum service. Of its type, this was competently done: it evaluated the needs which would be met by the proposed site, the extent to which its programmes would be supported by visitor revenue, and went into some detail in looking at how the buildings should be converted and programmed, the staffing arrangements and the operating costs. The study did not, however, deal with the two most basic doubts about the proposal as seen by outsiders – councillors and officials of local government – whether another museum was not only a good thing but competitive in terms of the return on its social investment to the Borough, and whether the industrial history of the area was something worth drawing attention to. This was a failure not solely of presentation but of thinking the plan and its objectives through.

In comparison, consider the development plan done (by a consultant recommended by the English Tourist Board) for Dudley Metropolitan Borough Council on a scheme to link three existing visitor attractions (including two healthy industrial heritage trusts) on Castle Hill with new investment to make a theme park. By comparison with the Wandle study, many of the aspects of these proposals were crude: the cultural objectives and their museological underpinnings were given little thought and would not have passed muster in the museum world. The market analysis was no more sophisticated than in the other document and did not go much beyond indicating how many people lived within a certain travelling distance. But the proposals duly reflected the concerns of the commissioning body to create a major pole of new employment and investment, and indicated how this could be achieved with significant public subsidies. Within this approach, industrial heritage was seen as an instrument of regeneration, not as an irrelevance or obstacle.

However, the Castle Hill proposals were no more successful than the Wandle proposals – and for the same underlying reason: they failed to take into account the interests and perceptions of key potential collaborators: in this case the existing trusts themselves. The one rule that seems to emerge here is that, when briefing a consultant or asking for advice concerning development proposals, it is important to make sure that all parties are clear about whom proposals are being prepared for and what decisions will be made on the basis of recommendations. Secondly, it is rare for any consultant or advisory body to be able to satisfy all the key audiences for a proposal – so it is necessary to edit and amend accordingly.

The experience of preparing a proposal document is now widely recognised as valuable to a project for the service such a document can provide in clarifying objectives and priorities, putting the project in the round and in the public eye. Projects which have continued to rely primarily on internally generated resources and which do not need to go through this process may avoid this important kind of reflection. They may thus fail to recognise significant problems or opportunities. There are even examples of well-established institutions which only undertook such an exercise when they needed to make a major funding application, and derived more benefits from the re-evaluation than they did from the funds received. Therefore, whether the proposals are successful or not in winning the necessary support – which may simply be beyond reach – they should still serve as an important point of reference.

Often, planning is done one stage at a time, because certain problems have so filled the horizon that it is difficult to look further. In the case of the House Mill at Bow, discussed above in the section on support structure, a long effort to secure the conservation of the building was undertaken on the assumption that it would be used as a museum as originally envisaged. However, in the ten-year interval since the original restoration proposals had been drawn up, expectations of what a museum might be able to do for the community by interpreting industrial heritage had increased while the financial resources of the local government had contracted. Large sums of money had been committed to the restoration of the mill without a viable plan for its use.

In 1988 a new curator who brought experience in establishing community museums in other London boroughs joined the Museum Service and realised the need for a development plan. As there was no time or resources for an elaborate study she presented the management committee with a revised version of the previous design brief which incorporated new objectives and recognised the new constraints. While it was still accepted that the restored mill would help house the Museum Service's industrial collections, greater emphasis was to be given to the mill itself as a working industrial monument. However, instead of literal restoration as a working flour mill, it would interpret the tide-mill power technology used locally by a variety of industries and thus link the interpretation of the site with its local context, both past and present. The Committee of Management was persuaded to accept this outline programme, which balanced an awareness of the integrity of the site with an appreciation of its links in the local landscape, but fundamental problems about how this was to be realised remained unresolved.

The restoration of a timber-framed structure subject to changing tidal forces must be phased over several years. It involves problems of finance and management outside the experience of the museum staff or the Museum Trust. The Committee of Management was persuaded to appoint a consultant project manager with experience of fundraising in 1989. The Museum Trust has had to confront difficult choices as to how the House Mill is to be run when it opens in 1992. Although members would like to continue a free access policy, they are forced to recognise that the local authority is presently forced to reduce expenditure in a way which threatens even the existing Museum Service. In this situation the Museum Service governors cannot consider opening a new branch museum without secure funding, although they would dearly like to see their industrial collections on display in the House Mill. Even the current stage of the project has placed severe strains on museum staff, who must strive to co-ordinate the goals and efforts of bodies over which they have no control. Unless there is a dramatic change in the financial position of local government or a suitable collaborator can be found to run the museum, the Museum Trust will have to plan the operation of the House Mill on a self-financing basis, with charges for admission. As the Museum Trust has so far been unwilling to employ staff on a continuing basis, an operating company which covenants its profits to the Museum Trust, or even a new Trust of a different character, may have to be established to run the museum.

The consultant project manager has consequently had to turn his attention to the viability of the site as a visitor attraction. With 4 million people within 40 minutes travel time, potential income is substantial, but so are the obstacles to be overcome:

- partial and constrained access to the mill
- lack of interpreted features on site and surrounding area
- the low esteem of the area as a destination
- difficulties of developing an interpretive programme which would meet community needs and also attract a fee-paying public

The most immediate bottleneck is the conflict between the need to offer a revenue-earning visitor attraction and the protracted restoration of the building. This will be overcome by reconstructing the adjacent miller's house as a visitor centre which provides services, offices and improved access. Its display space and meeting rooms can serve the wider and longer-term aims of the project while the mill is gradually restored and interpreted as a working tide mill. This break-through, which will allow the museum to open in 1992, could not have been achieved without securing a grant from the European Regional Development Fund for a tourism-related new building project in a decayed industrial area. Newham, along with other London authorities and the Department of the Environment, had been seeking suitable proposals and the project manager did well to secure this opportunity for using grant-aided new development to secure and extend a con-servation project. This European funding, in contrast with much current British practice, could only be obtained through the local authority, which provides finance until the grant can be claimed on completion.

Much remains to be resolved at the House Mill site. For all the ingenuity and effort expended, many parameters of a development scenario are still uncertain. The challenge which remains to be addressed lies in its relationship to the local environment, past and present. Even with its new building programme, the mill is vulnerable as a substantially self-supporting visitor attraction without promotion of linked attractions in the Lower Lea/North Docklands region. The project team looks especially to heritage-related redevel-opment on some nearby industrial sites, and is currently holding exploratory discussions. Some of the more likely possibilities include:

- a substantial enlargement of the small museum of the gas industry on the major gas distribution and stores site to the south of the mill
- restoration and opening of a visitor centre at the Victorian pumping station belonging to Thames Water a mile to the north-east of the mill
- re-use of the restored Clock Mill as restaurants and shops for the sale of former local products whose premises have long disappeared, e.g. Bow porcelain, Lloyd Loom chairs, basketry, Congreve fireworks
- development of an archival centre for business records, trading on convenience to financial centres, low rentals and the large number of industries which have had connections with the area, or others related to nearby financial centres

The establishment of such a complex of related projects would help secure the future of the restored House Mill. Beyond this they offer the prospect of animating the 'friches' and reviving the complex industrial heritage of the area. Such a project will require complex co-ordination if it is to be realised even in part. If it succeeds the result will be far from what was envisaged in the initial project to conserve the House Mill. Many projects develop along similar lines, feeling their way one step at a time, survive and even thrive. But projects would be more secure and more effective if the whole range of issues raised in this case study were appraised at the outset.

Such a strategic overview would not exhaust all the planning that is required to bring a project to fruition. When, after some delays, a package of support is put together and work begins in some haste, a series of decisions about who is going to do what and when must be made, and these decisions have implications for the future viability of the project. Quite often, some sort of 'operational plan' is established on the fly. Job roles are defined and deadlines and initial budgets set for an initial phase of work.

In the short term, when 'opening' is the primary consideration, the most important aspect of planning appears to be 'critical path' analysis – working backwards from the result to ensure that all the elements required for each stage will be ready when they are needed. In the medium term, however, these operational plans must be linked with a reconsideration of the initial objectives and proposals, in order that 'management by objectives' can become possible. Otherwise there is a real risk of loss of direction, and this can be fatal in a project which has mobilised many efforts around what appeared at one time to be a common purpose. Either energy seeps away, or competing futures mass on the horizon.

Many industrial heritage organisations have only formulated a development plan in this roundabout way, perhaps having encountered difficulties in their development. They come to recognise that maintaining a development plan which links objectives with operational requirements is necessary, on the one hand to keep up momentum, and on the other to forestall fragmentation. Entropy is a risk to apparently established heritage projects, whether they are value-based enterprises, associations or in the public sector, and industrial heritage projects are at greater than average risk, owing to their diverse facets and types of involvement.

Budgetary structure and strategy

Implementing a development plan requires a budgetary structure and strategy. The budgetary problems of industrial heritage projects are often complicated by a diversity of sources and objectives as well as complexity of operating programmes. The problem of devising adequate accounting objectives and procedures for hybrid organisations in particular is often underestimated – elements of voluntary, public expenditure and enterprise models can become entangled in a confusing or question-begging way.

Industrial heritage organisations exhibit a variety of levels of sophistication and types of approach to budgetary strategy. Two commonly occurring problems are a weak monitoring of operating costs and income in institutions which have become more dependent on earned income and, more serious, weak or missing links between such monitoring and development planning, with limited analysis of alternatives and how resources should be optimally allocated to realise strategic objectives (Lord, Lord and Nicks 1989).

Industrial heritage projects typically have complex financial inputs which cannot just be represented as contributed vs. earned income; they must balance the claims of unified management and spreading responsibility. They typically involve work with different objects and time scales: building conservation, collections management, public programmes and community relations, for example, have different patterns of inputs and outputs, as well as different kinds of objectives. The project may draw on diverse sources of support, each with its own conditions and criteria, as well as earned income. One strategy links specific sources of support with specific kinds of programme. This can help ensure that qualitatively different programme objectives are met and can strengthen involvement of supporting interests. Each body makes its own estimation of the value of its commitment and of the benefit it derives from the project as a whole. Large responsibilities can be divided into discrete and manageable commitments in a partnership. Many such arrangements, for example where buildings are looked after by government and collections maintained and interpreted by voluntary bodies, have proved stable for many years.

Often it is only possible to proceed on this disaggregated basis, as the whole project would be too much of a burden on public revenues, too much responsibility for a voluntary group, and unviable as an enterprise. The community museums of Scandinavia, for example, which have substantial assets which are open – and intensively utilised – for only a small part of the year, would be difficult to run on any other basis. The problem with disaggregating responsibility, however, is that it makes a strategic overview of effectiveness impossible in financial terms. Heritage trusts and foundations have to produce annual accounts, and trustees with business experience will want to see how accountability is to be established, efficiency appraised and optimal allocations of resources determined. This involves viewing the project as an integrated enterprise whose efficiency in meeting its objectives can be evaluated.

Some trusts try to tie different kinds of support to different parts of their accounts, so that all new development, for example, must be contributed or sponsored. In the early stages of a project this can appear a way of avoiding over-commitment by tying expansion to new sources of support, but it does not protect against taking on new commitments with incalculable operating consequences. Separating financial and operating considerations in this way makes it difficult to control development commitments and allocate resources for optimal effectiveness. If no evaluation of the likely, or actual, effects of alternative commitments on resources available for future use is made then there is a serious risk that investments which are crucial to long-term viability – in publicity or conservation, for example – will not be made, that commitments are made which threaten the viability of the whole project, that developments are undertaken in the wrong order, or that insufficient provision is made for reserves or endowment.

Planning and running an industrial heritage project can require quite complex calculations, with a considerable degree of risk. These may be illustrated in the problems of running a restored railway. Many of the practices of modern management, including several key accounting distinctions, first emerged as railways grew (Pollard 1959; Chandler 1977). On the one hand they required large initial investments in civil engineering which could only be recouped and replaced gradually over many years; on the other there were the related problems of scheduling and pricing journeys, which required a different set of calculations. In between, it was necessary to invest in rolling stock whose rate of depreciation was variable.

The same kinds of considerations emerged when the Ffestiniog Railway in Wales was extended to again connect with its original terminal at Blaenau Ffestiniog. Like many other restored railways, the Ffestiniog was a combination of an enthusiasts' project and a visitor attraction. The enthusiasts worked for years to restore the service to its original upland terminus, which required extending the line by a third and establishing a new route skirting a reservoir established since the closure of the line. This was eventually achieved but added substantially to its long-term responsibilities. Operating over the longer route also involved dilemmas – it increased the wear on the line's historic rolling stock, an already serious conservation issue. What was possibly worse, operating scheduling became much more complicated: the longer line opened up a local passenger traffic, but this was limited because of journey times and costs; many tourists were uninterested in taking the longer trip or paying the increased costs involved.

It took a considerable amount of analysis and experiment before it became clear how the Ffestiniog could best use its extension – if at all. Attention had also to be given to the most cost-effective marketing strategies and ticket pricing – the line had been giving off-season discounts which had effectively been subsidies to wealthier people taking additional holidays without children, whereas income could be increased through incentives to families and other forms of group travel.

Whatever the support strategy or institution type, a high level of variability in funding and expenditure is common, arising from different levels of grants, donations and subventions, and also from earned income – this is as true of ordinary operating budgets as of different capital projects. As most institutions have very little as endowment or reserves to call on, this unevenness can become a serious problem. Downturns in the economy affecting tourism and the level of public grants, together with taxation reform which is less favourable to charities, are currently causing serious problems even for well-established museums in the United States, with retrenchment to two-thirds of previous expenditure indicated. Some museums will close and the fate of their collections is in doubt.

Provision against such contingencies, and identifying adverse trends in good time, should be part of every organisation's budgetary strategy. Plural funding or a diverse support structure which utilises non-cash contributions can help, as well as making sure that increasing assets are properly valued, so they can be used as security, that items which can legitimately and cost-effectively be sold are identified. A substantial proportion of revenue should be capitalised, and held as appreciating endowment or invested strategically in publicity, to draw increased support and income. Operating plans should incorporate an element of flexibility, with a balance between different modes and periods of employment.

Staffing strategy

Most industrial heritage projects that have been at all successful have become so through extraordinary personal talent, imagination and energy – of both employed staff and volunteers. The planning of appropriate capacities to undertake the different aspects of a project as it develops is a matter of central importance and without it time phasing or work planning will prove unrealistic.

The range of relevant experience and knowledge required by the industrial heritage is substantially wider than in traditional heritage fields, embracing the knowledges and skills employed in the subject industries and their dependent cultures, multidisciplinary research capabilities, project development and communications skill, and an array of expertise relevant to conservation and interpretation. The opportunity to meet and share experience and perspectives is one of the most exciting aspects of managing the industrial heritage.

Equally, what makes it a challenging area for curatorship is the diversity of perspectives which are brought to it, so long as they can be made to converge; there is a tendency for the fragmentation of perspectives which industrial culture itself produces to be reproduced in industrial heritage projects – usually to the detriment of the project. In particular, division between supposedly academic historical disciplines and the hands-on practical and technical skills can undermine the achievement of each (see above, chapters 2 and 4).

The Industrial Heritage

Most projects will need to draw on human resources beyond those possessed by their core staff and thus will need to engage specialist help at various points – on a temporary, part-time or voluntary basis. Projects have provided for this in various ways: by choosing key staff wisely, by incorporating some specialist help on a voluntary basis or by collaborative agreement with other institutions, and by allowing for consultants and temporary help in budgetary estimates.

Most projects, however set up, have at some point to make their first professional appointments, often on a limited and insecure funding basis and with a development plan that has yet to be fully worked out. This is often true even in public sector projects, as for instance opening a museum at an old industrial site. Given these circumstances of appointment, the choice will often be between a young person of limited experience and knowledge of the industrial culture in question, but a professional formation in some heritage-related discipline, and an older person with substantial industrial experience in some capacity and a strong avocational interest in the type of project in question, but without academic or professional formation in heritage management.

Appointing committees have to balance compatibility of outlook with relevance of skills and experience in making their selection. Some of the more conspicuously successful, if apparently risky, appointments have been deliberately made to complement the existing resources on which the project could draw: an amateur historian trained as a mechanician to establish a new collection of machines in a national museum, an ethnography curator to be in charge of interpreting a major technical monument, a political sciences academic to institutionalise a community museum network, a retired engineer to interpret an industrial site on behalf of a trade union.

This same principle needs to be employed by the newly appointed in rounding out the team; for example, managers of the Tide Mills project in the London Borough of Newham recognised at an early stage that they lacked key entrepreneurial and communications skills and 'producing experience' so hired an ex-television producer to carry out fundraising consultancy. Serious staffing gaps or imbalance may lead to neglect of essential areas of work – often through underfunding but also through imbalance.

In making early appointments people often look for a jack of all trades and there is no doubt that a wide variety of skills is important. But the ability to enlist and orchestrate the efforts and resources of others is essential if a project is to grow. At the most basic level, effective delegation is also essential – perhaps less likely to be done by the sort of person who thinks they can do anything and everything. This ability is likely to be more important than administrative experience or relevant historical knowledge as such. A museum where the director has made a significant collection but is unable to delegate or sell the project to others is headed for trouble, and the realisation of this has sometimes made it difficult for people from curatorial or academic backgrounds to develop careers in heritage management today.

Our model of balance makes certain assumptions about what is necessary to cultural resources management; it gives quite a central place to curatorial roles. The future of curatorship in industrial heritage projects has been the subject of much recent discussion – as indeed has the future of curatorial roles in cultural resource management generally. This discussion is part of a wider debate about the role of cultural institutions and their sources of support.

The recent uncertainty about what constitutes the essential elements of professionalism in heritage management has been particularly marked in the UK (see Clark 1990 and Middleton 1990b), partly because the governors of museums both private and public have become determined that museum users should pay a more substantial share of their costs, and curators – or the sort of administrator who would have risen from the ranks of curators – were not perceived as being able to adequately exploit these markets. There are two kinds of issue tangled up here: one has to do with a grasp of the range of competences which are necessary to run projects and the other has to do with qualities of leadership. The people who are doing the hiring are aware that no occupational or professional background has a monopoly on the qualities that are needed to run projects successfully. The search for the appropriate blend has even led to the idea of appointing 'pure administrators' – accountants who would, as it used to be believed in the universities, optimise the conditions in which others could do the real work of the institution. Given the immature development of accounting techniques appropriate to heritage institutions, such a move is understandable, if hopeful.

In the course of preparing this study we have encountered quite a variety of different styles and practices of heritage management. What emerges most strongly from a comparative examination of projects is the centrality of a curatorial role which can relate resources and uses. Institutions which

are not capable of locating, amassing, studying and interpreting cultural resources to meet a variety of needs do not
have a secure future. Investment in theatrical and pre-
sentational effects or in high-quality visitor services will have
diminishing returns unless backed by programmes which
make cultural resources accessible to an ever more demanding
array of publics. 'Curatorship' in this sense includes all those
who can 'unlock' cultural resources, not only those with
professional museum qualifications – it includes those who
organise the restoration of canal boats or the recording of
watercress beds, as well as those who piece together the
history of the industrial landscape or select monuments for
protection.

In an expanded heritage, curatorial roles must continue to
become more supple and sophisticated in putting resources at
the disposal of users. The central positions will be held by
people who can create constituencies and oversee the strategic
use of resources to serve them, but they can have all manner
of backgrounds and interests: object-oriented curatorship
differs in some respects from that which is oriented around
the documentation of human activity, but that does not mean
it is necessarily either opposed to activity or opposed to the
user. Curators of all persuasions must also be more bold and
confident about what they have to offer. Industrial museums
have always recruited leadership from a variety of industrial
as well as museological backgrounds and they are bound to
experiment to try to correct what they perceive as established
biases. Whereas one set of arguments can be made in favour of
an engineering background as combining some management
experience with a knowledge of the resource, so equally can
arguments be made about the pertinence of experience in
arts administration, leisure management or community
curatorship as combining management experience with an
understanding of potential users.

Relations between volunteers and employed staff

The involvement of volunteers in heritage projects has been
characteristic of the early – and, in many cases, the only
continuing – phase of a project. The diversity of contact which
it makes possible is one of the things which makes it vital and
interesting.

Projects need to develop a professional approach to a variety
of matters: academic, managerial, technical. All these things
can be learnt to the extent that they are important, but there
are specific problems in organising voluntary effort which

arise from its contributed nature and the fact that it is offered alongside other commitments. To a certain extent these problems can be overcome through careful organisation and through objectifying the roles which volunteers are to perform in a handbook to which different people undertaking the same function may refer. Most industrial heritage projects however have established a paid staff, and different relationships are then possible between volunteers and employees, depending chiefly on who is ultimately responsible for the project but also on its objectives and the scale of its operation. Confusion and conflict can arise about the respective roles of volunteers and professionals when both work on, say, a restored railway which is a charitable company with a paid director but whose trustees are predominantly drawn from the volunteers working on the line. These can be partly solved by clear division of responsibilities but must also be grounded in a shared understanding about the nature of the organisation – to what extent is it a hobby club, a tourist attraction, a public service?

Where there is a clear understanding both of common purpose and of the specific responsibilities of each role and position, it has been possible for volunteers and professionals to work together closely. At Fourmies Ecomuseum, for example, the growth of the project and the elaboration of its division of labour has been planned to include opportunities for voluntary work with varying degrees of responsibility in all areas of the museum's work. It has been necessary to distinguish between work of support groups which is designed to fit in with their other commitments and ongoing museum functions which demand a different kind of commitment. Certain site and central management posts are occupied by appropriately experienced and dedicated volunteers, who are able to give a substantial proportion of their time.

Where, as is more common, growth and success meant a substitution of professional for voluntary effort and a marginalisation of the latter to the point of exclusion, there have been attempts to correct the balance. It is recognised that volunteers may have a strong contribution to make to industrial heritage projects by extending and improving the quality of their support, as well as bringing their own unique resources: specific connections with the interpreted industries, skills, knowledge, collection and documentary resources, energy and enthusiasm. But incorporating volunteers in a structure of work designed for professional staff involves careful delineation of boundaries of responsibility. Making effective use of voluntary effort is an important task in its own right, which has to be incorporated in professional job descriptions and work planning. If working with volunteers is not given an important place in museum objectives there is the danger that their presence may be seen by staff as a hindrance or even a threat to their livelihoods.

Changing relations between volunteers and professional curators are well illustrated at the Merseyside Maritime Museum where programmes of voluntary work within its Friends organisation are gradually becoming more closely integrated with the professional museum service. Merseyside provides a particular kind of case study: where, in the face of recent decline of an area encompassing a complex of related occupations, there has been a strong and diverse voluntary wish to become involved in industrial heritage. In these circumstances one might have expected the main conservation and interpretation initiative to have come from the voluntary sector. In Merseyside, however, the regional and national political response to the decline of the port has led to increasing state support for the Maritime Museum project as part of a showcase heritage and leisure rehabilitation of an architecturally distinctive part of the historic waterfront.

Merseyside's industrial history – and the character of the conurbation – has been shaped above all by Liverpool's growth and decline as the major deepwater port in the west of Britain. Only in the last thirty years has that decline been precipitate and apparently irreversible. Most people of middle age or older have held work which is directly or indirectly maritime and many younger people still identify with maritime history. Over 100,000 people – many of them young – turned out to see the Queen Elizabeth II liner when she paid her first visit to the Mersey to commemorate the one hundred and fiftieth anniversary of Cunard's transatlantic service from Liverpool. It was this sentiment which was behind the decision of the county Museums Service to open a Maritime Branch in 1976, and from the very beginning voluntary interest in the project was strong, leading to the establishment of a separate Friends organisation which soon became both more numerous and more active than the parent organisation which served the generality of the county's museums.

Whereas in many industrial heritage projects a few enthusiasts face the challenge of winning a wider constituency, and many populations affect amnesia with regard to their declining or departed industries, voluntary interest in Merseyside's maritime history has continued to spread (to 2,500 Friends in 1990), and to grow as active involvement (over 200 people are engaged in voluntary work in visitor services, boat maintenance and restoration or in the running of the Friends organisation itself). Members of the Friends have founded a legally separate but associated trust which restores and operates historic vessels characteristic of the area.

There has thus been a continuing dialectic between the growth of a publicly funded professional museum, and voluntary support through the medium of the Friends organisation; this is of interest especially for the way in which the division of responsibility between the two has been redefined, as each has grown and changed. The very popularity of maritime heritage leads to a certain amount of jostling over whose heritage it is, which can be positive as long as an impasse doesn't develop (either between or within organisations) to block development or frustrate involvement.

When the museum first opened, the boundary of responsibility between professionals and volunteers was not very clearly defined. Many Friends worked hard in a variety of jobs alongside paid staff to get things ready for the opening; in fact, it is hard to imagine how this would have been possible otherwise, given the very small budget provided by the County at this point.

Once the museum had opened the small curatorial staff turned their attention to building and ordering the collection. The continuing commitment of the active Friends was channelled in particular directions: boat restoration and the guiding of special parties. In part, this reflected patterns of interest and experience among active Friends who had worked in marine engineering or served on ships, or had a knowledge of aspects of Liverpool's maritime history which they wished to share. But it also reflected a policy of excluding volunteers from categories of work and areas of responsibility which could be confused with those of paid staff, because of union objections, the job-creation policies of the employing authority, and a desire to maintain overall managerial and curatorial control.

Thus the Friends did not assist with curatorial work and with what were judged essential visitor services; they were not authorised to take initiatives on behalf of the museum on an experimental basis, nor did they play an important role in fundraising. When the Metropolitan County was abolished, and the museum became a grant-aided trust as part of the National Museums and Galleries on Merseyside, there was no Friends representation on the museum board; Friends' guiding services have been kept outside the museum's new main building in the restored Albert Dock.

Thus channelled, the Friends organisation has developed a

four-part pattern of activity. On one level, it operates as a club, with assigned premises, opportunities for responsibility and participation in organising a programme of social and educational events – in which the less active members participate. In the areas of boat maintenance and visitor services, it provides organised support to the museum. Through the associated Preservation Trust, active members have 'their own' heritage project pursued in association with the museum.

To some extent this pattern of activity reflects the diversity of Liverpool's maritime associations; a diversity of programmes helps realise the potential and reduce the friction between Friends with different views, interests, temperaments and experience. However, these different foci need to be defined and related in such a way that it is possible to realise complex museum objectives.

The boat maintenance team goes back to the early days of the museum. Here, because the scale of work to be done is so large and the experience of many volunteers is relevant, Friends have worked closely with museum staff, in some cases right alongside on the same or similar jobs. It has always been accepted that a paid conservation staff is necessary but that it could never be sufficient to the museum's needs. There is competition to get on to the boat team, which is selected and directed by museum staff, who must assess what volunteers are capable of and provide training where feasible. Most of the work has been fairly basic maintenance, although some use has been made of specialist skills. Currently about 5,000 volunteer days a year are provided this way – an invaluable resource. Although there is no formal sanction if the quality of work is not good, a well-organised group of experienced people provides its own motives and sanctions.

Visitor services has grown from the handling of pre-arranged special parties to encompass a variety of functions. The general pattern, however, is quite different from the boat team. Friends generally take on work separate from that of museum staff, and the Friends' visitor services organisation operates its own recruitment and training. While the museum is keen to ensure the accuracy and appropriateness of what is said to visitors, it is monitoring rather than directly establishing and controlling the training programme. Responsibility for organising the increasingly differentiated visitor services support programme is delegated to a member of the Friends' committee who chooses suitable programme heads and establishes and monitors the appropriate training and a rostering system to ensure reliable turn-out.

Following a museum assessment of a dip in visitor figures in 1989, the Friends have been asked to try out 20-minute on-site guiding at fixed times and with a roving guide commission at weekends. In addition, leafleting is being tried around the docks and this will be put into costume, standardised to 1914 after initial enthusiasm to present various periods was rejected by the museum as providing too much of a free heritage attraction on the dock itself. In this case, the museum initiated a consultative process; on the other hand, the introduction of programmed school visits was suggested by the Friends, and is administered by them.

The scope of activity for the Friends is increasing, as their self-organisation is professional and directed towards well-defined goals, and as the museum begins to think more about mobilising additional voluntary resources, especially in labour-intensive areas of work. These developments have prompted a search for a new way of defining appropriate spheres, particularly in relatively unexplored areas where an important contribution could be made – fundraising, research and documentation. How much the latter is taken up depends on the cost–benefit estimation of the curatorial input required, and evaluation of alternatives. Whatever is decided on this particular issue, there is no doubting either the value of the contribution the Friends can make to the work of the museum, or the depth of opportunity which can be seized by mobilising it.

Caring for resources

In this section we are concerned with the *management* of conservation, not its techniques, which are the subject of other volumes in this series. We have to begin by frankly admitting that industrial heritage projects – which have often been started to 'save' things – do not have a particularly good conservation record by traditional museum standards. Industrial heritage has enormously increased the scope of what can be considered as a heritage resource. While this is an enrichment from the point of view of what it is possible to do with heritage, care of these resources poses some serious challenges for the management of industrial projects and for the industrial heritage movement as a whole.

As interest in this heritage has grown up rapidly and in a relatively uncoordinated way, the problem arises of the appropriate choice of landscapes, sites, buildings, artefacts and documentary records to be recognised and registered as heritage. As we argued above in chapter 3, inventory programmes – in addition to their value as a knowledge resource, contributing essential perspective to any understanding of industrial culture – are a necessary corrective to the 'rescue' response which has been the basis of many initiatives to assume care. They have also proven invaluable in, for example, optimising the expenditure of public funds on industrial monuments. Inventory work is an essential element in establishing initial project feasibility, detailed development planning and ongoing monitoring and management. Aspects of inventory work depend on, and help develop, the basis for good inter-institutional collaboration.

However, inventory work involves a cost and can become systematic enough to be valuable only over a period of time; this implies operating with rules of thumb which are more than usually subject to revision, so that many decisions to extend care (whether or not to assume ownership) must be properly regarded as provisional. This has one sort of implication in extending protection in the built environment, where the decision is only one element in the future considerations – anyway subject to re-evaluations – and another sort of implication in, say, museum collection, which is often made under assumptions of perpetual care. In these areas too it needs to be accepted that care decisions are subject to re-evaluation.

Taken together with the other points raised in this section, this argues not only for greater collaboration between institutions in making care decisions, but for the formulation of policy and instruments of temporary or provisional care, subject to review. It suggests the usefulness of collectively supported facilities for storage and assessment of both artefacts which may be taken into collections and those which, from the point of view of one institution, have been downgraded to low priority. This amounts to some kind of reception or assessment centre – an indoor scrapheap.

Even with a perfect state of knowledge to support prioritisation there would be too much industrial heritage to take into direct care. The rarity value of objects of the pre-industrial period, or of non-industrial production in the industrial period, provides a basis for rationalising care decisions which is of limited use in managing the industrial heritage. As we have seen discussed in chapter 3 the issues of degree and kind of protection necessarily come into play, as also does the question of sharing responsibility for care; this approach can usefully also be applied to artefacts, and was developed to do so at the Ecomuseum of Le Creusot-Montceau-Les-Mines in the early 1970s. Here property of cultural value from a scientific or community perspective was not collected but was maintained formally or informally in the care of its existing owners (see above, chapter 4).

In the built environment the question of re-use of buildings and sites is dominant, though not to the same degree in all countries, whereas with artefacts simple disposal is the more usual option. By preserving an artefact there is seldom an important opportunity cost to the owner, and use of space for other purposes is the main issue. This implies that a policy of underpinning care for cultural heritage in the community could be successful without much expenditure; with some documentation the main cost is initial, and is incurred in putting the experience or record into a form in which it can be conserved and used subsequently.

Such strategies of conditional, partial and collaborative or community care challenge some of the most fundamental assumptions of conservation practice and are therefore somewhat controversial. However, the care and conservation record to date leaves no doubt that hard thinking, and a willingness to try fresh approaches, are required. Publicity for, and publications about, the industrial heritage movement of the later twentieth century extol its achievements with buildings, sites, landscapes, monuments, collections and new museums, and one would not want to deny the significance of what has been achieved. However, there are few respects in which one can say that this record provides an adequate basis for the future.

First, many decisions have been reactive rather than based on a well-defined and defensible strategy. Many institutions even lack clear prioritising criteria or have failed to apply them in collections management or other aspects of conservation policy: many care commitments have been entered into without a sound justification (Robbins 1988).

Second, many care commitments which have been entered into are at risk. Sadly, many projects which have been instigated through the desirability of preserving certain resources have not been able to provide adequately for their future. The storage conditions for industrial collections – particularly mechanical ones – are mediocre at best; they get second- or third-class treatment in many established public sector museums – the storage situation in several of the best-known independent industrial museums is clearly inadequate, with little or no environmental quality control. The organisation and documentation of industrial collection storage are also often poor, with a substantial risk of loss of or damage to key items and parts. Knowledge of appropriate conservation techniques is also patchy, and the quality of both preventive and remedial work highly variable. There is a very large backlog of conservation work, with the majority of items in most collections currently needing attention, although the proportion in a crisis state or rapid deterioration is probably quite small (Ramer 1989).

Third, few managements have taken the measure of the care problem or devised a strategy to cope with it. There is a serious under-investment in care, which to a certain extent reflects the weak financial position of many projects; better-endowed institutions, like the Museum of American Textile History, have a superior conservation record. Other projects which also often have a good record in this respect are operating railways, which, although accused of 'using up' their resources, have higher standards and more active programmes of resource management. At the opposite extreme, it is clear that many care commitments have been entered into without any clear plan as to how they can be fulfilled. Although most projects have a conservation budget of some kind, few have carried out a thorough assessment of conservation responsibilities, established priorities and incorporated a programme of preventive and remedial work into an ongoing development plan. Conservation training of employed and volunteer staff is seldom planned in any systematic way.

There is every reason to think that these problems will get worse. Collections are being added to at a much greater rate than preventive, let alone remedial, measures are being undertaken. Many projects have had the benefit of relatively recent investment, especially in building rehabilitation and installations, and are enjoying a temporary holiday from major maintenance. The recent stress on heritage uses, and the priority given in management profiles to sponsor- and audience-related performance, draw attention and investment away from the backroom and into the shop-window. Unless there is a significant change in average current practice, a conservation crisis lies in store for many projects – one which may affect the credibility of the whole industrial heritage movement. The authorities who have pump-primed many projects by grant aiding or undertaking building and site restoration for interpretive uses will be among the first to notice if projects are not carrying out their care responsibilities.

As we have suggested, project management can attack the conservation problem on many fronts. The starting point must be an assessment of the conservation needs of existing collections, and the devising of a programme of work and environmental improvements which can match those needs. Given the slippage of responsibility in this area, there is something to be said for this assessment, and the scope if not the detail of the plan, being done externally to the project, by either an independent consultant or one provided by an advisory service, a group of peer projects, or a specialist society. Quite apart from the question of specialist knowledge which may be helpful in certain cases, it is more likely that a problem which has been objectified in this way will receive its due attention.

Although there is no doubt that more money needs to be spent on the conservation of industrial collections and that it occupies too small a percentage of expenditure in many projects, the scale of the problem is beyond the resources of most institutions unless its basic parameters are changed. Projects can multiply the effectiveness of their limited resources by concentrating on environmental improvements and training; apart from a few areas in which special knowledge and skills are required, staff are best employed in the recruitment, training and supervision of suitable volunteers, both those with relevant industrial experience and those who are interested in learning. Much of the best work in industrial heritage conservation has been done by volunteer groups, and, while it is easy enough to produce stories of misguided work, on the whole the amateurs have at least as good a record as the professionals.

Here, it has to be accepted that, while working as part of a group on a particular restoration project – which will then be in the public eye – is very satisfying, much routine preventive maintenance is not particularly edifying. Volunteer working groups must have their experience checked and may require training, but they also have to be organised and motivated. One good example in this context is the Merseyside Maritime Museum's boat team: it is not easy to get into the team and there is a good *esprit de corps* owing in large part to the careful planning of a developing relationship between work and workers, with work taking place only in supervised groups at appointed times. In some such programmes there is the potential to pass on skills and experience which are themselves part of the industrial heritage – something worth doing in its own right. The question of the specialist skills and knowledge essential for conservation work – as well as conservation training generally – is another aspect of the problem which needs a co-ordinated approach by heritage agencies, museum networks and specialist societies. There are many areas of industrial collections which are losing their connection with living experience – mechanical horology is one; it is as important to pass on that experience as it is to document it or collect its products, tools and effects.

Experience with unemployment relief schemes has been patchy from a conservation point of view, although participation in these may be justified by other objectives, for example playing a positive community role or desiring to get work done which would not be otherwise. In a slump in Sweden in the early 1980s, some quite skilled building and machinery conservation projects were carried out by teams with substantial knowledge and experience, but youth training schemes of the sort more commonly seen in Britain have been difficult to lead effectively. Conservation projects need also to be set up as genuine training opportunities – in this respect they may have more to offer some other categories of work. It is important to identify discrete goals which are not essential to ongoing operations, as schemes are wound up or changed by policy and economic circumstances unrelated to the needs of projects. Therefore, while at best such schemes have helped establish or develop certain installations, they have not been helpful in an overall conservation strategy – in fact they have had a disruptive and distracting effect, in Britain at least. This is not to say that there is not scope for a different type of unemployment training scheme devised to be more closely related to the needs of the heritage industry. A substantial proportion of museum volunteers are not in regular paid employment and although most are not seeking employment some come seeking skills, knowledge and opportunities.

Even if the base of conservation work is enlarged in this way, as it has been successfully in some projects, there is likely to continue to be a gap between intention and reality. This can really only be resolved by reviewing collection policy and existing collections. This may involve both the disposal and the dispersal of certain objects from an overloaded care system. Documentation and recording can ensure that they remain recognised as a cultural resource, and the opportunity for periodic or occasional public access is not necessarily lost. Inventory projects linked with care in the community policies and appropriate interpretive programmes could motivate a major extension of involvement in conservation appreciation and work, and a greater sense of public responsibility. Secondly, existing collections need to be evaluated from the point of view of potential use as well as that of provenance and costs of conservation. Explicit decisions must be made about which artefacts are to be used in one way or another through display, demonstration, etc., which will be used as spares, which maintained and or documented as reference copies, which have what sort of rarity value. Frank Atkinson's work at Beamish open-air museum showed how important such collection management policies could be to interpretation – they can also play a role in cutting the conservation problem down to size.

Managing design

Many design problems have to be resolved in bringing a heritage project to fruition – problems of communication design, often of installation design for visitors, staff and collections, and possibly of architecture and landscape design. In most cases specialist assistance will be engaged with the design and subsequent execution, either on a contract basis or from somewhere else in the organisation if it is a large one, e.g. a multi-department museum. The advice given in this section is not a substitute for these professional design services, but guidance in how to manage design.

Design decisions are crucial to the implementation of conservation and interpretation strategies; the choices about how a resource is to be protected, used and its potential communicated depend on design. As discussed elsewhere in this book, it is impossible to use or interpret a heritage resource without changing it, or what it means, and there are different, often conflicting, views about how these problems should be resolved. On one side stand those who would make the work performed by heritage management on the resource clearly visible, and on the other those who would obscure it either to create a sense of continuity with the past or to create some dramatic effect. In exhibition and publication such reworking of historical resources is largely a question of selection and arrangement in a new order, but the editing of buildings, sites and landscapes often destroys part of the resource and substantially alters its character. Much regret has been expressed over irreversible changes which were subsequently judged to have diminished rather than enhanced the resource.

Design work may privilege certain ways of regarding the resource and thus indicate how it is to be used. Design often brings out aesthetic qualities by stripping away workaday context. This may result from a decision that the aesthetic qualities represent the most important resource in question (or one most likely to be appealing to users), as at Cressbrook Mill in Derbyshire or Le Grand Hornu in Belgium, from the exigencies of conservation, or from the desire to create a monument to important achievement. Taken together, these considerations can entail both substantial destruction and new building on an historic site, as at the former works of the Coalbrookdale Company, now part of the Ironbridge Gorge Museum. When such decisions are made, it is essential to consider how thereby dislocated facets of industrial heritage can be documented, selectively conserved and adequately represented elsewhere in the interpretive design; otherwise loss is compounded by distortion.

While architecture is often set up against, or as a substitute for, other dimensions of industrial heritage such as technology and working life, the potential of industrial remains to communicate essential features of past ways of life to future generations sometimes goes unrealised. Bringing out the implicit meaning of, for example, the walls in a factory compound requires both historical understanding and spatial and symbolic imagination. In the view of a Norwegian team of architects who specialise in industrial adaptation, this potential resource needs special attention alongside that given to more obvious resources and the functional requirements of new uses (Corneil, personal communication, 1989). Recognising and using inherent resources can be more effective and a good deal cheaper than adding new elements, as demonstrated by the re-use of the pithead tower at Norberg in Sweden as a theatre.

New building may be indicated, however, when the essential functions of proposed uses conflict with the essential features of the existing resource. It is by no means the case that the easiest form of adaptive re-use is to make a museum, as is often suggested. The kind of accommodation necessary to give a rounded interpretation of a site or surviving feature may not be compatible with respect for the integrity of the structure or its equipment, without taking into account other visitor services, offices and stores. Sometimes, as in the case of the tide mill at Bow, it is possible to accommodate such functions in new building which re-creates or restores the facades of derelict or previously destroyed buildings on the site. It is impossible to evaluate the relative effects of interior alteration or new building on the site without reference to the basic strategy linking resources and uses, and the same goes for most other design decisions.

To judge by both the results and accounts given of the process, the track record of professional designers working in heritage organisations is an uneven one. While there have been some happy collaborations and brilliant results, there are many stories of persistent misunderstanding, with results at odds with stated objectives and diminishing rather than augmenting the resource. A recurrent problem (according to heritage managers) is the failure of some designers – especially architects – to understand and respect what heritage managers are trying to do with the resource. From the other side, some heritage managers expect too little or too much of the designer; they either expect 'an original concept' without having provided a thorough brief, or they are inflexibly committed to a particular result from the beginning.

It is possible to avoid these pitfalls by providing for two-way communication in several stages. Before seeking any design assistance it is important to have prepared a strategy based on an assessment of resources and their potential uses for key constituencies. Without this there is no basis for entering into a discussion. It is also necessary to be able to outline the likely scope and time scale of a development plan; together these will throw up the most important design problems. On this basis it is possible to sound out possible designers – these should be people whose work is known to be relevant to the project's needs.

The degree of packaging of different design services varies. In some localities it is possible to engage teams who offer a comprehensive interpretation service; this can offer important advantages, as there are good reasons to believe that design for interpretation is best done by bringing together different perspectives, skills and experience. However, the range of skills offered varies considerably and should be examined to see how well it fits project needs; the work of such a team still needs to be guided by a strategy of resources and uses, and care taken to avoid general formula solutions.

A leading American museum consultant has the following to say about the role of different specialisms in the design process:

> Design, program, management; teams providing all of these are needed. However, I am leery of the ability of a design firm to provide the right kind of integration. All too often the historical content – either best new interpretations or historical richness – are neglected in a dramatic design solution. Only rare designers are sensitive to presenting history. On the other hand, few historians know how to ensure both that the important messages are the ones the designer communicates and that they are communicated in an appropriate way. The best solution to these problems may have to be a history or content driven approach. In such an approach, a public history team, working with subject-matter specialists as consultants and with current staff of the institution, outlines the thematic and program outline. Only after that outline is clearly accepted by staff

and trustees does the design process begin. And the history team participates in a significant way throughout the design and fabrication process. (Victor, personal communication, 1991)

The availability of suitable consultant groups depends on both the supply of expertise and the typical forms in which work is offered. In some localities teams of experienced people get together on an ad hoc basis to bid for particular jobs; in others little design for interpretation work is offered on contract, or the dominant commissioning groups, local government for example, give a higher priority to design or leisure management professionalism than to an understanding of the historical resources and their cultural potential. Many projects choose or are constrained by limited finance to carry out much of the design work internally. In all cases, however, some form of partnership is required between different kinds of experience and this association develops best in response to a clearly stated brief, developed by the project from the exploratory discussions. The brief states the work to be carried out, the evaluative criteria which must be met, and the time and budgetary constraints.

The scope and detail of the brief may vary considerably depending on the work to be done; it might be to develop concepts and implementation proposals for a fundraising document, a detailed study for the conversion of a building, signage for a network of sites, an installation or temporary exhibition, storage system or publications and publicity. All briefs should specify how work in progress is to be monitored and when and how approval is to be given to preliminary studies, detailing and final results. In more involved jobs it will be necessary to oversee the scheduling of both design and making, even if these are contracted out. When opening dates are to be met, critical path analysis should be used, tracking back the essential ingredients of the final result (Miles 1988).

Points and criteria of approval are important. At each stage a consideration of design work provides an opportunity for evaluation of the project of which it is a part. This evaluation should include, directly or indirectly, the key constituencies which the project aims to serve. However, confusion can result if the body which has to give later approval is substantially different from that which set it going. In fairness to the designers, if criteria are modified while the job is in progress, this must be acknowledged as additional work.

As we discuss elsewhere (see chapter 5), there are a number of different strategies of design for interpretation. It is worth noting, however, that there has been a trend towards uniform solutions to certain standard problems, and that this may erode the specific character and value of the resource. This character is that which figures in local memory and identity, and that which people from elsewhere will travel to experience.

Monitoring effectiveness

A working development plan, as distinct from a prospectus, should indicate the setting of specific objectives or targets – financially, in the use of time, in the quality of achievement – which allow a regular monitoring and review of all aspects of a project's operations. There are three kinds of evaluation which may be carried out:

- evaluation of programme effectiveness in relation to objectives
- evaluation of changes in resource significance (as defined in chapter 4)
- operational efficiency (inputs/outputs)

These are logically nested. Resource assessments depend on use criteria – even scholarly assessments of historical significance are embedded in assumptions about the documentary or monumental significance of certain kinds of resources or the interest in knowing the answers to certain kinds of historical questions. Assessments of operational efficiency inputs/outputs can be defined in a number of different ways but their significance depends on the relevance of the particular operation being evaluated to programme effectiveness and resource or asset enhancement.

In certain areas of heritage management, such as adaptive re-use, calculations are made which contain proxies for all these variables, for instance, initial asset value, cost of conversion, sale or rentability in relation to proposed uses (Eley and Worthington 1984; Reichen 1985). In many cases adaptation or conservation can produce acceptable development values although not necessarily the highest. Although there are cases – for example at King's Cross, London, or some other nexus sites – where competing uses are of a different order of magnitude, focused discussion about inherent architectural quality or historic interest has been shown to affect actual and potential asset value and thus alter the range of re-use projects undertaken, although there are always problems about balancing the tangibility of rehabilitation costs against shifting assessments of cultural value (O'Neill 1989). But at least developers are used to subjective and shifting assessments of eventual development value – professionals are employed to make those judgements. Historic building trusts have to deal with the possible non-correspondence between their own enthusiasms and those of potential buyers, and to manipulate culturally specific sources of funding.

If one takes the example of Calderdale, heritage-sensitive rehabilitation can be shown to have had impact on property values, immigration employment and quality of life perceptions, and there is the possibility of arguing about links between some kinds of conservation policy and crime, vandalism and other sorts of social problems (Patten, Whelan and Dixon 1989). While the links are there for examination, the extent to which local planning authorities take them into account is probably negligible and there is minimal exchange of information let alone common policy formation between different departments or authorities. Therefore the link between such phenomena as vandalism and environmental perception, if seen at all, is construed in a narrow way, around control values, defensibility, activity channelling and not often related to sense of place, sense of identity, heritage, etc. (but see Oliver 1982).

Nevertheless models of environmental quality assessment have been established – notably in environmental psychology and parts of social geography, and by architects/urban designers – and related to policy questions such as designation of amenity, or special character landscapes, conservation, townscape management, and most especially the assessment of the relationships of multiple deprivation in synthesised environments, public housing, estate and neighbourhood design, etc. (Gold and Burgess 1982). In these contexts there are a lot of tools for defining environmental qualities and scaling evaluations of them, as well as correlating such responses with a wide range of other variables. So far as we know these research tools – which cost money – have not been routinely used in conservation policy, but only in special studies, nor has any thought been given to finding simple proxies which could be referred to as a matter of course.

As far as museums, sites and other visitor attractions are concerned, measures of operating efficiency have become increasingly discussed in recent years but we still lack generally agreed measures of effectiveness (Bud, Cave and Hamney 1991). Visitor figures are the main proxy, even – perhaps especially – where they are indirectly related to income (Hooper-Greenhill 1988: 213–32). Audience surveys of varying kinds have been done, to determine composition of visitor populations as much as their evaluation of different aspects of public programmes. Depending on organisational objectives, visitor profiles can be used to maximise income through adjusting marketing strategies or to identify imbalances. Experience profiles can examine typical patterns of use, and determine levels of utilisation and quality of response to particular aspects of programme – results which may also be obtained by observation programmes. By comparison with the models and literatures about environmental evaluation, assessment of visitor experience is underdeveloped, nor are such evaluations used regularly in assessing effectiveness for grant purposes or even in a product development sense, much less in the service sense we have argued for in chapter 3. The reasons for this include professional reluctance to have to analyse the museum's cultural role in a way that would directly impact on museum practice, and the difficulty of finding suitable proxies for qualitative discriminations.

Qualitative and quantitive analysis of visitor experience gives only one dimension of project output. What is required is to identify and measure the full contribution of curatorial output to a comprehensively specified cultural management strategy. This would include, for example, the contribution to asset value (through both conservation and interpretation), to a diversified 'goodwill' (through peer group and other constituency feedback), to knowledge (scholarly and educational output), to the success of particular interpretive projects (defined in terms of their programme objectives), to more effective use of resources within the institution, and the indirect contribution of building heritage awareness to meeting other cultural and social objectives.

Given the specificity of project objectives, attempts to devise universal formulae for monitoring project effectiveness are quixotic and open to abuse by single-minded policy-makers. There is no doubt, however, that each and every industrial heritage project would benefit from thinking hard about how it would define and measure effectiveness in the three senses indicated at the head of this section. Locally valid proxies can be found for most objectives. For example, the number of person-hours spent in exhibitions is a proxy for their capacity to involve; cost divided by time spent by visitors (and/or other outputs) is a proxy for operational efficiency (Walden 1991: 28). Policy objectives like amenity, tourism and regeneration have qualities which may in turn be quantified: for example, amenity surveys indicated above may be extended to connect with other areas of social policy like care for the environment; visitors' experience can be similarly elaborated. Tourism quality may be seen from different perspectives – project revenue and area revenue, public relations and area image – and these may be related dynamically to quality of visitor experience and profile of visitor populations. Demonstrating effectiveness can help make the case for industrial heritage projects, and measuring it is important to their viability.

Recognising blockages

A major purpose of managing in relation to a development plan is that it forces recognition of obstacles and blockages in the project's development. Such blockages often occur through changes in circumstance or flaws in the basic strategy of the project, which have not become evident because they have been left implicit. An example where such blockage has recently become acknowledged is the American Precision Museum, a small museum of the machine tool industry established in the late 1960s in the old building of the Robbins and Lawrence manufacturing company in Windsor, Vermont – one of the key sites where the tools and techniques of manufacture with interchangeable parts were developed. The founder director established just enough support from the industry, public grants and his own resources to acquire and partially restore and adapt the building for museum use. Building on his long experience as an amateur historian and contacts established while he was a curator at the Smithsonian, he gradually assembled the most important collection of machine tools in the United States and, arguably, the world, which was simply displayed as a 'machine tool hall of fame'. Chiefly through publishing a newsletter which consistently presented new scholarship and valuable documentation, the museum developed an international Friends network, which, taken together with the meagre seasonal attendance income, provided enough income to keep the museum going, paying only part salaries to the retired director, a secretary and custodial/maintenance help.

This is a project with some outstanding resources: a fine building and historically important site, an important collection and a distinguished autodidact historian as director. All these qualities are acknowledged by those 'in the know', but the project's shaky viability is maintained only by the semi-voluntary efforts of its retired director. Although various fundraising initiatives have been taken, and from time to time grants or donations have given cause for hope, although small improvements are made in facilities and conservation is not neglected, the museum's support has not been on an upward path for some considerable time.

Even large-scale investment would not transform the American Precision Museum into a volume visitor attraction. Given its Vermont location – not isolated, and in a quietly fashionable holiday area, but far from major population centres – and the nature of its subject matter, it was always wise to seek specialist support over a wide area. Even so, more could certainly have been done over the years to make visiting the museum interesting for the non-specialist – the family groups, for example, which predominate among the holidaymakers. The Museum publishes an exemplary booklet 'From Muskets to Mass Production' introducing its 'story', and has staged video demonstrations for the BBC, but has virtually no interpretive aids helping the visitor to understand the machines in the collection – how they were made and operated, what they were used to make – and how they changed the nature of manufacturing, or their contribution to the making of the local industrial landscape.

That this situation has remained unchanged for many years says something about the convictions and predilections of the director, and indeed it is clear that to his way of thinking there are worse fates than the present difficulties – to become an 'amusement park' or to be swallowed up into the US National Park Service, for example. But it also says something about the museum's board, who seem willing to allow things to continue along these lines, and are in any event chiefly responsible for its support strategy. How could this be?

The American Precision Museum board has had preponderant representation from the American machine tool industry. Since the museum's foundation, this industry has been devastated by rapid technological change and international competition, so it has been chiefly individual interest and support rather than corporate funds which people from the industry have been able to bring to the museum. In fact this has become virtually the sole element of support. Public institutions and local or regional government do not contribute substantially nor do they play an active role on the board. In what some see as the original home of rugged individualism, this lack of subvention is not surprising, but the lack of any positive relationship at all is a problem, not remedied by the presence of one or two residents of the area. One or two historians of technology and the director of a related museum in government hands add a slightly different note, but these links have produced no significant collaboration between their institutions nor any broadening of the support base of the museum.

It has become difficult to avoid the impression that the last vestiges of a once great and pioneering mechanical engineering culture have circled their wagons at Windsor, Vermont. A development plan which provided criteria for monitoring would have long since focused attention on these weaknesses in programme and support which have recently been acknowledged to block the development of this potentially important project.

New directions

Blockages in development are not the only reason why industrial heritage projects come to reassess their basic strategy. Changes in the resource, evolution of the support structure and the emergence of new opportunities may lead to a redefinition of responsibilities. The Museum of American Textile History provides a good example of how this may happen.

This project had been established in 1959 as the Merrimack Valley Textile Museum, an offshoot of the North Andover, Massachusetts Historical Society. Mrs Caroline Rogers and her husband, who had been interested in hand spinning and weaving, persuaded relations who owned the Stevens woollen company, established in the locality since 1813, to provide a substantial endowment for a new museum which would collect historical records and materials pertaining to woollen textile manufacture in America in its craft and factory stages.

In 1959 the woollen industry, including the Stevens firm, was already in full retreat from New England and this timely initiative was well placed to build important collections and archival resources whose scope was subsequently extended to all the textile industries of America. Throughout the 1960s the trustees of the foundation, made up of Stevens family representatives, members of the local historical society and invited academic advisers, concentrated on building the resource and supporting research. The directors of the museum have all been historians and the annual reports of the 1960s and 1970s show how the scholarship and curatorship of the staff and the increasingly impressive resource became better known among those interested in textile history, although the number of visitors to the museum's little building on the village green remained under 10,000 per year. Carefully designed displays in the small industrial and pre-industrial galleries remained relatively unchanged in this period, although occasional temporary exhibitions mounted by the museum in urban centres showed the potential to engage larger publics.

During the 1970s, however, the growth of collections and programme threatened to exceed income from endowment which was held in check by a stagnant stock market. Towards the end of the 1970s key founding trustees retired or died. The new trustees had to consider how the museum's resources, which were attracting increasing attention, and its responsibilities could be maintained. The tone of annual reports shifted away from that of an antiquarian/philanthropic project towards that of a non-profit corporation, with a higher profile for public presentation and winning new support, and programme-effectiveness evaluation of curatorial programmes.

The challenge of grant conditions and an arts administration student's 1979 report on use-effectiveness of resources led to an identification of audiences, programmes and services for which the museum was responsible, ranked in order of importance. It was felt that the most important audiences were residents of the Merrimack valley, teachers, students and scholars, and that the important services were exhibits, publications, collections, research, reference, textile conservation, grants in aid and scholarly conferences. As a result, it was decided to work on a series of printed guides to the collection, to establish temporary exhibition space, to make the exhibit of early industrial technology more relevant to the social and economic context of industrialisation, to establish a travelling exhibition, and to rearrange storage space.

These changes began a change of emphasis towards using the museum's resources to broaden the basis of support and involvement, which was to include the reorganisation of education and interpretation into a public programmes function on the one hand and community relations on the other.

The idea that the museum needed support on a broad scale was not accepted overnight, but such support was forthcoming because of the quality of its resources and programmes, and it steadily increased throughout the 1980s. The annual report itself has become an agent as well as a register of this support, combining representations of a sense of purpose, efficient management and achievement of high standards with a note of personal vigour and commitment. Reorienting the museum towards its constituencies has not, however, simply been a matter of presenting better what was there before, but has involved rethinking its basic responsibilities. As the project gradually moved out of the orbit of a local historical society to become an institution of national scope and international reputation, its neat little colonial-style building site on the village green at North Andover, isolated from the millscape of the textile industry, became increasingly anomalous. The irksomeness of having most of the collection in store away from the eyes of the public and the offices of curators had long been evident, but it was the new orientation of the museum towards creating constituencies which made consideration of a move to larger accommodation in a major population centre possible.

The terms of this challenge were influenced also by the increasing recognition of industrial heritage and its possible role in the regeneration of communities, dramatically demonstrated by the implantation of national and state heritage parks in Lowell and efforts in the same direction in nearby Lawrence. Without widespread interest in industrial environments and buildings and the working lives of people as well as decorative arts, technology or economic history, it wouldn't have been possible for the museum to contemplate moving to the centre of a desperately depressed mill city. Even with these developments and assistance from the state and the city of Lawrence in acquiring a disused mill building, the trustees found the scale of the new commitments difficult. To preserve their independence they had scouted involvement with others in Lowell, but in Lawrence an independent gamble on visitor income could have lost enough to threaten the security of the museum. This prospect prompted the trustees to establish a working party with senior staff to re-evaluate priorities: why the museum collects extensively, how and for whom its results should be used, and the specific programmes needed to realise these objectives.

This process of detailed self-examination consolidated the re-orientation begun ten years earlier. The museum had established practices of 'curatorial autonomy', but now, with major risks to be taken, trustees had to learn how things really worked. Doubts were expressed about the detrimental effects of depending on visitor income on standards of scholarship and interpretation. Involvement in the city might mean they had to meet expectations for which they were not prepared. Soundings were taken on the willingness of potential sponsors to support an expanded public role. Eventually a tightly argued statement of objectives was adopted which supported a move into Lawrence, and a move has been agreed to a smaller former textile warehouse near motorway access, a site less dependent on the results of other redevelopment efforts.

The ambitious programme now adopted by the Museum of American Textile History attempts to come to terms with the implications of the growth of awareness of industrial heritage since it was founded a generation ago. It will take its outstanding collections and curators to an industrial building and participate in the remaking of the industrial landscape. It will aim to involve larger numbers of visitors by evoking the working life of the industry as well as indicating its key. While success of the new programmes will depend on a number of factors, the work done on prioritisation and re-evaluation will stand the museum in good stead in undertaking new responsibilities.

Many other industrial heritage projects are, or will soon be, approaching similar points of reassessment and renewal. They will have to cope with different patterns of change in their heritage resources, key support structures and responsibilities.

Bibliography

Aérospatiale, Comité d'établissement de (1985) *Mémoire d'usine*, Chatillon-sous-Bagneux: Aérospatiale.

Alfrey, J. (1986) 'Archaeology or architecture? The Nuffield archaeological inventory of the Ironbridge Gorge', in Inventaire Général des Monuments et des Richesses Artistiques de la France, *Les Inventaires du Patrimoine Industriel: Objectifs et Méthodes*, Paris: Inventaire Général.

Alfrey, J. and Clark, C. (forthcoming) *The Landscape of Industry: Patterns of Change in the Ironbridge Gorge*, London: Routledge.

Alzen, A. (1979) *Arbetarbostader i Vallvik*, Uppsala: Uppsala Universitet.

Ambrose, T. (ed.) (1987a) *Education in Museums, Museums in Education*, Edinburgh: Scottish Museums Council.

Ambrose, T. (1987b) *New Museums: A Start-Up Guide*, Edinburgh: Scottish Museums Council.

Ambrose, T. (ed.) (1988) *Working with Museums*, Edinburgh: Scottish Museums Council.

Backlund, A.-C. (ed.) (1988) *Bokem om Bergslagen*, Stockholm: Förlaget Rubicon.

Bamberger, M. (1984) 'Shape and microstructure of copper produced in a reconstructed ancient smelting process', *Historical Metallurgy* 18, 1: 31–4.

Bann, S. (1984) *The Clothing of Clio: A Study of the Representation of History in Nineteenth Century Britain and France*, Cambridge: Cambridge University Press.

Basalla, G. (1981) 'Musées et utopie technologique', *Culture Technique* 4: 19–27.

Beaudry, M. C. and Mrozowski, S. (1988) 'The archaeology of work and home-life in Lowell, Mass: An interdisciplinary study of the Boott Cotton Mills Corporation', *Journal of the Society for Industrial Archaeology* 14, 2: 1–22.

Belhoste, F., Cartier, C. and Smith, P. (1987) 'Industrial heritage inventories in France', in The International Conference for the Conservation of the Industrial Heritage, *Industrial Heritage – Austria 1987: Transactions 2*, Vienna: Federal Office for the Protection of Monuments and Department for Industrial Archaeology of the Technical University of Vienna.

Berckmans, P. (1990) 'Work and discipline: A new look at industrial architecture', paper given at Seventh International Conference on the Conservation of the Industrial Heritage, Brussels, September.

Berliet, P. (1985) 'An approach to conservation of the industrial heritage: Marius Berliet Foundation', paper given at Council of Europe Conference, 'The Industrial Heritage: What Policies?', Lyons, October.

Bettum, O. (1989) 'The Aker River Environmental Park, Oslo. Re-use of industrial and riverside built heritage as part of a comprehensive conservation plan', in Council of Europe, *Heritage and Successful Town Regeneration: Report of the Halifax Colloquy*, Strasbourg: Council of Europe.

Bigmore, P. (1990) 'Gentry, antiquarianism and the origins of county history in Suffolk', unpublished paper, Middlesex Polytechnic.

inel, C. (1986) 'Inventaire expérimental en hampagne-Ardenne', in Inventaire Général es Monuments et des Richesses Artistiques de France, *Les Inventaires du Patrimoine dustriel: Objectifs et Méthodes*, Paris: ventaire Général.

inney, M. (1984) *Our Vanishing Heritage*, ondon: Arlington.

inney, M., Machin, F. and Powell, K. (1990) *right Future: The Re-use of Industrial uildings*, London: SAVE Britain's Heritage.

onnet, E. and Cortois, F. (n.d.) *Sentiers observation à Wignehies*, Fourmies: comusée de la région Fourmies-Trelon.

ott, V. (1985–6) 'Collecting the twentieth ntury', *Social History Curators Group urnal* 13: 12–15.

ott, V. (1990) 'Beyond the museum', *useums Journal* 90, 2: 28–30.

ottomley, V. (1988), speech to the Council of urope Conference, 'Heritage and Successful own Regeneration', Halifax, October.

ourdieu, P.-P. (1984) *Distinction*, London: outledge.

ourdieu, P.-P. (1985) 'The aristocracy of lture' *Media, Culture and Society* 2.

owditch, J. (1988) 'Collecting the big, the bad d the ugly: industrial artefacts in history useums', paper given at American ssociation of Museums Conference, ttsburgh, June.

audel, F. (1981) *Civilisation and Capital fteenth Century to Eighteenth Century: The ructures of Every-day Life*, London: Collins.

echer, J., Lombardi, J. and Stackhouse, J. 982) *Brass Valley: The Brassworks History oject*, Philadelphia: Temple University Press.

elot, C.-I. and Mayaud, J.-L. (1982) *Industrie en Sabots*, Paris: Editions arniers.

uchanan, R. A. (1980) *Industrial Archaeology Britain*, London: Allen Lane.

ud, R., Cave, M. and Hamney, S. (1991) Measuring a museum's output', *Museums urnal* 91, 1: 29–31.

ursell, B. (1975) *Träskoadel*, Stockholm: ordiska Museet.

Bursell, B. (1987) 'In search of the human element: An empirical example', in The International Conference for the Conservation of the Industrial Heritage, *Industrial Heritage – Austria 1987: Transactions 2*, Vienna: Federal Office for the Protection of Monuments and Department for Industrial Archaeology of the Technical University of Vienna.

Bursell, B., Morger, K. and Nisser, M. (1990) 'Companies and society in transition. A study of two industrial communities 1945–1985', paper given at Seventh International Conference on the Conservation of the Industrial Heritage, Brussels, September.

Burton, V. (1989) 'Museums, research and display', *Museums Journal* 88, 2: 77–9.

Butt, R. (1989) 'Auditing your heritage assets', in Council of Europe, *Heritage and Successful Town Regeneration: Report of the Halifax Colloquy*, Strasbourg: Council of Europe.

Camusat, P. (1985) 'The experience of the Fourmies Trelon Region', paper given at Council of Europe Conference, 'The Industrial Heritage, What Policies?', Lyons, October.

Camusat, P. (1987) 'La mise en valeur du patrimoine industriel de la Région Fourmies-Trelon', in Actes du VIIIième Colloque sur le Patrimoine Industriel, *L'Archéologie Industriel en France*, Paris: CILAC.

Casanelles, E. (1987) 'Industrial heritage in Spain: The process in Catalonia', in The International Conference for the Conservation of the Industrial Heritage, *Industrial Heritage – Austria 1987: Transactions 2*, Vienna: Federal Office for the Protection of Monuments and Department for Industrial Archaeology of the Technical University of Vienna.

Casanelles, E. (1990) 'Water, technology and labour. The "Museu de la Ciencia i de la Tecnica" of Catalonia: a museum-system', paper given at Seventh International Conference on the Conservation of the Industrial Heritage, Brussels, September.

Cedrenius, G. (1987) 'Collecting today for today and tomorrow', in T. Ambrose and G. Kavanagh (eds), *Recording Society Today: Papers from a Seminar, October 1986*, Edinburgh: Scottish Museums Council.

Bibliography

Centre de Recherche sur la Culture Technique (1981) *Manifeste pour la développement de la culture technique*, Paris: CRCT.

Chabal, J. S. and Sclafer, J. (1981) 'Culture – technique – éducation', *Culture Technique* 4: 29–37.

Chandler, A. (1977) *The Visible Hand*, Cambridge, Mass.: Harvard University Press.

Civic Trust Regeneration Unit (1989) *Draft Burslem Action Plan*, Civic Trust.

Clark, R. (1990) 'In search of an industrial museum', paper given at the Scottish Museums Council conference on industrial museums, Glasgow, November.

Clement, B. (n.d.) *Lectures du Paysage Industriel: Le Creusot Plaine des Riaux*, Le Creusot: Ecomusée de la communauté Le Creusot-Montceau-Les-Mines.

Coles, J. (1973) *Archaeology by Experiment*, London: Hutchinson.

Combier, J.-C. (1977) 'La Mémoire collective d'un territoire', *Aménagement Local* 5: 15.

Conradson, B. (1984) 'Don't forget the white-collar workers!', *Industrial Heritage '84 Proceedings: The Fifth International Conference on the Conservation of the Industrial Heritage*, Washington: Society for Industrial Archaeology.

Cossons, N. (1975) *The B.P. Book of Industrial Archaeology*, Newton Abbot: David & Charles.

Coutts, H., Clark, H. and King, E. (1989) 'Telling the story', *Museums Journal* 89, 11: 30–3.

Cranstone, D. (ed.) (1985) *The Moira Furnace: A Napoleonic Blast Furnace in Leicestershire*, Coalville, England: North West Leicestershire District Council.

Crowther, D. (1989) 'Archaeology, material culture and museums', in S. Pearce (ed.), *Museum Studies in Material Culture*, Leicester: Leicester University Press.

Curti, R. (1988) *La Casa dell'Innovazione e del Patrimonio Industriale*, Bologna: Museo-laboratorio Aldini-Valeriani.

Curti, R., Guenzi, A. and Poni, C. (1988) 'Richerche storiche e museografia del patrimonio industriale', *Scuolaofficina* 2 (Bologna: Museo–laboratorio Aldini-Valeriani).

Davies, S. (1983) 'Change in the inner city', *Social History Curators Group Journal* 11.

Davies. S; (1984) 'Museums and oral history', *Museums Journal* 84, 1: 25–7.

Davies, S. (1985) 'Collecting and recalling the twentieth century', *Museums Journal* 85, 1: 27–9.

Davies, S. (1987) 'Social history collections: disposal', *Museums Journal* 87, 3: 124–36.

De Corte, B. (1990) 'A history of technical museums in Belgium: the absence of tradition' paper given at Seventh International Conference on the Conservation of the Industrial Heritage, Brussels, September.

Deligianni, O. (1990) 'Expériences de valorisation du patrimoine industriel de la ville de Thessalonique', paper given at Seventh International Conference on the Conservation of the Industrial Heritage, Brussels, September

Delony, E. (1990) 'Documenting the industrial and engineering legacy: twenty years of the Historic American Engineering Record', paper given at Seventh International Conference on the Conservation of the Industrial Heritage, Brussels, September.

de Noblet, J. (1981) 'Chroniques', *Culture Technique* 4: 11–16.

Department of the Environment (1988) *Creating Development Trusts: Good Practice in Urban Regeneration*, London: HMSO.

Desvallées, A. (1985) 'Technical museums: sector reborn', paper given at Council of Europe Conference, 'The Industrial Heritage: What Policies?', Lyons, October.

de Varine-Bohan, H. (1973) 'Un musée "éclaté": Le Musée de l'Homme et de l'Industrie: Le Creusot-Montceau-les-Mines', *Museum* XXV, 4: 242–9.

de Virvelle, M. et al. (1977) *Système descriptif des objets domestiques français*, Paris: Editions des musées nationaux.

De Villiers, C. and Huet, B. (1981) *Le Creusot Naissance et Développement d'une Ville Industrielle 1782–1914*, Macon: Champ Vallon.

octer, R. (1987) 'Les Pays Bas: veloppement d'une politique uvernementale pour l'inventaire et la otection des monuments et des paysages bains de l'époque contemporain', Inventaire néral des Monuments et des Richesses rtistiques de la France, Les Enjeux du trimoine Architectural du XXième Siecle, ris: Ministère de la Culture et de la ommunication.

ey, P. and Worthington, J. (1984) Industrial habilitation: The Use of Redundant ildings for Small Enterprises, London: chitectural Press.

rard, M. (1977) 'Les gens fouillent mémoire grenier. . . .', Aménagement Local 5: 6–9.

geborg, E. (1984a) 'When is a chair not a air? Considerations on the acquisition of efacts', Industrial Heritage '84 Proceedings: e Fifth International Conference on the nservation of the Industrial Heritage, ashington: Society for Industrial chaeology.

geborg, E. (1984b) 'Har var di ingenjorer lve', Fataburen, Stockholm: Nordiska useum.

geborg, E. (1987) 'In search of the human ment: A methodological approach', in The ternational Conference for the Conservation the Industrial Heritage, Industrial eritage – Austria 1987: Transactions 2, enna: Federal Office for the Protection of onuments and Department for Industrial rchaeology of the Technical University of ienna.

lconer, K. (1986) 'Inventories of the dustrial heritage: an English perspective', in ventaire Général des Monuments et des ichesses Artistiques de la France, Les ventaires du Patrimoine Industriel: Objectifs Méthodes, Paris: Inventaire Général.

lconer, K. (1987) 'Recent initiatives in the cording of industrial buildings in the United ingdom', in The International Conference for e Conservation of the Industrial Heritage, dustrial Heritage – Austria 1987: ransactions 2, Vienna: Federal Office for the otection of Monuments and Department for dustrial Archaeology of the Technical niversity of Vienna.

Falk, N. (1987) 'Baltimore and Lowell: Two American approaches', Built Environment 12, 3: 145–52.

Fenton, A. (1988) 'Industrial heritage and contemporary documentation: Considerations from Norway', Museums Journal 88, 2: 71–3.

François, P. (1982) Itinéraires industriels, Le Creusot: Ecomusée de la Communauté Le Creusot-Montceau-Les-Mines.

Gaudin, T. (1981) 'Ethnotechnologie: Pour une analyse des interactions objets/sociétés', Culture Technique, Cahiers Special Ethnotechnologie 2: 119–21.

Geijerstam, J. (1990) Arbetets Historia i Sverige: En guidebok til museer och miljoer, Norrköping, Sweden: Arbetets Museum.

Gold, J. R. and Burgess, J. (eds) (1982) Valued Environments, London: Allen & Unwin.

Goujart, M. (1988) Ecomusée de la région Fourmies-Trelon: Contributions au Plan 1989–1993, Fourmies: Ecomusée de la région Fourmies-Trelon.

Green, O. (1985) 'Our recent past: The black hole in museum collections', Museums Journal 85, 1: 5–7.

Greene, J. P. (1983) 'Independent and working museums in Britain', Museums Journal 81, 1: 25–8.

Greene. J. P. (1987) 'Independent museums: problems', Museums Journal 86, 4: 191–2.

Greenwood, J. (1990) 'It was a sheer pleasure to do this occupation', Oral History 18, 2: 58–63.

Gross, L. (1984) 'Workers and artefacts: New uses, new purposes', Industrial Heritage '84 Proceedings: The Fifth International Conference on the Conservation of the Industrial Heritage, Washington: Society for Industrial Archaeology.

Harvey, D. (1990) 'From space to place and back again: Reflections on the condition of post-modernity', paper given at a symposium on Futures, Tate Gallery, London, November.

Hay, G. D. and Stell, G. D. (1986) Monuments of Industry: An Illustrated Historical Record, Edinburgh: Royal Commission on Ancient and Historical Monuments in Scotland.

Bibliography

Hendricks, J. E. (1990) 'Museums for unpopular industries: alcohol, tobacco, nuclear energy, and other industrial museums in the face of public opposition', paper given at Seventh International Conference on the Conservation of the Industrial Heritage, Brussels, September.

Hewison, R. (1987) *The Heritage Industry*, London: Methuen.

Hills, R. (1977) 'Museums, history and working machines', *History of Technology* 2: 157–68.

Hindle, B. (1978) 'How much is a piece of the true cross worth?', in I. M. G. Quimby (ed.), *Material Culture and the Study of American Life*, New York: Norton.

Hobsbawm, E. and Ranger, T. (eds) (1983) *The Invention of Tradition*, London: Routledge.

Hoel, K. (1982) *Fabrik og Bolig ved Akerselva*, Oslo: Norsk Teknisk Museum.

Hooper-Greenhill, E. (1988) 'Counting visitors or visitors who count?', in R. Lumley (ed.), *The Museum Time Machine*, London: Comedia.

Hooper-Greenhill, E. (1989) 'The museum in the disciplinary society', in S. Pearce, (ed.), *Museum Studies in Material Culture*, Leicester: Leicester University Press.

Hough, M. (1990) *Out of Place: Restoring Identity to the Regional Landscape*, New Haven, Conn.: Yale University Press.

Hudson, K. (1975) *A Social History of Museums*, London: Macmillan.

Hudson, K. (1980) *Where We Used to Work*, London: John Baker.

Hudson, K. (1987) 'High technology and mass consumerism. Interpreting the history of the modern period through museums', in M. Stratton (ed.), *Interpreting the Industrial Past: Papers from a Short Course, February 1986*, Ironbridge: Ironbridge Institute.

Hume, I. N. (1978) 'Material culture with the dirt on it: A Virginia perspective', in I. M. G. Quimby (ed.), *Material Culture and the Study of American Life*, New York: Norton.

Hume, J. (1985) 'Industrial architecture and structures: Retention and re-use. The Scottish case', paper given at Council of Europe Conference, 'The Industrial Heritage: What Policies?', Lyons, October.

Hutchinson, G. and O'Neill, M. (1989) *The Springburn Experience: An Oral History of Work in a Railway Community 1840 to the Present Day*, Edinburgh: Polygon.

Jenkins, J. G. (1974) 'The collection of ethnological material', *Museums Journal* 74, 1: 7–11.

Jenkins, J. G. (1989) 'The collection of material objects and their interpretation', in S. Pearce (ed.), *Museum Studies in Material Culture*, Leicester: Leicester University Press.

Jenkinson, P. (1987) 'A taste of change: Contemporary documentation in inner city Birmingham 1983–1894', in T. Ambrose and G. Kavanagh (eds), *Recording Society Today: Papers from a Seminar, October 1986*, Edinburgh: Scottish Museums Council.

Jenkinson, P. (1989) 'Material culture, people's history and populism: Where do we go from here?' in S. Pearce (ed.), *Museum Studies in Material Culture*, Leicester: Leicester University Press.

Johnson, A. and Moore, K. (n.d.) *The Tapestry Makers: Life and Work at Lee's Tapestry Works, Birkenhead*, Liverpool: University of Liverpool.

Jones, S. and Major, C. (1986) 'Reaching the public: oral history as a survival strategy for museums', *Oral History* 14, 2: 31–9.

Jordanova, L. (1989) 'Objects of knowledge: A historical perspective on museums', in P. Vergo (ed.), *The New Museology*, London: Reaktion.

Kavanagh, G. (1983) 'SAMDOK in Sweden: Some observations and impressions', *Museums Journal* 81, 1: 85–8.

Kavanagh, G. (1987) 'Recording society today', in T. Ambrose and G. Kavanagh (eds), *Recording Society Today: Papers from a Seminar, October 1986*, Edinburgh: Scottish Museums Council.

King, E. (1987) 'People's Palace, Glasgow', in T. Ambrose and G. Kavanagh (eds), *Recording Society Today: Papers from a Seminar, October 1986*, Edinburgh: Scottish Museums Council.

Bibliography

nsthogskolans Arkitekturskola (1983)
rgslagen: Arbetsplatser och Bostäder Under
undra År, Stockholm: Konsthogskolans
kitekturskola.

use, S., Smith, R. and Starling, K. (1988)
perimental casting of silver ingots',
storical Metallurgy 22, 2: 87–92.

lik, G. and Bonham, J. C. (1978) Rhode
und: An Inventory of Historic Engineering
d Industrial Sites, Washington: US
partment of the Interior, Heritage
nservation and Recreation Service and
fice of Archaeology and Historic
servation, Historic American Engineering
cord.

nge, U. (1984) Älvkarleby: Kulturhistorisk
byggelseinventering, Uppsala:
plandsmuseet.

rson, A., Follin, A. and Ganslandt, M. (1987)
otal surveys of production-units as a basis
· industrial archaeology and town and
untry planning', in The International
nference for the Conservation of the
dustrial Heritage, Industrial Heritage –
stria 1987: Transactions 2, Vienna: Federal
fice for the Protection of Monuments and
partment for Industrial Archaeology of the
chnical University of Vienna.

maire, G. (1990) 'De la Compagnie des
onzes à la Fonderie: une contribution à la
odification du paysage urbain', paper given
Seventh International Conference on the
nservation of the Industrial Heritage,
ussels, September.

niaud, J.-M. (1985) 'Provision for the
otection of the industrial heritage in France',
per given at Council of Europe conference,
he Industrial Heritage: What Policies?',
ons, October.

wis, P. (1979) 'Axioms for reading the
ndscape', in D. W. Meinig (ed.), The
terpretation of Ordinary Landscapes, New
rk and Oxford: Oxford University Press.

ght, J. D. (1984) 'The archaeological
vestigation of blacksmiths' shops', Journal
the Society for Industrial Archaeology 10,
55–68.

ndqvist, G. and Karlson, B. (1980)
mbygdsgårdar, Jönköping: Jönköpings
ns Museum.

Lindqvist, S. (1981) 'How to research a job',
in Marie Nisser (ed.), The Industrial Heritage:
Proceedings of the Third International
Conference on the Conservation of the
Industrial Heritage, Stockholm.

Lindqvist, S. (1982) Grav hvor du star.
Handbog i at udforske et arbejde,
Copenhagen.

Lindsley, S. (1980) 'Preservation in industrial
archaeology', Industrial Archaeology Review
V, 1: 41–50.

Lindsley, S. and Smith, S. (1973) 'On site
preservation of industrial monuments',
Transactions of the First International
Congress of the Conservation of Industrial
Monuments, Ironbridge, England: Ironbridge
Gorge.

Lockwood, J. (1988) 'The Calderdale Fair
Shares Inheritance Project', in Calderdale
Council, Calderdale Heritage Review.

Lord, B., Lord, G. D. and Nicks, J. (1989) The
Cost of Collecting: Collections Management
in UK Museums. A Report Commissioned by
the Office of Arts and Libraries, London:
HMSO.

Loyer, F. (1987) 'La Modification de critères
dans l'évaluation du patrimoine contemporain
préalables à une politique de protection', in
Inventaire Général des Monuments et des
Richesses Artistiques de la France, Les Enjeux
du Patrimoine Architectural du XXième
Siècle, Paris: Ministère de la Culture et de la
Communication.

Ludvigsen, P. (1990) 'Trade unions and
museums', paper given at Seventh
International Conference on the Conservation
of the Industrial Heritage, Brussels,
September.

Lynch, K. (1972) What Time is This Place?
Cambridge, Mass.: MIT.

McNulty, R. (1989) 'Lessons from North
America', in Council of Europe, Heritage and
Successful Town Regeneration: Report of the
Halifax Colloquy, Strasbourg: Council of
Europe.

Malcolm-Davies, J. (1990) 'Keeping it alive',
Museums Journal 90, 3: 25–9.

Malone, P. (1986) 'Present and potential value
of American inventories', in Inventaire

Bibliography

Général des Monuments et des Richesses Artistiques de la France, *Les Inventaires du Patrimoine Industriel: Objectifs et Méthodes*, Paris: Inventaire Général.

Mattingly, J. (1984) *Volunteers in Museums and Galleries*, Berkhamstead: The Volunteer Centre.

Mende, M. (1987) 'Adapting an industrial landscape', in The International Conference for the Conservation of the Industrial Heritage, *Industrial Heritage – Austria 1987: Transactions 2*, Vienna: Federal Office for the Protection of Monuments and Department for Industrial Archaeology of the Technical University of Vienna.

Merriman, N. (1989a) 'The social basis of museum and heritage visiting', in S. Pearce (ed.), *Museum Studies in Material Culture*, Leicester: Leicester University Press.

Merriman, N. (1989b) 'Museum visiting as cultural phenomenon', in P. Vergo (ed.), *The New Museology*, London: Reaktion.

Middleton, V. (1990a) 'Irresistible demand forces', *Museums Journal* 90, 2: 31–4.

Middleton, V. (1990b) *New Visions for Independent Museums in the U.K.*, Chichester: Association of Independent Museums.

Miles, R. S. *et al.* (1988) *The Design of Educational Exhibits*, London: Unwin Hyman.

Moreton, A. (1988) 'Tomorrow's yesterdays: Science museums and the future', in R. Lumley (ed.), *The Museum Time Machine*, London: Comedia.

Morger, K. (1985) *Skebo Bruk*, Stockholm: Stockholms Universitet.

Mullins, S. (1985) 'Market Harborough: Building a collection', *Museums Journal* 81, 1: 20–1.

Mullins, S. (1986–7) 'Beyond collecting: projects as policy at the Harborough Museum', *Social History Curators Group Journal* 14: 20–2.

Museum of American Textile History (1984) *Annual Report*, North Andover: Museum of American Textile History.

Museums Documentation Association (1981) *Practical Museum Documentation*, Cambridge: Cambridgeshire Museums Documentation Association.

National Trust for Historic Preservation (1976) *A Guide to Delineating Edges of Historic Districts*, Washington DC: Preservation Press.

Nijhof, P. (1990a) 'Cultural heritage: The Netherlands', *European Environmental Yearbook*, Milan: Institute of Environmental Studies.

Nijhof, P. (1990b) 'A new wave of museal steampumping engines in Holland', paper given at Seventh International Conference on the Conservation of the Industrial Heritage, Brussels, September.

Nilsson, S. (1983) *Bryggerier i Sverige: En Kulturhistorisk Inventering*, Uppsala: Riksantikvärieambetet och Statens Historiska Museer.

Nisser, M. (1986) 'Industrial heritage in Sweden: Objectives and methods', in Inventaire Général des Monuments et des Richesses Artistiques de la France, *Les Inventaires du Patrimoine Industriel: Objectifs et Méthodes*, Paris: Inventaire Général.

Norsk Kulturrad (1988) *Bevaring av Tekniske og Industrielle Kulturminner i Norge*, Norsk Kulturrad.

Nystrom, B. and Cedrenius, G. (1982) *Spread the Responsibility for Museum Documentation: A Programme for Contemporary Documentation at Swedish Museums of Cultural History*, Stockholm: Nordiska Museet.

Oliver, K. (1982) 'Places, conservation and the care of streets in Hartlepool', in J. R. Gold and J. Burgess (eds), *Valued Environments*, London: Allen & Unwin.

O'Neill, D. (1989) 'The use of heritage in the Kings Cross redevelopment', unpublished MA dissertation in History of Design, Middlesex Polytechnic.

O'Neill, M. (1987) 'Recording modern Springburn', in T. Ambrose and G. Kavanagh (eds), *Recording Society Today: Papers from a Seminar, October 1986*, Edinburgh: Scottish Museums Council.

Neill, M. (1990) 'People as a driving force', *useums Journal* 90, 2: 21.

isby, I. (1990) *The Englishman's England: ste, Travel and the Rise of Tourism,* imbridge: Cambridge University Press.

ven, D.E. (1987) *Setting up and Running a w Museum,* Chichester: Association of ependent Museums.

rrick, J. (1990) 'Representations of food', published MA dissertation in History of sign, Middlesex Polytechnic.

tten, R. H., Whelan, J. and Dixon, M. (1989) me economic consequences of heritage nservation: The case of Calderdale', in uncil of Europe, *Heritage and Successful wn Regeneration: Report of the Halifax lloquy,* Strasbourg: Council of Europe.

atman, J. (1989) 'The Abbeydale Industrial umlet: History and restoration', *Industrial chaeology Review* XI, 2: 141–54.

nn, T. Z. (1980) 'The Slater Mill Historic e and the Wilkinson Mill Machine Shop hibit', *Technology and Culture* 21: 56–

cival, A. (1978) *Understanding our rroundings,* London: Civic Trust.

llard, S. (1959) *The Genesis of Modern anagement,* Harmondsworth: Penguin.

ni, C. et al. (1980) *Maccine Scuola Industria: l Mestiere alla Professionalita Operaia,* logna: Il Mulino.

rter, G. (1988) 'Putting your house in order: presentations of women and domestic life', R. Lumley (ed.), *The Museum Time ichine,* London: Comedia.

tkonen, L. (1984) 'Re-use of old industrial ildings from the preservation point of view', *lustrial Heritage '84 Proceedings: The Fifth ernational Conference on the Conservation the Industrial Heritage,* Washington: Society Industrial Archaeology.

tnam, T. (1987) 'The changing context for lustrial heritage initiatives in Britain', in e International Conference for the nservation of the Industrial Heritage, *lustrial Heritage – Austria 1987: ansactions 2,* Vienna: Federal Office for the otection of Monuments and Department for

Industrial Archaeology of the Technical University of Vienna.

Putnam, T. (1988) 'The theory of design in the second machine age', *Journal of Design History* 1, 1.

Putnam, T. (1990) 'The crafts in museums: consolation or creation', *Oral History* 18, 2: 40–3.

Putnam, T. and Newton, C. (1990) *Household Choices,* London: Futures Publications.

Quimby, I. M. G. (ed.) (1978) *Material Culture and the Study of American Life,* New York: Norton.

Raistrick, A. (1972) *Industrial Archaeology: A Historical Survey,* London: Eyre Methuen.

Ramer, B. (1989) *A Conservation Survey of Museum Collections in Scotland,* Edinburgh: Scottish Museums Council.

Rehnberg, H. and Sörenson, U. (1987) 'A Swedish ecomuseum: The art of engineering a landscape', in The International Conference for the Conservation of the Industrial Heritage, *Industrial Heritage – Austria 1987: Transactions 2,* Vienna: Federal Office for the Protection of Monuments and Department for Industrial Archaeology of the Technical University of Vienna.

Reichen, B. (1985) 'The economic aspects of conversion projects', paper given at Council of Europe Conference,' The Industrial Heritage: What Policies?', Lyons, October.

Richards, J. M. (1958) *The Functional Tradition in Early Buildings,* London: Architectural Press.

Riksantikvärieambetet och Statens Historiska Museer (1983) *Att Uppratta Program for Kulturminnesvård,* Stockholm: Riksantikvärieambetet.

Riksantikvärieambetet och Statens Historiska Museer (1989) 'The Swedish Report to the Twenty-third International Congress on Comparative Law, section IV.D.1 "The Protection of the Cultural Heritage"', Stockholm.

Rivière G. H. (1989) *La Muséologie,* Paris: Dunod.

Rix, M. (1955) 'Industrial archaeology', *Amateur Historian* 2: 225–9.

Bibliography

Robbins, M. (1988) 'What must we keep?' *Industrial Archaeology Review* VI, 2: 81–8.

Rosander, G. (1980) *Today for Tomorrow*, Stockholm: SAMDOK.

Roth, M. (1981) *Connecticut: An Inventory of Historic Engineering and Industrial Sites*, Washington: Society for Industrial Archaeology.

Roth, M. (1984) 'The Re-use of historic industrial sites in New England: an evaluation', in *Industrial Heritage '84 Proceedings: The Fifth International Conference on the Conservation of the Industrial Heritage*, Washington: Society for Industrial Archaeology.

Roth, M.(1986) 'The goals and methodologies of industrial heritage inventories: A comparison between the comprehensive and intensive approaches', in Inventaire Général des Monuments et des Richesses Artistiques de la France, *Les Inventaires du Patrimoine Industriel: Objectifs et Méthodes*, Paris: Inventaire Général.

Roux, A. (1985) 'The national Museum of Science, Technology and Industry, Paris, La Villette', paper given at Council of Europe Conference, 'The Industrial Heritage: What Policies?', Lyons, October.

Rydberg, S. (1985) 'A key factor: industrial firms', paper given at Council of Europe Conference, 'The Industrial Heritage: What Policies?', Lyons, October.

Saumerez Smith, C. (1989) 'Museums, artefacts and meanings', in P. Vergo (ed.), *The New Museology*, London: Reaktion.

Scalbert Bellaigue, M. (1981) 'Industrial archaeology in industrial anthropology: The ecomuseum of the community of Le Creusot-Montceau-Les-Mines, France', *Industrial Archaeology Review* V, 3: 228–36.

Scottish Museums Council (1985) *Museums are for People*, Edinburgh: Scottish Museums Council.

Sekers, D. (1987) *The Role of Trustees in Independent Museums*, Chichester: Association of Independent Museums.

SHIC Working Party (1983) *Social History and Industrial Classification: A Subject Classification for Museum Collections*, Sheffield: Centre for English Cultural Tradition and Language.

Shrimpton, D., Chambers H. T. et al. (1986) 'Some new working textile museums', *Textile History* 17, 2: 181–96.

Silvester, J. W. H. (1975) 'The fragmented museum project at Le Creusot', *Museums Journal* 75, 2: 83–4.

Skramstad, H. K. (1978) 'Interpreting material culture: A view from the other side of the glass', in I. M. G. Quimby (ed.), *Material Culture and the Study of American Life*, New York: Norton.

Smith, D. (1974) *Amenity and Urban Planning*, London: Crosby, Lockwood Staples.

Smith, S. B. (1979) 'The construction of the Blists Hill Ironworks', *Industrial Archaeology Review* III, 2.

Smith, S. B. and Gale, W. K. V. (1987) 'Wrought iron again: The Blists Hill Ironworks officially opened', *Historical Metallurgy* 21, 1: 44–5.

Sommestad, L. (1983) *Sagverksarbetarna i Strukturomvanlingen*, Gävle: Lansmuseet i Gävleborgs Lan.

Sörenson, U. (1987) *Jarn Bryter Bygd: Ekomuseum Bergslagen Berattar i Landskapet*, Stockholm: Ekomuseum Bergslagen.

Stockholms Stadsmuseum et al. (1984) *Vardefulla Industrimiljoer i Stockholm*, Stockholm: Stockholms Stadsmuseum.

Stratton, M .J. (1990) 'Industrial archaeology: a case study of Stanley Mill', paper given at Seventh International Conference on the Conservation of the Industrial Heritage, Brussels, September.

Suddards, R. (1988) *Listed Buildings: The Law and Practice of Historic Buildings, Ancient Monuments and Conservation Areas*, London: Sweet and Maxwell.

Svenska Turistforeningen (1989) *Mest om Järn*, Uppsala: Svenska Turistföreningen.

Swade, D. (1990) 'Long live the Babbage difference', *Guardian*, 8 November.

Sylvan, B. et al. (1984) *Industrilandskapet Vid*

ömmen i Norrköping, Norrköping:
mmunstyrelsen Norrköping.

bo, M. (1986) *Some Aspects of Museum
cumentation*, Stockholm: Nordiska
seet.

lbot, M. (1986) *Reviving Old Communities:
Manual of Renewal*, Newton Abbot: David
Charles.

mpleton, M. (1981) 'Centres de Science et
Technologie', *Culture Technique* 4: 39–43.

n Hallers, F. (1985) 'Protection and special
tures of industrial heritage: Experience and
iciencies in several European countries',
er given at Council of Europe conference,
e Industrial Heritage: What Policies?',
ns, October.

omas, R. (1990) 'Port in a storm', *Museums
urnal* 90, 4: 24–7.

ompson, J. M. A. (ed.) (1984) *Manual of
ratorship: A Guide to Museum Practice*,
ndon: Butterworth.

uring Club Italiano (1983) *Archaeologia
ustriale*, Touring Club Italiano.

inder, B. (1973) *The Industrial Revolution
Shropshire*, Chichester: Phillimore.

inder, B. (1981) 'The open village in
ustrial Britain', *Industrial Heritage:
ansactions of the Third International
nference on the Conservation of the
ustrial Heritage*, Stockholm.

inder, B. (1982) *The Making of the
ustrial Landscape*, Gloucester: Alan
ton.

an, Y.-F. (1977) *Space and Place: The
rspective of Experience*, Minneapolis:
iversity of Minnesota.

plandsmuseet and Lansstyrelsen (1984a)
gd att Varda I*, Uppsala: Upplands
rnminnesforenings Forlag.

plandsmuseet and Lansstyrelsen (1984b)
gd att Varda II*, Uppsala: Upplands
rnminnesforenings Forlag.

n Aerschot, S. (1986) 'Communauté
mande de Belgique: Patrimoine industriel
nventaire du patrimoine architecturel', in
entaire Général des Monuments et des
hesses Artistiques de la France, *Les*

*Inventaires du Patrimoine Industriel: Objectifs
et Méthodes*, Paris: Inventaire Général.

Vasström, A. (1987) 'Preservation of industrial
heritage – what purpose?', in The
International Conference for the Conservation
of the Industrial Heritage, *Industrial
Heritage – Austria 1987: Transactions 2*,
Vienna: Federal Office for the Protection of
Monuments and Department for Industrial
Archaeology of the Technical University of
Vienna.

Vergo, P. (1989) 'The reticent object', in P.
Vergo (ed.), *The New Museology*, London:
Reaktion.

Viane, P. (1990) *Industriele Archaeolgie in
Belgie*, Ghent: Strichting Mens en Kultuur.

Victor, S. (1981) 'Skill, museums and the
industrial heritage', in *Proceedings of the
Fourth International Conference on the
Conservation of the Industrial Heritage*, Paris:
CILAC.

Vincent, J.-M. (1987) 'Les législations de
protection des espaces et le patrimoine
architectural du XXième siècle', in Inventaire
Général des Monuments et des Richesses
Artistiques de la France, *Les Enjeux du
Patrimoine Architectural du XXième Siecle*,
Paris: Ministère de la Culture et de la
Communication.

Vlaamse Verenignen voor Industriale
Archaeologie (1990) *Handen Te Kort*, Ghent:
VVIA.

Walden, I. (1991) 'Qualities and quantities',
Museums Journal 91, 1: 27–8.

Weslowski, P. L. (1984) 'Analysis of industrial
sites inventory data and use in public planning:
Innovative strategies in Massachusetts',
*Industrial Heritage '84 Proceedings: The Fifth
International Conference on the Conservation
of the Industrial Heritage*, Washington:
Society for Industrial Archaeology.

West, A. (1990) 'Museums and the real world',
Museums Journal 90, 2: 24–6.

West, B. (1988) 'The making of the English
working past', in R. Lumley (ed.), *The
Museum Time Machine*, London: Comedia.

Whincop, A. (1986) 'Using oral history in
museum displays', *Oral History* 14, 2: 46–50.

Bibliography

White, P. (1990) 'English industrial cities: A new look at protecting their historic buildings', paper given at Seventh International Conference on the Conservation of the Industrial Heritage, Brussels, September.

Williams-Davies, J. (1990) 'The changing role of the rural blacksmith', *Oral History* 18, 2: 68–9.

Woolaghan, G. (1982) 'The origins of scientific tyre design', unpublished MA dissertation in History of Design, Middlesex Polytechnic.

Wraith, A. E. (1978) 'The performance of an experimental charcoal fired crucible furnace', *Historical Metallurgy* 12, 1: 44–6.

Wright, P. and Putnam, T. (1989) 'Sneering at the theme park', *Block* 15.

Index

Index

Index

Index

Index